THE SEA WOLVES

LORIMAR presents

A EUAN LLOYD PRODUCTION
AN ANDREW V. McLAGLEN FILM

GREGORY ROGER DAVID
PECK MOORE NIVEN

in

THE SEA
WOLVES

with
TREVOR HOWARD
BARBARA KELLERMANN
and
PATRICK MACNEE

Screenplay by
REGINALD ROSE
(Based on the book "Boarding Party" by
James Leasor)

Executive Producer
CHRIS CHRISAFIS

Producer
EUAN LLOYD

Director
ANDREW V. McLAGLEN

Made by Richmond Light Horse Productions Ltd for
Varius A. G.

THE SEA WOLVES

JAMES LEASOR

With a Foreword by
Admiral of the Fleet,
the Earl Mountbatten of Burma

Originally published as The Boarding Party

*This low-priced Bantam Book
has been completely reset in a type face
designed for easy reading, and was printed
from new plates. It contains the complete
text of the original hard-cover edition.*
NOT ONE WORD HAS BEEN OMITTED.

THE SEA WOLVES

*A Bantam Book | published by arrangement with
Houghton Mifflin Company*

PRINTING HISTORY

Originally published as The Boarding Party
Houghton Mifflin edition published January 1979
2nd printing .... *January 1979*
Bantam edition | October 1980

ISBN 0–553–13304–7

Published simultaneously in the United States and Canada

PRINTED IN THE UNITED STATES OF AMERICA

0 9 8 7 6 5 4 3 2 1

CONTENTS

ILLUSTRATIONS

IN TEXT

From *Gallop*, Vol. III, No. 2 (June 1937)

Some of the Allied shipping losses in the Indian ocean in late 1942

Kit required by members proceeding to Ranchi "on special course"

IN INSERT

Proclamation Parade, January 1, 1936

The Calcutta Light Horse Rugger Team 1939

A paperchase 1939 – the first fence

Annual Camp Exercises

Another time the Calcutta Light Horse took to the water

Colonel W. H. Grice, ADC, ED

The house in Goa from which Trompeta was kidnapped

Only *Phoebe* of the Hopper Barges was used as an assault craft in the Far East

The Calcutta Light Horse regimental silver

The CLH Club House as it is today

Ehrenfels

Drachenfels

Braunfels

Ehrenfels and *Braunfels* in Marmagoa harbor

The Axis ships burning in Marmagoa harbor, March 9, 1943

Settling into the water
Drachenfels after the raid
"Mutinous Axis crews burn their ships in Goa"
As reported in *The Times of India*

FOREWORD

by Admiral of the Fleet,
the Earl Mountbatten of Burma,
KG, GCB, OM, PC, GCSI, GCIE, GCVO, DSO

As the last British Viceroy and Governor-General in India, I was also, by long tradition, Honorary Colonel of the Calcutta Light Horse.

This regiment owed its origins to the first British Governor-General, Robert Clive, who in 1759 raised a formation of irregular cavalry from Europeans in Calcutta to frustrate a Dutch attack on what was then a new British settlement.

In more recent years, members of the Calcutta Light Horse served with distinction in both world wars. But not all could be accepted into the services because of their age, or their value to India and the war effort as civilians. This book tells how fourteen of them, with four colleagues from the Calcutta Scottish, another Auxiliary Force unit, volunteered for a hazardous task which, for reasons the author makes plain, no-one else was able to undertake.

This happened shortly before my arrival in India in 1943, as Supreme Allied Commander, South East Asia, and I immediately saw how valuable were the results of this secret operation.

I am pleased that at last credit may be given to those who planned and carried it out.

Mountbatten of Burma
A.F.

ACKNOWLEDGMENTS

I would like to thank many people who helped me
with my enquiries in Britain, Germany and India. I am
especially in the debt of Mr. W. E. Catto, Mr. Dan
G. Haigh, and Major-General Lewis Pugh, CB, CBE,
DSO, for their kindness in supplying me with rec-
ollections, anecdotes and incidents concerning the
Calcutta Light Horse and Operation Creek.

I would also like to thank the following people for
their assistance:

Mrs. J. P. Archer-Shee;

Herr W. Asendorpf, Stadtbücherei, Kiel;

Captain P. N. Batra, Director, Marine Department, Calcutta Port Trust;

Mrs. Dorothy Bardock;

Mrs. Jill Bebbington;

Herr Reinhard Bettzuege, Embassy of the Fed-
eral Republic of Germany, London,

Mr. W. D. Bryden;

Sir John Burder;

Captain A. N. Chackerbutty, Deputy Director,
Marine Department, Calcutta Port Trust;

Miss S. A. Coombes, Lloyd's Register of Shipping;

Mr. R. N. Coppock, Ministry of Defence, Naval
History Branch;

Major John F. F. Crossley;

Mr. Samir Datta, *The Statesman*, Calcutta;

Mr. T. K. Datta, Calcutta Port Trust;

Commander Bernard Davies, RN;

Mr. R. W. Dennis;

Herr Fritz Dimzak;

Mr. T. M. Dinan, Librarian, Lloyd's, Lime Street,
London;

Mr. Desmond Doig, *The Statesman*, Calcutta;

Mrs. A. E. Duffield, Department of Printed Books, Imperial War Museum, London;

Mr. Robert Dugvid;

Mr. Lindsay Emmerson, *The Statesman*, Calcutta;

Herr Walter Esskuchen;

Mr. F. D. Farmer;

Mr. K. R. Fergie;

Mrs. Gisella Ferrari;

Mr. H. Fowler;

Mr. Roland Gant;

The Rt. Hon. Lord Glendevon, PC;

Mrs. Doris Grice;

Mr. R. Groom, Foreign & Commonwealth Office Library and Records Department;

Mr. A. B. Gupta;

Mr. D. J. Hawkins, Naval History Branch, Ministry of Defense;

Lt. Col. J. D. S. Henderson;

Mr. Sidney Herbert;

The directors of the Hansa Line, Bremen;

Herr C. Jansen, Schiffsfotos, Hamburg;

Mr. Roger W. Jordan, MAIE, Editor, Lloyd's Log;

Mr. Y. P. Kamat, Hotel Mandovi, Panjim, Goa;

Mr. M. K. Kavlekar;

Herr Arnold Kludas, Stiftung Deutches, Schiffarts-museum Bremerhaven;

Mr. Kolhatkar, *The Times of India*, Bombay;

Frau Kossack, Marineschule Mürwik, Flensburg-Mürwik;

Mr. P. Radha Krishnan, *The Reader's Digest*, Bombay;

Sir Gilbert Laithwaite, GCMG;

Mrs. Joan M. Leasor;

Mrs. Janet Lodge;

Mr. Colin Hercules Mackenzie, CMG;

Mr. Douglas Matthews, the London Library;

Dr. Maiehöfer, Bundesarchiv, Militärarchiv, Freiburg;

Herr Mirow, Deutsche Dampfschiffahrts-Gesellschaft, "Hansa";

Herr Heinz Marx;

Mr. Ron Mellor, Public Record Office, London;

Mr. K. S. K. Menon, Editor, *The Navhind Times,* Goa;

Admiral of the Fleet, the Earl Mountbatten of Burma, KG, GCB, OM, PC, GCSI, GCIE, GCVO, DSO;

Mr. Denis Mullick;

Mrs. Eileen Paterson, John Moore Public Relations Ltd;

Mr. T. Parameshwar, *The Reader's Digest,* Bombay;

Mr. and Mrs. Partap Sharma;

Mr. Alexander Peterson, OBE;

Mr. Charles Pick;

Mrs. Barbara Pickering;

Mr. C. Stan Pinto, Manager, Aguada Beach Resort, Goa;

Herr Kurt Reimers (Deutscher Marinebund e.B);

Professor Jurgen Rohwer, Bibliothek für Zeitgeschichte, Stuttgart;

Miss Leesa Sandys-Lumsdaine;

Mr. P. G. Sandys-Lumsdaine;

Mr. V. M. Salgoacar, Chairman and Managing Director, V.M. Salgoacar & Brothers Pvt., Ltd., Goa;

Dr. Sareyko (Auswärtiges Amt, Bonn);

Mrs. Joan St. George Saunders, Writer's and Speaker's Research;

Mr. N. K. Sen;

Dr. Maurice Shellim;

Mrs. Jill Sherratt;

Mr. Ruhul Singh;

Mr. Derek Smith, Museum Assistant, Department of Ships, National Maritime Museum, London;

Sir Nicol Stenhouse;

Mr. Colin Burton Stewart;

Mrs. Bridget Stoddart;

Mr. J. D. Tanner;

Herr Kurt Thamm;

Mr. C. Tharoor, *The Statesman,* Calcutta;

Mr. Ian Turcan;

Herr R. Voigt;

Herr Ludolf Timm, St. Pauli Landungsbruechen 3;

Colonel J. L. Wardle;

Dr. Weinandy, Foreign Ministry, Bonn;

Herr Johann Wellhausen;

Mrs. Jean Whitburn;

Mr. A. H. d'A. Willis;

Herr J. Witthöft, Hapag-Lloyd Aktiengesellschaft, Hamburg;

Mr. P. G. Wood, Assistant Private Secretary to Permanent Under-Secretary of State, Ministry of Defense;

Mrs. Margaret Wylie.

I would also like to acknowledge my indebtedness to *Gallop,* the magazine of the Calcutta Light Horse; *The Calcutta Scottish Regimental Chronicle; 85 Years of Shipping Under the Maltese Cross* by Leonard Gray of the World Ship Society in cooperation with R. Pöpper of Hansa Lines, Line Drawings by Frau E. Pöpper, published by the World Ship Society, Kendal, 1967; Files of *The Statesman,* Calcutta; *The Times of India,* Bombay; *The Sphere,* London; *The Illustrated Weekly of India,* and *Calcutta Light Horse, A.F. (I.) 1759–1881–1947,* published by Kale & Polden Ltd., Aldershot, 1957.

FROM THE WRITER
TO THE READER

This is a true story.

At the request of several people—British, German and Indian—involved in the events described in this book, I have changed or omitted some names and altered certain physical characteristics. Also, at their request, a few incidents have been paraphrased.

James Leasor

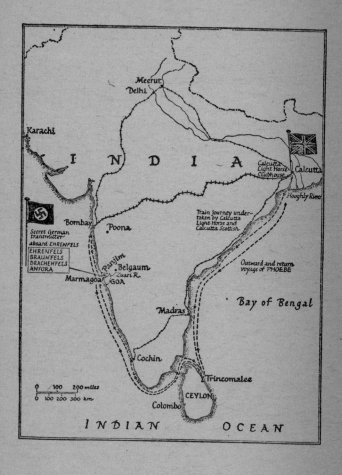

Meerut
Delhi
Karachi
I N D I A
Calcutta
Light Horse
Clubhouse
Calcutta
Hooghly River
Bombay
Poona
Train journey under-
taken by Calcutta
Light Horse and
Calcutta Scottish
Secret German
transmitter
aboard EHRENFELS
EHRENFELS
BRAUNFELS
DRACHENFELS
ANFORA
Panjim
Belgaum
Zuari R.
Marmagoa
GOA
Outward and return
voyage of PHOEBE
Madras
Bay of Bengal
Cochin
100   200 miles
0   100 200 300 km.
Trincomalee
CEYLON
Colombo
I N D I A N   O C E A N

ONE

Against the evening swell and sweep of rollers half a mile long, where flying fish skimmed from one foam-capped mountain of water to another, the U-boat periscope stood no higher than a small shark's fin.

A million tons of seawater streamed over the outside lens. Inside the U-boat the rubber eyepieces trembled against the lookout's skull as he half-crouched, half stood, in the control room lit by dim red bulbs to accustom the crew's eyes to darkness.

The weight of water shifted restlessly. He saw a deep green haze, then bubbles of salty foam, then blue evening sky above the Indian Ocean, between Ceylon and East Africa.

He moved the handlebar controls slowly, two degrees at a time. More water, more sky, a further froth of waves, and then, 500 meters to the south, the tossing outline of a cargo ship, her shabby gray hull streaked with rust.

For a second he held her, and then she was gone in an uneasy rolling trough of water a hundred feet deep. He found her, perched on the long creaming crest of a wave, her funnel pouring smoke, before she disappeared again. He turned to the commander of U-181, Leutnant Wolfgang Lüth.

"In position, sir," he reported.

Lüth bent over to peer through the lenses; there she was right enough, steaming west. He thumbed through his vessel recognition book, and checked the ship's outline with the printed silhouette. A caption gave details of speed, power, owners and tonnage.

Just before daybreak, he had surfaced at an agreed time to accept a radio signal from an unknown station. This had informed him he should ex-

1

pect to intercept a Greek cargo ship at around 07:30 hours, and a British freighter at approximately 20:30 hours, and had given him certain bearings and courses.

At 07:37 precisely Lüth had sunk the Greek ship *Mount Helmos* of 6,481 tons at 26.38 south and 34.59 east. Now, he was surfacing to sink the British *Dorington Court*, bound from Calcutta to Lurenço Marques and Durban. His bearing was 27.00 south and 34.45 east. According to his radio and the recognition book, she should be a 5,281 ton vessel, built in 1939 by J. L. Thompson and Son of Sunderland, England, and owned by Court Lines Ltd., of London.

Lüth marveled at the accuracy of the information the radio signal had contained. He did not know who sent it or exactly where the transmitter could be, although from the direction and strength of the signal he guessed it must be sited somewhere along the west coast of India, probably well south of Bombay.

Every night, at a different time specified in a previous message, he would surface his U-boat, and while the generators charged batteries and hatches were opened for fresh air, the radio operator would listen for his next instructions.

These came in a regularly changed code. Such-and-such a ship, bound from this port to that, would be at such-and-such a bearing at a certain time. Lüth guessed that the person who gathered this information must also know the speed of that ship, the time she left port and other details of cargo and power before he calculated their point of interception.

But how could a German spy be working so calmly and efficiently in British India, literally surrounded by the enemy, yet still able to transmit almost every night without being discovered? It seemed incredible, and yet it was true, and he wondered at the courage of this unknown agent.

In Germany, when on leave, Lüth had often heard of heroism at sea, in the air, in North Africa or on the Russian front, but for him the real heroes were men, or maybe women, like these who gathered pieces of

2

specialized information in ways about which he could not even begin to guess, and then deliberately beamed them out, night after night after night.

Since the beginning of that month, these messages had predicted for him the whereabouts of three American ships, *Alcoa Pathfinder*, *Excello* and *East Indian*, and two Norwegian freighters, *Gunda* and *K.G. Meldahl*, and the Greek *Mount Helmos*. He had sunk them all. Now he would add *Dorington Court* to the list.

The lookout carefully turned the periscope handles through a full circle, in case any other vessels were in the vicinity, for Lüth was a careful and experienced commander. He had won the Knights Cross and the Iron Cross in 1940, and then had been awarded Oak Leaves to add to this; and for this month's work he would later receive a further award of Oak Leaves with Swords.

The sea stretched wide and empty as the sky; they were safe from any retribution. Lüth gave orders to fire two torpedoes, and followed their tracks. A green wall of water lifted as they hit *Dorington Court*. An orange circle of flame erupted around her stern. He gave orders to surface and, as *Dorington Court*'s crew frantically tried to lower boats, and the helmsman put her hard over to port to present less of a target to another salvo, the U-boat's gun opened fire.

Dorington Court began to sink quickly, stern first, bows up out of the water, looking at that distance like a child's boat sinking in a bath. A great gout of sea water billowed up and subsided. Then there were only floating spars and boxes, and heads bobbing up and down as survivors swam desperately toward the lifeboats.

Lüth surveyed the scene for a moment. It was difficult to think of the men out there as human beings with homes and families. They were simply the enemy to him, as he was to them. Some would survive and some would not; that was the chance of fate. In his position they would doubtless have acted as he had done. He nodded to his number two. U-boat 181 crash dived. Lüth checked his watch with the chronometer.

3

Some of the Allied shipping losses in the Indian Ocean in late 1942

Atlischer Ozean

1 2 3	4	5	6	7	8	9	10 11 12	13	14	15
October 1942 (Fortsetzung)										
8/0140 dt U 172	Emsmann	GR 5649	-D 3400+	T	.	8/	gr -D Pentella	3283+	34.20 S/ 17.40 E	
9/0021 dt U 68	Merten	GR 5689	-D 5000+	T	.	8/	gr -D Koumoundouros	3588+	34.10 S/ 17.07 E	
8/0340 dt U 68	Merten	GR 5932	-D 6000+	T	.	8/	al -D Gaasterkerk	8679+	34.20 S/ 18.10 E	
8/0903 dt U 159	Witte	GR 5656	-D 5300+	T	.	8/	br -D Clan Macterlab/	7031+	34.53 S/ 16.41 E	
8/1731 dt U 179	Sobe	-------		T	.	8/	br -D City of Athem,	6551+	33.40 S/ 17.01 E	
8/7051 dt U 68	Merten	GR 5939	-F: 8207+	T	.	8/	ae -27 Selfsauve	8207+	34.40 S/ 14.25 E	
8/2222 dt U 68	Merten	GR 5963	-D 6000+	T	.	8/	br -D Sarthe,	5271+	34.50 S/ 18.40 E	
9/0344 dt U 68	Merten	GR 5645	-D: 4981+	T	.	9/	br -D Ezmaila	4061+	34.52 S/ 18.30 E	
9/0454 dt U 68	Merten	GR 5965	-D 6000+	T	.	9/	br -D Belgian Fighter	5+3+	35.00 S/ 18.30 E	
9/1150 dt U 159	Witte	GR 8144	-D: 8557+	T	.	9/	bs -D Calembyn	6557+	35.47 S/ 14.34 E	
10/1028 dt U 172	Emsmann	GR 7335	-D:0:23456+	T	.	10/	br -D Orenden/	23456+	31.51 S/ 19.40 E	
13/1337 dt U 159	Witte	GR 6996	-D:0:0113+	T	.	13/1449	br -D Empire Wood/	7167+	37.50 S/ 18.16 E	
13/1920 jp I-162	Shinone	O06/ 826	-D	T	.	13/	br -D Karzaban,	-161+	05.31 N/ 62.03 E	
17/0615 dt U 504	Poske	JJ 1313	-D 5000+	T	.	17/	br -D Empire Chaucer/	5970+	40.10 S/ 18.30 E	
22/ jp I-27	Kitsuna	22n/ 4co	-D . +	T	.	22/	br -D Ocean Vintage/	717+	21.37 N/ 60.06 E	
23/2312 dt U 504	Poske	KZ 1972	-D: 5600+	T	.	23/	br -D City of Johannesburg	5666+	33.20 S/ 29.30 E	
26/1643 dt U 504	Poske	KZ 1864	-D 12000+	T	.	26/	an -D Anne Hutchinson	7178+4	33.10 S/ 28.20 E	3)
29/1226 dt U 159	Witte	JJ 2511	-H: 4978+	T	.	29/	br -D Ross	4978+	38.51 S/ 21.40 E	
29/2118 dt U 159	Witte	JJ 2755	-D: 7327+	T	.	29/	br -D Leplace/	7327+	40.25 S/ 21.35 E	
31/0903 dt U 504	Poske	KZ 9187	-D: 8000+	T	.	31/	br -D Empire Guidon/	7041+	40.10 S/ 33.50 E	
31/1718 dt U 504	Poske	KP 9843	-D: 5113+	T	.	2/	br -D Reynolda	5113+	29. S/ 41. E	2)
31/2223 dt U 172	Emsmann	GP 3211	-D: 4091+	T	.	31/	br -H Aldington Court	6091+	30.20 S/ 08.10 W	

Indischer Ozean

1 2 3	4	5	6	7	8	9	10 11 12	13	14	15
November 1942										
1/1530 dt U 178	Dhoken	KF 8011	-D: 8400+	T	.	1/	br -D Hendra/	0233+	29.20 S/ 32.13 E	
2/2340 dt U 172	Emsmann	GO 4769	-D: 4908+	T	.	2/	br -D Llandilo/	4908+	27.03 S/ 02.59 W	
2/2145 dt U 177	Gysae	GR 1715	-D- 8000+	T	.	31/	gr -D Aegeus	4538+	32.20 S/ 03.05 E	1)
3/ dt U 181	Lüth	GR 7835	-M: 8139+	T	.	3/	c -M Sat India	6159+	37.23 S/ 13.34 E	
3/1947 dt U 504	Poske	KZ 4549	-D: 5187+	T	.	3/	br -D Porto Alegre	5187+	35.27 S/ 28.07 E	
4/1452 dt U 178	Dhoken	KF 5355	-D: 3000+	T	.	4/	br -D Mai King	2864+	25.55 S/ 33.10 E	

1	2	3	4	5	6		11	12	13	14
6/Aug8 dt	U 178	-Ibbeken	KP 5355	-Dt	5200+ T		6/	hr -D. Trefriew ✓	5200+	25.46 S/ 33.48 E
8/2138 dt	U 68	Merten	GF 3811	-Dt	803++ T		8/	hr -D City of Cairo	603++	23.30 S/ 05.30 W
7/2250 dt	U 159	Witte	GR 7359	-Dt	8500+ T		29/	sn -D La Salle	9463+	40.00 S/ 21.20 E 23
8/2055 dt	U 181	Lüth	KP 6982	-D	6000+ TA		8/	pd -D Plandit	5050+	36.00 S/ 26.32 E
10/0027 dt	U 181	Lüth	KZ 4681	-Dt	3799+ T		30/	hr -D X.G.Swisaki	3799+	34.59 S/ 29.43 E.
13/2020 dt	U 178	Ibbeken	KP 9885	-Dt	376++ T		13/	hr -D Louise Moller	378++	30.50 S/ 35.34 E
13/0801 dt	U 181	Lüth	KZ 1918	-Dt	9959+ T		13/	sn -D Sunniis	4959+	52.23 S/ 30.07 E
13/ dt	U 159	Witte	GG 5811	-Si	2290+ A		13/	sn -S Star of Scotland	2290+	26.33 S/ 00.30 W
15/0145 dt	U 178	Ibbeken	KZ 2385	-D	6000+ T		15/	hr -D Adviser	5348+	32.03 S/ 33.52 E
15/2125 dt	U 181	Lüth	KP 132t	-D	2000+ T		13/	hr -D Zada	2243+	25.40 S/ 33.53 E
19/2307 dt	U 177	Gysae	KP 9720	-T	10000+ T		13/	hr -DT Scottish Chief	700+	30.36 S/ 34.84 E
20/012m dt	U 181	Lüth	KP 5327	-Dt	3562+ T		20/	hr -D Corinthiakos	3563+	25.43 S/ 33.27 E
20/1140 dt	U 177	Gysae	KP 9910	-Dt	7191+ T		20/	sn -D Fierce Davies	7191+	29.40 S/ 35.35 E
22/2033 dt	U 181	Lüth	KP 5372	-Dt	6700+ T		21/	sn -D Alcoa Pathfinder	6797+	26.45 S/ 33.10 E
22/2153 jp	I-158	Tanaka	08n/ 77e	-D	+ T		23/	hr -D Cranfield ✓	-5332+	08.26 N/ 76.42 E
23/ jp	I-29	Izu	07n/ 61e	-D	+ T		23/	br -D Tisaa ✓	1000S+	07.38 N/ 61.06 E

Column 1 refers to date and time of attack

Column 2 gives nationality of the attacking submarine; dt for German (Deutsch); jp for Japanese

Column 3 gives the number of the attacking submarine

Column 4 gives the surname of her commander

Column 5 refers to position of attack

Column 6 the target of the submarine; D = Dampfer (Steamer); M = Motor-ship; DT = Steam Tanker

Columns 11 and 12 type and name of target ship

Column 13 gives her size

Column 14 geographical position of attack

Twenty-thirty-four precisely, on the evening of November 24, 1942.

Twelve men in middle-age sat grim-faced around a horseshoe-shaped table covered in black baize, in a cellar 150 feet below the British Admiralty in London. Some wore the uniform of naval officers, and others were in civilian suits. Their complexions had the curiously gray color of people who for too long have had too little sunlight and fresh air.

Bare electric bulbs in china shades cast a harsh light as unnatural as the dim red bulbs in Lüth's U-boat. Here, as there, day and night had no meaning; it could be any hour of the twenty-four.

The cellar walls were distempered green. Red steel girders reinforced the roof. Metal ventilating ducts under the ceiling and a gray steel door with screw bolts like a warship's watertight door, all contributed to the sensation of being below decks in an old ironclad. This background was in keeping, for these men were members of a secret Admiralty committee called to suggest an answer to the serious and increasing shipping losses in the Indian Ocean. Even more disturbing were frequent reports by survivors from these vessels that German U-boats and not Japanese submarines were responsible. In roughly six weeks, U-boats had sunk 46 Allied ships in the Indian Ocean—more than 250,000 tons. How could they operate so effectively, so far from home?

Allied cargo ships sailed across the Indian Ocean from so many separate ports to so many different destinations that the convoy system could not be used, even if Allied navies could spare warships to escort them, which they could not. Two British and three Dutch submarines were all the Allies had to patrol 28,000,000 square miles of disputed sea. Cargo vessels thus had to trust mainly to their individual speed, and to frequent changes of course.

Sometimes, the captains of ships carrying cargoes of vital importance to the war were issued with sealed orders to open only when many miles out to sea. These would contain instructions for taking evasive action, involving detours of hundreds of miles from their original route. But no matter where they sailed or when, a German U-boat would too often rise from the depths and engage them. For the U-boat commanders appeared to know their courses and their speeds with uncanny accuracy.

During the earlier part of 1942, Japanese submarines had been predominant in the Indian Ocean, but most had now apparently withdrawn east of India, to concentrate on shipping in the Bay of Bengal and south towards Burma and Malaya.

This was presumably by design and not by chance, for the Germans clearly had access to an espionage network of extreme efficiency in India, which was not available to the Japanese.

"German information is so good that when a U-boat confronts two or three of our cargo ships, and her captain doubts he has time to sink them all, he will invariably select the one carrying the most urgent cargo," a commander pointed out now. "That must mean he has details of all their cargoes—and their priority to us. And how the hell do the Germans find that out?"

A rear admiral across the table shuffled some papers.

"I have already sent a request, through the usual channels, to the government of India, for their Central Intelligence Bureau, asking them to discover this leakage as a matter of the highest priority."

"Not much else we can do, I suppose," agreed a captain halfway down the table, "but I must say I don't hold out much hope from them. They have their time cut out arresting subversives and others agitating against us and what they call an imperialistic war. What about Naval Intelligence?"

"It's not really up their street. And they're already fully stretched with the Japs. They report some loose talk about shipping in the Taj bar in Bombay and at the Galle Face in Colombo. But no instances of people saying much more than generalities. And the Germans couldn't possibly pick up details of cargoes, alternative routes and so on from that kind of eaves-

7

dropping. They must have far more sophisticated sources of information."

A civilian was the next to speak. He had gray hair and thick bushy eyebrows, and before the war he had been a Cambridge don. Now he worked for one of several Intelligence agencies nominally under the control of the Ministry of Economic Warfare.

"I propose, sir, that we send a copy of this signal to SOE in India. They have just set up an office out there."

"Special Operations Executive," said the captain reflectively. "Think they can do anything? Sound rather a mixed bag to me, from what I hear. Business men, schoolmasters, merchants."

"You know something about them, then?" asked the commander.

"Should do," replied the captain. "Got a relative in that lot. Pugh. Lewis Pugh. He's changed about a bit himself. Used to be a soldier, then went into the Bengal Police. Now he's arranging all kinds of odd things supposed to help the war. I would have thought they were a bit remote for our particular problem."

"How do you mean, remote?" asked the rear admiral.

"Physically remote, sir. Their office is in Meerut, 40 miles north of Delhi. Right in the center of India. And about 1,800 miles from the west coast."

"Maybe they'd like a breath of sea air," replied the rear admiral drily. He turned to the professor.

"I'll inform SOE, as you propose. Now, gentlemen, has anyone any other proposals pertinent to the situation?"

He glanced around the table at his colleagues. They shook their heads.

The captain checked his watch with the electric clock on the wall, which had four hands to give the time in Washington as well as in London. He had never been particularly close to Pugh, and he had not seen him since before the war. Now for the first time in years, he wondered what he was doing at that moment.

8

He was, in fact, sitting in a cane armchair in Calcutta in the upstairs bar of the Light Horse clubhouse, overlooking the garden. Lewis Pugh wore British army uniform of khaki drill bush shirt and trousers, with the crown and star of a lieutenant colonel on his shoulder straps. He was a slim man in his late thirties with sandy hair and blue eyes.

He also kept glancing at the clock above the bar, where two Indian barmen wearing smart white linen uniforms, with brass buttons and turbans and belts in the maroon, gold and blue Light Horse colors, were busily polishing glasses.

It was Sunday, just before lunch. Soon the bar would be crowded with the businessmen, jute merchants, bankers, brokers, solicitors and accountants who formed the membership of the Calcutta Light Horse.

Pugh was not a member. As a professional soldier —from Woolwich, he had been commissioned into the Royal Horse Artillery—he was not eligible, but his family had long links with India stretching back for generations, and most of the members were his friends. Pugh had served in Germany when he was first commissioned, and then on the northwest frontier in India. But he soon grew impatient with the slow promotion of peacetime, for some officers in his regiment were still subalterns after 17 years.

He answered an advertisement for men with knowledge of India to join the Special Branch Intelligence Department of the Bengal Police. In this capacity, he had been stationed for some time at Howrah, a teeming suburban slum on the far side of the Hooghly River along which Calcutta had been built, and so had become a regular guest of club members.

At the outbreak of war Pugh returned to the army, and when SOE came to India he was a natural recruit. Now he was Director of Country Sections, which handled various clandestine undercover operations. He had been in Calcutta for two days, discussing one of these missions to be made behind the Japanese lines in Burma with the men of Force 136,

9

who would carry it out. This was one of SOE's most successful units. They had their headquarters in Calcutta, and specialized in placing agents and trained saboteurs deep inside Burma and Malaya.

Pugh was now on his way back to his own office in Meerut, and had several hours to kill before the evening train was due to leave. He had thus been pleased to accept an invitation to have a curry lunch with Bill Grice, the present colonel of the Light Horse, and another friend, Dick Melborne, an up-country tea planter, making one of his rare visits to the city.

The Calcutta Light Horse was technically a part-time auxiliary regiment with a history going back for about 183 years. But many of its members believed that military activities should take second place to social and sporting interests. Everyone was expected to attend a fortnight's annual summer camp, and a certain number of evening parades throughout the year. These were loosely defined. An evening in the clubhouse bar could often be dignified in the regimental ledger as a parade.

Young men in business or the professions, out from Britain on their first tour of duty in India, joined for several reasons. First, they could live cheaply in the clubhouse, and within days of arriving would be introduced to far more congenial people of their own age and outlook than they could usually hope to meet in as many years back home. One reason for this was the Victorian system of calling to leave cards which was still the fashion among Europeans in India to a greater extent than in Britain. A new arrival in Calcutta would have visiting cards engraved with his name and address and his company. A friend would then provide him with a list of residents, and he would spend an afternoon touring round their houses, to deposit these cards.

After due time, if the people on whom he had called decided they wished to make his acquaintance, they would ask him to dinner. Parents with unmarried daughters were generally among the first to respond with such invitations. Having accepted this initial hospitality, the newcomer was then at liberty to invite them back.

Another inducement to join was the prospect of subsidized riding. In order to encourage proficiency in riding—for the Indian Army before the war was not fully mechanized—the government of India allowed each Light Horse member 32 rupees a month (about £2.50p.) towards the upkeep of his horse. At the prices prevailing, this provided for the animal's fodder and also went some way towards paying the wages of its groom.

The experience of one young accountant, Mark Hilliard, who arrived in Calcutta early one Easter Monday morning on the Blue Train, which met the steamers at Bombay, was typical of many Light Horse members.

On Tuesday, through a friend in the Light Horse, he found a room in a chummery, the name given to a house run as a mess for bachelors.

On Wednesday, another Light Horse member, going home to England, sold him a passable horse.

On Thursday, Hilliard joined the Light Horse himself, so that he could draw the horse allowance.

On Friday, a third member heard of his interest in sports cars and sold him a two-seater M.G.

On the Saturday, Hilliard drove in the car to a party, where he stayed until the early hours of Sunday morning—when he left for a dawn canter on his new horse. His first week in Calcutta was over—and an infinity of similar activities lay ahead.

Perhaps the greatest attractions of the Light Horse were friendship and fun. The unit was totally democratic. Everyone joined as a trooper, and all promotion was from this rank, by popular vote. Thus an extremely rich merchant might remain a trooper for years, while a more enthusiastic but less successful accountant could be promoted sergeant within a matter of months.

Pugh remembered wild Light Horse parties and paper-chases, when riders would race across the

11

AFTER THE BALL

Doff the motley, Oh! my
horseman,

Clear your head of Rhenish
vapours.

You have had your dance,
and liked it,

Cut your measured ballroom
capers,

You have sat in "kali
jagahs,"

Graced the bar, that flat-
foot's haven,

Now your supper party's
ended,

You must start, unslept,
unshaven,

Bound for Jhow and grass and Nullah, Ganges Khadir, sand and thorn,
      Hone your spears to razor sharpness, Mount at dawn.
Bacchus held his feast, my horseman, Held his feast, and you were there.
      Now the pleasant jest is ended, Now you face the cold grey air.
Guests and hosts and jazz-musicians, All alike are gone to bed ;
      Theirs the Europe morning, Theirs the Sunday pudding-head ;
Yours, where Jhow and grass and Nullah, Ganges Khadir, sand and thorn,
      Stretch black-purple in the gloom, to Mount at dawn.

(Acknowledged to The "Statesman")

(D. C. HAIGH)

countryside in the early morning, following a trail of pieces of paper. He recalled gymkhanas when friends rode racehorses which appeared solemnly in the regimental records as "Charger, Military, Trooper for the use of." Many races were run at Tollygunge, a private course, near the golf course of the Tollygunge Club. This club was so exclusive that at one time it had a waiting list of more than five years for member-ship.

All "Tolly" races were for Gentlemen Riders, the definition of a G.R. being one who had never won a race worth more than rupees 99, about £7.50. Usually, winners were awarded rupees 50 in cash and a cup valued at rupees 49.

Racing was extremely sophisticated and well organized, frequently with elaborate "arrangements" between Gentlemen Riders, which equally often, did not come off as planned. Professional English jockeys in Calcutta had a low opinion of all this.

"Tolly?" one remarked. "G.R.s? Ain't safe to have a bet on the *sunrise* there."

There was plenty of time and opportunity for sport, for office hours in Calcutta could be pleasantly elastic, and the weekend could be not much shorter than the working week. This was the tail end of a 19th-century tradition when Thursday was mail day. The packet would leave for English every Saturday, and so all letters had to be despatched by train in time to catch this vessel in Bombay or wait until the next one was due to sail. As a reaction to such last minute activity, little work was done on Fridays, less still on Saturdays and, of course, none on Sundays.

Now, the majority of members were away in the services and only a few remained, most too old or too important in their firms to be allowed to volunteer.

They were coming into the bar now, in twos and threes, middle-aged men with thickening waists and thinning hair, calling for gins and limes, and telling the barmen to be *jaldi* about it.

Dick Melborne, one of Pugh's hosts, arrived, and sat down thankfully at Pugh's table. An Indian barman brought him a drink before he could give his order. The barmen prided themselves on knowing what every member liked to drink before lunch; his choice for Melborne was a large gin fizz. Pugh thought this apt; everything about Dick Melborne was large. He was burly, beginning now to run to fat, but in his day a fine rugger player, and still a hard rider to hounds—the jackal in Bengal, not the fox. Melborne ruled his tea-gardens as he rode—in an autocratic and individualistic way. Just before the war, several Light Horse colleagues spent a weekend with him there. Gin flowed freely, and after a hot curry lunch on the Sunday they concocted a rude telegram to the head of one of Calcutta's most important companies. Melborne handed this telegram to his senior bearer,

13

with instructions to send it off from the nearest telegraph office in the village, several miles away.

But after a siesta, and several cups of strong tea, Melborne's guests did not find this idea so funny as it had appeared before lunch. They knew the man to whom it was addressed was as influential as he was humorless, and his displeasure could conceivably affect their careers. On reflection, it would be wiser not to send it.

Accordingly, they hastily called Melborne's bearer and asked him to return to the telegraph office and retrieve the cable. Transmission was only made in the early evening, and so it would not have been despatched. But the bearer steadfastly refused to act on the orders of anyone except his master, so the Light Horsemen rather grumpily set off to walk to the telegraph office themselves.

To their amazement, their progress was barred at the tea estate gates. Six hefty Indians carrying long poles known as *lathis*, of the type used by police when dealing with riots, barred their way. They were as adamant as the bearer. No one left the compound without Melborne sahib's permission. He was still asleep, and so they had to wait fuming until he awoke, and gave his gracious permission for them to leave.

"Don't often see you here," said Melborne now. "How are things in Meerut?"

"So-so," said Pugh guardedly.

No one really knew the nature of his duties, and on his occasional visits to Calcutta he always had to parry well-meaning questions.

Bill Grice came into the room, nodding to friends at the bar, and sat down at Pugh's table. Grice was a stocky, firm-faced man in his late forties, going thin on top, but with a serious, rather grave face. As a schoolboy during the First World War, Grice ran away from home, added two years to his age and joined up in the Royal Navy. While still in his teens, he served as a junior officer in a coal burning warship at Zeebrugge. After the war, he left the navy, but lacking academic qualifications, found it difficult to

14

find a worthwhile job in England during the depression. He used his gratuity and savings to sail to East Africa, and after a short time, went farther east to India. Here, he joined the Calcutta office of a British owned chemical company, and by sheer application and hard work had received regular promotion. Now he was managing director with a seat on the boards of other companies, and in due course, no doubt, in line for a knighthood on his retirement.

Grice had joined the Light Horse as a trooper, and rose quickly through the ranks, for he was both efficient and popular. As colonel for a couple of years before the war, he had done his utmost to increase the efficiency of the military side of the regiment's activities, while never losing sight of social and sporting needs.

He still looked more like a naval officer than a managing director or a colonel. His speech was as direct as his general outlook. He was well known for the brevity of the traditional naval grace which he used when asked to officiate at a guest night or official dinner. While others might deliver a long blessing in Latin, Bill Grice would simply stand up, survey the company, and say, "Thank God," and then sit down.

"Seen *The Sunday Statesman* today?" he asked as he shook hands.

The others said they had not yet read it.

"Not missed much good news, then. Things look bad in Burma. At the present rate of progress the Japs should be over the border and in Calcutta in weeks rather than months."

"Can't understand their success," said Melborne. "They've gone through Hong Kong, Malaya, Burma and the Philippines like a dose of salts—while we've hardly stopped long enough to take breath to start retreating again."

"The best barometer of Allied success is how the local Bengalis react," said Grice drily. "Right now they are all for non-cooperation, and say they would welcome the Japs here, because they would liberate India from the British imperialistic yoke."

15

"Remember when those same liberating Japs dropped a couple of tiny bombs on Calcutta?" asked Pugh. "Next morning, Howrah Bridge was jammed so close with rich Bengalis running away, you couldn't have pushed a piece of paper between them. And those who had shouted the loudest were in the biggest cars, fleeing the fastest."

Melborne signaled for more drinks.

"The best description I ever heard about Bengal, was when I was at school in a geography lesson," he said. "Bengal is a low-lying country, inhabited by low, lying people."

"Well," said Grice reasonably, "we are not putting up such a good show, are we? If I were a Bengali I wouldn't think there was much to be proud of in our performance. Only wish I could do something to help. If I was 20 years younger, I'd have volunteered the day war broke out. But—there it is."

He shrugged.

"You're lucky, Pugh. At least you are in uniform. But what do you actually *do* in Meerut? Push a pen, like the rest of us?"

"We do all sorts of odd jobs," Pugh replied with deliberate vagueness. "Odd things other people don't want to touch."

"How odd?" asked Melborne. "Be specific." He prided himself on his directness. Once, when he was on a long, up-country tour for his company, a colleague in Calcutta, wanting to know his whereabouts on a certain day, cabled, "Please send details of your movements." Melborne replied shortly, "Once yesterday. Twice today. Why?"

"We carry out unusual operations," explained Pugh.

"Sounds like a bloody abortionist, the way you put it," retorted Melborne.

Grice frowned. He did not always appreciate Melborne's bluntness.

"Well, Lewis," he said. "If ever you hear of anything so odd no one else wants to get involved with it, remember the Light Horse."

"I don't think I'm likely to," Pugh told him frankly.

"Don't care a damn what it is. I admit we are a

16

bit thin on top, just as we are a bit thin in numbers now. But the spirit's like it always was. And the higher the odds against us, the better the Light Horse likes it. So remember that too, will you?"

"I will," promised Pugh, and raised his replenished glass.

TWO

Special Operations Executive headquarters in Meerut was housed in a Victorian bungalow in a road known as the Cavalry Lines. In peacetime, this bungalow had been used by the brigadier commanding the British cavalry brigade on garrison duty in Meerut. It had a front garden, with a long wall facing the road, and stone gate posts. To the right-hand gate post was bolted a small black wooden board on which an Indian sign writer from the bazaar had painted in white letters: *Ministry of Economic Warfare*. Since SOE was under the control of this ministry, the notice seemed as good a cover for their activities as any other.

On the morning Pugh returned to Meerut, an urgent meeting was called in this bungalow to discuss the most immediate instructions they had received from London through the government of India, in Delhi, to deal with shipping losses in the Indian Ocean.

The meeting was held in what the brigadier had used as a family dining room. It was the custom for the British Army in India then to furnish married quarters for regular officers and other ranks, and this room still bore strong traces of official taste in furniture and decoration. The walls were cream and the doors painted brown. An old-fashioned sideboard had been cleverly copied from an original photograph by an Indian carpenter in the bazaar. Above this hung Snaffles prints showing thin-faced English country gentlemen riding to hounds, or, in acceptably well-worn uniforms, leading horse-drawn gun teams into action in Flanders during the First World War.

A fan creaked above the heads of the five officers

sitting around what had been the dining room table. The controller of SOE in India, Colin Hercules Mackenzie, sat at the head of the table. He was a director of one of Scotland's largest cotton thread firms, but he had the gentle, sensitive face of a scholar. Mackenzie had lost a leg in action with the Scots Guards during the last weeks of the First World War, and bore his affliction with such dignity that to strangers he simply appeared to be only slightly lame. He was an unusual combination of litterateur and business man. A scholar at Eton, he went on to Cambridge, where he won the Chancellor's Medal for English verse. His financial acumen in his firm was equally respected.

Before the war, one of Mackenzie's fellow directors in this company had been a firm friend, Lord Linlithgow. Now, in 1942, Linlithgow was Viceroy and Governor-General of India. In the previous year he had sent a senior member of the government of India's Intelligence Bureau, to Singapore for a liaison visit. On his return, this officer recommended that a branch of SOE similar to one already operating in Singapore should be established in India. The viceroy was short of qualified men to run this operation, and suggested that Colin Mackenzie would be ideal to do so.

Mackenzie was then in Scotland. He had recently married, and, as the father of a baby daughter, was not over eager to accept, but felt it was his duty to do so. Accordingly, he traveled to London to Baker Street, where SOE had their headquarters. Here he was introduced to Gavin Stewart, a giant of a man, over six feet three inches tall, and built to match, whose family controlled an engineering business with a branch in India. Stewart had served for three years in Calcutta and knew India well. He was an ebullient character with great enthusiasm for this assignment, and greatly attracted by the audacity of some of SOE's schemes.

Mackenzie and Stewart had set off together for India from Liverpool by ship. Their instructions were to commence operations as speedily as possible, but the ship was old and slow and took three weeks to reach Freetown, in West Africa. Here, they disembarked and explained their urgent need for swifter transport to the local authorities, who found places for them on an RAF transport plane.

The aircraft came down in Khartoum to refuel, where they had to spend the night. Mackenzie accidentally dropped his artificial leg on the tiled floor of his bedroom—and the main goose-neck joint snapped completely. He had sent the leg for overhaul before he left home, and this part had presumably been replaced by one with a flaw in the metal. Without this vital joint, Mackenzie could not walk a step.

Stewart, as an engineer, examined the break, and realized it could not be repaired. A completely new joint must be fashioned before they were due to take off at dawn next day—but how?

With the artificial leg under his arm, Stewart took a taxi to the local RAF base and explained the gravity of the situation to two Scottish engineers. They immediately volunteered to work all night, and by morning had produced a completely new joint. Their reward was the only bottle of very special Talisker whisky that Mackenzie and Stewart had been able to bring on the trip with them.

Next to Pugh sat Alex Peterson. They had been to preparatory school together in England, but had not met since then until they arrived in Meerut to join SOE.

Peterson was a schoolmaster in civilian life. He had taught English, French and Geography at Shrewsbury. When he came to join the army, a friend of his from Oxford days, Lionel Hale, a literary critic and broadcaster, who was then working in SOE headquarters in Baker Street, arranged for Peterson to be seconded to SOE.

For the first six months of Peterson's stay in India, he had traveled around the country with Gavin Stewart, setting up an underground organization to continue resistance if the Japanese invaded India.

In this connection, Peterson had worked closely with

Indian communists and other subversives, on many of whom Pugh had ironically collected detailed police dossiers before the war.

One of Peterson's tasks in Meerut was to write items of propaganda camouflaged as news, and place them with newspapers and radio programs in India.

He lived in a bungalow which was unusually shabby and unkempt. A very popular name for suburban bungalows in England was "Mon Repos," and mindful of the wretched condition of his quarters, Peterson named his bungalow, "Mon Debris."

The fifth man at the table, Walter Fletcher, was physically the largest—he weighed 19 stone. As with many fat men, he had a cheerful, rubicund countenance. He wore spectacles, and when he beamed, which was often, he looked like a larger-than-life Mr. Pickwick.

Fletcher was in his early fifties, and for many years had been chairman and managing director of a large firm that supplied all grades of raw rubber to the trade. He held a degree from Lausanne University, and before the First World War had worked in Paris, Budapest and Hamburg. During the war he served as a major in East Africa, and afterwards stayed on there for several years building up his business. Later, he traveled extensively between the Far East and the United States.

Because of Fletcher's wide variety of interests—from painting to farming—and his equally wide range of contacts and friends in government and industry in so many countries, he always seemed to know the name of the very man who could help SOE with some strange and esoteric enquiry. And if he did not know him personally, then he certainly knew someone else who did. Fletcher's ability as an organizer also meant that he could translate some of SOE's more outlandish propositions into feasible projects, with the certainty of no comeback to anyone in authority should anything go wrong.

His talents in smoothing ruffled official feathers were very valuable, for, since SOE was a new organization in India, its formation had caused some jealousy among more established intelligence departments. Life for them had gone on smoothly for fifty or sixty years. They did not approve of rumors they had heard about SOE's unorthodox way of working—of kidnappings, political assassinations, the deliberate planting of forged documents on people and organizations they needed to discredit, and the rest.

This coolness meant that SOE had to rely on personal contacts and friendships more than on official backing. It was also one reason why they worked from a bungalow, 40 miles north of New Delhi, the capital of India, and the home of GHQ (India). Suitable offices there were hard to find in the overcrowded official buildings, but Mackenzie realized the advantages of being independent physically and administratively from other government departments and the convoluted ramifications of India Command, which controlled armed forces in both India and Burma.

When Lord Louis Mountbatten became Supreme Allied Commander, South East Asia, in 1943, he moved his headquarters to Kandy, in Ceylon, out of the heat and inertia of Delhi. He believed that Europeans in the East worked far better in a cooler climate and a high altitude. As one member of the staff put it, "Kandy is dandy and handy. Delhi is smelly."

Also when Mountbatten became Supremo, the activities of SOE increased dramatically; by the war's end they had taken over all available office space in Meerut. But in December, 1942, they were still small enough to fit into this one bungalow.

Outside their dining room window, an Indian gardener, known as a *mali*, was diligently watering the square of dusty dried-up lawn from a glistening goat's skin of water. As he worked, the *mali* regularly hawked in his throat and spat in a mechanical, almost unconscious action.

"Must we endure that disgusting noise?" asked Fletcher at last.

"So long as we're in India, we have to," Pugh told him. "I call it the song of India."

"I don't care what you call it. It's a vile habit. Takes one's mind off the job in hand. What were you saying, Gavin?"

"That I've asked the radio monitoring people to listen for any unofficial broadcasts that could contain shipping information," said Stewart. "They report no clandestine transmitter operating on Indian soil on the west coast, from Karachi in the north, to Cape Comorin in the south, nearly 1,400 miles."

"You specifically say *Indian* soil," observed Fletcher pointedly, glancing at the huge map of India that covered one complete wall of the room. "But remember there is a neutral Portuguese colony on that coast, roughly 400 miles south of Bombay. Goa. Anything there?"

"I was coming to that," said Stewart testily, for he had wanted to break his news more dramatically.

"They report regular radio transmissions at night from the main port in Goa, which is Marmagoa. Here."

He stood up, crossed the room and pointed to the Portuguese possession, which was colored green on the map where the rest of India was shown in red, the traditional color for countries within the British Empire. "They transmit in German code, and at varying speeds and times."

"Have the codes been broken?" asked Pugh.

"Yes. They give details of various ships, and their destinations, and where they should be at certain times. But I'm damned if I know how they find the information, which is pretty detailed."

"I can tell you," replied Pugh. "Almost every European office employing Indians will have one or two who imagine they are serving their country—or Gandhi or the Congress Party, which to many of them is the same thing—if they pass on any information they can glean to the Axis."

"But for that to be of any use implies an Axis spy net across India!" interrupted Mackenzie.

"It would really only need to concentrate around the ports, Calcutta, Karachi, Madras, or most likely, Bombay," replied Pugh. He turned to Stewart.

23

"Our people are absolutely certain these transmissions are coming from Marmagoa?"

"Absolutely," said Stewart. "In fact, they've pinpointed them from somewhere in the harbor, rather than on land. I questioned that, but they were adamant."

"And?"

"Well, they're either mistaken—which I doubt—or the Germans are using a transmitter from a submarine in the harbor, which I also doubt. That leaves a third possibility. They have a transmitter aboard a ship at anchor."

"Which gives us a choice of four possible ships," said Fletcher.

Everyone in the room knew that four merchant vessels, three German and one Italian, had sought refuge in Marmagoa, as the nearest neutral port, when war broke out. They had stayed in that harbor ever since, and now provided a focal point of interest for British visitors to Goa. Because of the war, it was difficult and sometimes impossible for British civilian families in India to take home leave or to visit South Africa as some preferred to do. Instead, as a substitute, they could spend a holiday in Goa, 24 hours by train from Bombay, and linked by a good motor road to Belgaum, the nearest large town in India, about 150 miles from the border.

Such families found the atmosphere of Goa, as a Portuguese colony, mildly continental and so a welcome change from India. The beaches were safe and sandy, and if hotels were small and sometimes a bit down-at-heel, and the water not always safe to drink, these drawbacks only accentuated the difference between Portugal and Britain and their overseas empires, and so were of themselves part of the attraction of "going continental."

From the upper rooms of the Gran Palacio hotel in Marmagoa—and how infinitely more exciting that name sounded than the prosaic palm court associations of the Grand Palace!—visitors could clearly see these four enemy ships at anchor. They could actually observe the Nazi flag unfurled, and might even brush shoulders with German and Italian sailors drinking in a café. When Japan entered the war, the captain of the Italian ship, *Anfora,* had defiantly run up the Japanese flag, until the Portuguese authorities requested he haul it down.

The fact that these ships were all anchored by chains from bows and stern and so could not move, was also somehow reassuring to British visitors. They were visible and comforting proof that no matter what disasters might affect Allied armies elsewhere, from Dieppe to Singapore and Pearl Harbor, here four valuable enemy cargo ships were being kept in virtual incarceration.

The officers in the bungalow in Meerut knew quite a lot about the ships. They were the 5,452 tons *Anfora* of the Lloyd-Triestino Company; and the 7,752 tons *Ehrenfels;* the 6,342 tons *Drachenfels,* and the *Braunfels,* of 7,847 tons, all owned by the German Hansa Line. Their cargoes included such unlikely items as cooked hams, sacks of flour and bags of explosives for mining purposes; marble slabs, bottles of mercury, locomotive spares, automobile batteries, and even a Mercedes sports car originally intended for an Indian princeling, with stocks of Chianti in the holds of *Anfora* and several hundred crates of best Bavarian beer in the others.

"If it's aboard any of them, my guess is it's *Ehrenfels,*" said Pugh.

"Why?" asked Peterson.

"The others are all old tubs caught on the high seas when war broke out. Their crews just painted out their colors on the funnels and dashed to Goa as the nearest neutral port, where we couldn't touch them. But *Ehrenfels* is different.

"She visited Calcutta when I was there in the police, on her way from Tokyo and Batavia, just before war started. We were tipped off that a German spy master was aboard, known to our intelligence people as Trompeta.

"We hoped he would come ashore, so we might nab him on some pretext, but he was far too careful. He stayed on board the whole time *Ehrenfels* was in

25

port, and Indian Nazi sympathizers visited him in-stead.

"On the day before war broke out I had a call from one of our people in the docks. He reported that *Ehrenfels* had left Calcutta during the night, with-out clearing her departure with the port authorities, or taking aboard a pilot.

"Her commander, Captain Röfer, is a pretty ex-perienced man. He was so eager to get away that he risked the 120 mile trip down the Hooghly, one of the worst navigational hazards in the world, rather than be interned and have his ship seized. He sailed direct to Goa and has been there ever since. And as far as I know, so has Trompeta."

"You think Trompeta could be sending the mes-sages?"

"More likely he's organizing the whole thing. He's lain very low for a long time. He could well have been quietly setting up an espionage system of sleep-ers, who he's now using, when all our energies out here are directed towards the Japs."

"Know much about the ship?"

Pugh crossed the room and opened a filing cabinet. He returned to the table with a sheaf of papers and began to read from them.

"She is powered by two six-cylinder two-stroke MAN diesels. Each engine develops 3,820 horsepow-er. They are the same type as the German Navy use in their pocket battleships, geared here to a single screw shaft.

"I put a man aboard her in Calcutta as a port fireman, and he reported that the decks are of special reinforced steel, and she carries concealed gun mountings. She was built by the Maschinenfabrik Augsburg-Nurnberg A.G. of Bremen, so that she could double as an auxiliary cruiser, and was launched in 1935.

"She is identical to another Hansa Line ship, *Kandelfels*, which the German navy successfully con-verted into the auxiliary cruiser *Pinguin*. And until HMS *Cornwall* sank her off the Seychelles last year, *Pinguin* had either captured or sunk 28 Allied ships, a total of 136,551 tons—*on her own*. Which gives you an idea of her speed and fire power—and the accuracy by which she was directed to her targets."

"So if *Ehrenfels* made a dash for Singapore, the Japs could fit her with guns from stores in the dockyard?"

"Easily. She has a cruising speed of 18 knots—and a maximum around 20. But I think she's more valuable as a floating radio station. She carries a powerful Deutz generator, for her transmitter and receiver have worldwide range."

"I've asked about transmitters, and our diplomatic people say the Portuguese insisted that all these ships' radios were dismantled before any of them could stay in the harbor," said Stewart.

"I'm sure they did," agreed Pugh. "But what's to prevent the Germans having a second radio that the Portuguese authorities in Goa know nothing about?"

The others sat in silence for a moment, then Stewart spoke.

"Let's go in and deal with all those ships," he said. "Surprises me we haven't thought of doing this before."

"We can't possibly do that," replied Mackenzie quietly. "How can we attack four apparently defenseless ships that have sought sanctuary in a neutral harbor belonging to our oldest ally?"

The others nodded reluctant agreement. Although Goa was physically only a tiny enclave on the western coast of India, with a coastline barely 65 miles in length, and a total area of less than 2,400 square miles, its international significance was out of all proportion to its size.

Goa was Portugal's oldest Eastern colony, and, in a world at war, Portugal was one of the most important neutral countries. This neutrality, however, was significantly biased in favor of the Allies for historical, traditional and other reasons. The Lisbon government allowed British and American aircraft flying the Atlantic to refuel in the Azores. This was an extremely valuable concession, for few aircraft could cross the Atlantic without refueling. Portugal also granted certain other facilities to the Allies in her Atlantic ports, and Lisbon, as a major neutral European city with an international airport, was extremely useful for Allied Intelligence purposes.

The Axis were, of course, fully aware of Portugal's importance to the Allied cause, and constantly strove to persuade the Portuguese government of the greater advantages to be gained by siding with them. If she would not associate by treaty, then, as with Spain, she should at least lean towards the Axis by inclination and attitude.

If this happened, the Allies would immediately lose all their facilities to the Axis. Worse, batteries of German coastal guns could be mounted near Sagres on the Algarve coast to command the approaches to the Mediterranean. This would complicate the defense of Gibraltar and Malta, and dramatically increase the losses in convoys bound for North Africa.

Portugal's neutrality was of such incalculable importance to the Allies that the British Foreign Office had given to the government of India the strictest and most specific categorical instructions that no action whatever must be taken which Portugal could conceivably consider to be an infringement of it.

"Well, if we can't get the ships out," said Stewart. "What about lifting Trompeta? The radio won't be much use without messages to send."

"Damned risky, if we made a mistake," said Fletcher cautiously.

"What if I prove that information is reaching Goa from Bombay—and being broadcast out again?" asked Pugh.

"It would still be damned risky, but then at least we'd know it might be a risk worth taking."

"Right," said Pugh, turning to Stewart. "If you can get our listening posts to monitor those signals, I'll tell you now what they'll pick up within the next few days. The news that we are moving bullion into Goa, for unknown reasons."

"But you aren't, I trust?" asked Mackenzie innocently.

All the others smiled knowingly at this, for Mackenzie had recently been called to answer some awkward questions about an earlier SOE scheme that Stewart had proposed. This was to install a Q-ship in the Bay of Bengal, which could engage unsuspecting enemy vessels.

Stewart had suggested that SOE purchase an Arab dhow from East Africa. They would arm her with concealed guns, install a powerful engine and put aboard a British naval crew. But the location, purchase, shipment to India and subsequent conversion of a suitable dhow had proved infinitely more complex and expensive than anyone had foreseen. And when the dhow was finally launched with all her new and extremely heavy equipment, a further depressing discovery was made.

The vessel's hull was so heavily infested with eel worm that many timbers were severely weakened. The first time the dhow's guns had fired a practice shot off Vizagapatam, on the east coast of India, the vessel virtually disintegrated and sank within minutes.

Stewart moved uneasily in his chair as the others smiled in his direction, for he knew what they were thinking.

Peterson now put forward the idea that he should contact the leaders of the Indian communist party, who might be willing to help the British—if only because Russia was an ally. He would see whether they could arrange some party or meeting or other diversion in Marmagoa that would bring the crews ashore, while others could sail the ships out of the harbor.

Then Fletcher made his proposal.

"Send an Indian SOE agent to Goa," he said. "We'll give him authority to offer Captain Röfer a bribe in any currency, to be deposited anywhere in the world, if he will sail his ship out of harbor beyond the three-mile limit, where we can seize it."

"A good idea," agreed Peterson. "How much do you suggest?

"Ten thousand pounds," proposed Pugh.

29

"For a ship worth at least 50 times as much?" asked Fletcher in amazement. "We've got to make it worth his while. He has to trust us, after all."

"*Can* he trust us?" asked Peterson. "Would you, in his circumstances?"

"I am, thank God, not in his circumstances," replied Fletcher diplomatically. "Let's give our man a chance by starting at 20,000 and going up to 30. After that, he reports back to us. We are still getting a phenomenal bargain if Röfer agrees. We silence the radio and we also acquire a ship, which, heaven knows, the Merchant Navy could use."

So it was agreed, and the discussion turned to other topics.

Afterwards, Pugh walked down to the bazaar in Meerut, a welter of streets lined with single-story, open-fronted shops where Indian tailors could run up a passable copy of a European suit or dress within hours, past shoemakers and sellers of herbal remedies for impotence and premature old age, to the yard of the Indian carpenter who had made the sideboard in their bungalow. Pugh gave him instructions to make a box, two feet square, of unpainted wood, fit this with rope handles, and deliver it to his bungalow that same evening. The crate arrived on the back of a bullock cart at about seven o'clock. Pugh paid the carpenter, and two orderlies carried the box into the hall. Here Pugh filled it with sand from several fire buckets, and stenciled black block letters on all six sides: *Bullion. Handle with Care.*

The next morning, in uniform, with a revolver at his belt and with two armed military policemen as escort, Pugh saw that this crate was loaded on to the Bombay train. At Victoria Station, Bombay, he ordered four coolies to place it on a luggage trolley, and wheel it to an army truck which he had arranged to be there, through the local SOE office in Bombay.

The crate was heavy and difficult to handle, and the coolies dropped it clumsily as they tried to maneuver it on to the truck. One corner splintered and sand began to pour out. Pugh held his hand over the hole to stop the flow, in case anyone should realize that the crate contained sand and nothing else. Finally, it was heaved into the back of the truck, and a small ring of people who had nothing better to do but watch this performance, heard him give clear instructions in Hindustani to the Indian driver to take the quickest and most direct route to the Goa frontier.

They set off at a great pace, but when Pugh was satisfied they were not being followed, he ordered the driver to drive back towards Marine Drive, a road that ran along the edge of the sea, and up Malabar Hill.

They turned into the gates of a stone house, built in Edwardian days with shutters and turrets and verandahs, a strange mixture of Eastern and Western architecture. This was formerly the home of a successful Parsi doctor, and now housed SOE's Bombay office. The truck was driven into the garage and the doors closed behind it.

Pugh and the two corporals then returned to Meerut by the next train. Three days later, at their regular weekly meeting, Stewart handed Pugh the decoded transcript of a radio message sent in German from the transmitter in Marmagoa harbor.

This reported that the British were openly sending considerable amounts of bullion into Goa for purposes of their own. It requested that funds should be sent as quickly as possible to counteract this enemy money.

Pugh looked around his colleagues at the table.

"I think that proves fairly conclusively, gentlemen, that the Germans *are* operating a spy ring, and information from it *is* going into Goa and out by this transmitter. Any news about Captain Röfer?"

"Nothing good," Fletcher admitted. "Our man made contact, but Röfer was totally unwilling to accept any bribe and would not even discuss the matter."

"I'd do the same in his shoes. What guarantee has he got we won't shoot him as soon as he's beyond the three-mile limit?" asked Stewart.

"We'd keep our side of the bargain," Mackenzie

31

assured him. "But it doesn't seem there is going to be one to keep."

Now Peterson reported on his suggestion to involve Indian communists.

"There is so much coming and going with them, arguing who does what and when, that we will never be able to arrange anything in such a short time," he said. "We will have to abandon that whole idea."

"Couldn't we put a time bomb aboard *Ehrenfels?*" suggested Stewart. "They must buy food and vegetables ashore. We could conceal one in a basket of mangoes or oranges or something of that sort."

"No problem," agreed Pugh. "But more than likely it would explode on deck, and so wouldn't harm the transmitter at all."

"Well, as I've said before," replied Stewart. "If we can't silence the radio, let's deal with the man behind it—Trompeta."

"How, exactly—remembering our orders about not infringing Portuguese neutrality?"

"Pugh and I can go into Goa as two civilians in a car we pick up in Bombay. We find out where Trompeta lives, call on him and bring him out in the back of the car under some blankets. Q.E.D."

"The risk of something going wrong is very high," objected Fletcher. "You'd have no excuse whatever if you were caught. Instead of that, couldn't we lean on the governor of Goa diplomatically? Say we hear that the Germans are insulting Portugal's neutrality by operating a secret transmitter aboard one of their ships, and then *they* would go and get it out?"

"Our consul in Marmagoa has already done that," said Stewart. "He reports that the Portuguese officials were rather offended by this information. They repeated they had removed vital parts of each ship's radio before they allowed the ships to stay. They have no reason to believe the Germans have any other radio."

"Of course they haven't," said Pugh irritably. "They have no equipment to locate it, and even if they had, the Germans are probably paying out hush money."

The five men sat considering the problem. A tonga

rattled along the road outside the window; bells jingled on the pony's harness like a sleigh. The fan creaked and ticked above their heads. Then Mackenzie spoke.

"All right," he said reluctantly. "As Cassio told Iago, 'I'll do it, but it dislikes me.' And I only agree because I can see no other way of solving the problem, except by kidnapping this German.

"But remember, infinitely more hangs on this than just abducting one man. If you two are caught and the real story ever came out, then heaven alone knows the trouble we'll be in, so—take care."

"We will," Pugh assured him. "I suggest Stewart and I meet in Bombay at the Taj, three days from now."

"Why not sooner?"

"Because I must go to Calcutta tonight."

"Calcutta?" repeated Stewart in amazement. "What for?"

"A friend of mine is involved with goodness knows how many companies there. He commands the Calcutta Light Horse, and told me only a few days ago how much he wants to help the war effort. I'll ask him for a letter to say we're in Goa for one of his companies."

"But why go all the way to Calcutta for that? I know half a dozen people in Bombay who'll give us such a letter. Calcutta's nearly a thousand miles from here and 1,500 from Goa."

"Which is why I'm going there," replied Pugh. "Because it is so far away, no one in Goa will be able to check out that letter if we are caught. With me?"

Stewart nodded.

"Let's meet on Thursday morning at noon in the bar of the Taj in Bombay, then. Civilian clothes, ten thousand rupees in cash to buy a second-hand car, and no identification papers. Right?"

So it was agreed.

THREE

Grice sat in the living room of his flat in Ballygunge, a suburb of Calcutta. The open windows overlooked miles of newly cut grass, known as the *maidan,* which presented a peculiar mixture of Indian and British life. Some small rowing boats were out on the ornamental lake, by the banks of which Indian *dhobis,* the washermen, were laundering clothes by beating them on rocks.

White cows, holy to Hindus, walked around the tennis courts, where mixed foursomes were at play. Elsewhere, big wooden cricket screens were set up for a friendly game. An Indian carrying a long pole on his shoulder, with bird cages of parakeets hanging from each end, hopefully hawked his wares to batsmen waiting their turn at the wicket.

Every so often, Grice glanced at his watch and frowned. The time was seven thirty-five. Lewis Pugh had telephoned him at his office that afternoon, and said he would like to see him at his flat at seven-thirty. Grice hated unpunctuality and could not understand why Pugh had been insistent on coming to his flat rather than meeting at the Light Horse club. He had put off a bridge four that evening in order to be at home, because Pugh had insisted that his business was urgent. Now the fellow hadn't even arrived. The evening was hot, and although the windows were wide open, the air felt like warm steam. Two whirring fans, turning this way and that, only stirred it. His wife, Doris, sat in an easy chair opposite him. She was a pleasant-faced woman, younger than her husband. She busied herself with a piece of embroidery on her lap.

34

"You have no idea at all what he wants to see you about, dear?" she asked at last.

"None," replied her husband. "I saw him only a few days ago, in any case. Seems damned odd for him to return to Meerut—and then come all the way back here again. Presumably, it must be *something* important—or at least what he thinks is important."

"I expect it is something to do with his work, dear," said his wife. She liked Pugh, and his cheerful personality, and was sorry he was so seldom in Calcutta. With Mrs. Pugh, they had so often made a foursome for dinner at Firpo's, an Italian restaurant on Chowringhee, Calcutta's most important main street, or for bridge, or a visit to the races. But now the war had changed everything and everyone. She sighed for days that had gone and which, deep down, she doubted would ever come again.

"Where are his wife and daughter?" she asked.

"Oh, in the hills, I expect. Don't really know."

It was the custom for husbands to send wives and young children to the hills in the hot weather. In Simla, in the foothills of the Himalayas, or in Ootacamund, in southwest India, they could avoid, for a few months, the heat of the plains or the humidity of Calcutta. Now some mothers with young children had moved there indefinitely.

Grice glanced at his watch again, and as he did so, their bearer entered, and bowed.

"Colonel Pugh sahib is just now arrived," he announced.

"Show him in, then."

"Sorry I'm late," Pugh apologized as they shook hands. "Had the devil of a job getting a taxi. City seems suddenly full of American troops."

"It is. They are waiting to go on to China, apparently. Bad enough with all the British troops here, and then the West Africans, and now Americans. And the way they've pushed up the prices!"

He poured out a chota peg of whiskey for his visitor.

"I'll leave you two to talk shop," said Doris Grice

35

tactfully. "But be sure to remember me to Wanda if I don't see you before you go."

"I will," Pugh promised. "I've a letter to her I haven't finished. I'll tell her I have seen you."

He waited until they were on their own, then he sat down gratefully, suddenly weary after his long train journey. Through the open window, the cries of street vendors, the incessant hooting of taxis, the ding-a-ling of bicycles and rickshaw bells sounded muted and far away.

"Well?" said Grice, with unconcealed impatience. "What's so important you have to see me here?"

"You told me the other day how you'd like to help the war in any way you can, Bill. I've come to take you up on that, and thought it safer to see you here than at the club. I need a letter on the notepaper of one of your companies to explain that Gavin Stewart and I are your employees. Preferably working for a company that does business with Goa."

"Goa!" Grice paused. "That's not difficult. The Midnapore Zemindary Company are interested in a ground-nut scheme there. I know the managing director well. I'll get a letter from him. But what's it in aid of?"

"I'm sorry, but I can't tell you yet. We need a letter so that if anyone in Goa suspected that Stewart and I were engaging in any nefarious purpose, it could show we were simply innocent traders."

"It would be dangerous—what you plan to do?"

"Yes."

"Then the Midnapore Zemindary Company should be the right one. At least you know the place if there are any questions."

Pugh nodded. He knew that area well. It had been one of his first postings in the Police, an area in Bengal as large as Wales, there they had grown indigo until chemical dyes killed the trade. Life had been generations behind the times. He did not tour his district on horseback, as was usual in country areas, but on a police elephant, with an Indian landowner riding on another elephant as his companion.

They traveled with retinues of servants. When they stopped for the night, their tents dotted the plain like a canvas village.

Another anachronism in Midnapore was the attitude of Indians towards Europeans. In many towns and villages throughout India, some Indians would always salaam a European in the street as a mark of respect. In Midnapore, they went much further. They would squat down at the roadside and put handfuls of earth on top of their bare heads in deference to them.

Midnapore had thrown up a few particles of print in newspapers around the world several years earlier when an Indian Christian priest had discovered two children who had apparently been adopted by wolves. Like Romulus and Remus, they had grown up with wolf clubs, running on all-fours and eating raw meat until he found them and taught them more orthodox habits.

The area had a most unpleasant climate, even worse than Calcutta. Humidity and temperature in the monsoon were generally up around the middle nineties. Fungus, known as Bengal rot, would grow overnight on shoes and leather belts, on bedclothes and sometimes even on human feet. In winter, mosquitoes swarmed in clouds so that Europeans lit little smoking charcoal fires in metal containers under their dinner tables at night to keep them away. If ladies came to dine, some might bring pillowcases with them to put their feet and legs inside, to frustrate the attentions of mosquitoes.

And there was another reason why Pugh remembered Midnapore. It had been the scene of a strange murder, constantly held up to him as a classic example of poor police detection. Years before, one of the company's employees, George Yonge, had quarreled with a colleague, Richard Aimes, who was never seen again. Rumors persisted that Yonge had murdered Aimes with the help of several Indians, and finally Yonge was brought to trial. But no body could be found, and although police opened a newly made

grave, they reported that it only contained the putre-
fying remains of a cart horse, so Yonge was released.
⟶ Many years later, long after Yonge's own death,
an old Indian confessed that he and several friends
had indeed helped Yonge to kill Aimes. Then they
disemboweled a dead horse and sewed up Aimes's
body inside the carcass, concealing the man within
the beast in the same giant grave.

"Don't worry about Aimes," Grice advised Pugh
drily, guessing his thoughts. "Concentrate on the
fellow who got off. I'll give you a letter tomorrow
morning that will get you off anything."

"Thanks, Bill. One day I'll tell you what it's all
about."

The night moths beat powdery fluttering wings
against the electric light bulbs, as the two men sat,
suddenly awkward.

"Is that all we in the Light Horse can do for you,
Lewis?" Grice asked in disappointment.

"For the moment," admitted Pugh. "Now, if you'll
excuse me."

"Do you mean to say you have come all the way
here from Meerut just for one letter?"

"It's that important," said Pugh simply. "Now I
must go."

Both men stood up. The bearer materialized in his
silent, well-trained way and showed Pugh out of the
front door.

Grice crossed to the window and watched him walk
through the garden of the block of flats to the main
road. A taxi was waiting for him. Its taillights disappeared towards the glow that hung like a strange am-
ber miasma above Calcutta, the second largest city
in the British Empire. Grice stood for a moment,
sipping his whiskey. He had hoped for some more active involvement in whatever Pugh and Stewart
were planning than simply to provide a forged letter,
for a purpose he was not even allowed to learn.

It seemed ironic that while some younger men he
knew were willing to be medically downgraded or
registered as being in essential jobs, to avoid active

service, he and his friends in the Calcutta Light Horse, many much older than those who set such store by their own safety, would give anything for action, and yet were denied the opportunity.

Perhaps it was that the Calcutta Light Horse's name was associated more with sporting and social activities than military prowess? They were, of course, keen on horses—India was sometimes called the Kingdom of the Horse. Perhaps that damned and dated them. The world had passed on to the age of the tank and the aircraft. In doing so, had it also left them impossibly far behind?

Grice recalled the 1930s, when social life in Calcutta appeared to be one long party; when a man could keep a horse for 30 odd rupees a month, with the wages of a full-time groom even less. Then, even a modest household would employ several servants— a cook, cook's boy, bearer, underbearer, an *ayah* if there were children, and one or two *malis* if they had a garden. Then they would need a driver for their car, and a groom for the horses.

So many memories concerned horses and their riders. The regiment had provided a traditional mounted escort for the viceroy, their honorary colonel, on the annual Proclamation Parade each New Year's Day. Here, the sovereign was solemnly proclaimed King Emperor of India, and the viceroy took the salute from 25-pounder guns and a *feu de joie* by a British infantry regiment.

By tradition, the Light Horse always led this parade, and occupied the right of the line, second only to the guns. This particular parade was compulsory for all members and their registered chargers. Any horse known to be temperamental—usually a former racehorse or a part-time racehorse—was put in the rear ranks. Oddly, these animals ignored the 25-pounders, but at the rattle of rifle fire some would invariably whip around and bolt. Tramlines were dangerously near, and the riders had to throw away their swords to take a two-handed pull on the reins. So many swords were disposed of in this way that a sword-picker-upper was posted to collect them. Once, he inexplicably found one more sword than there were scabbards.

Grice remembered Corporal Bill Manners, a businessman by profession and a rider by birth and inclination. Up in the lead on a paperchase one early morning, Manners had taken a heavy fall, and Grice and two others found him lying face down in the mud.

They rolled him over and were horrified to discover that he had lost an eye. Carefully, they covered the empty muddy socket with a handkerchief, and Grice waited by Manners' side, while his friends rode off frantically to fetch a doctor. Soon, Manners regained consciousness, brushed the handkerchief away and asked what had happened to his horse, which had wandered off.

"Never mind your horse," said Grice in a hushed voice. "What about your eye?"

"What about it?" asked Manners casually. "Don't you know, I *always* take it out when I'm paperchasing—in case I lose it?"

And he produced a glass eye from his jacket pocket. He explained he had lost the real one years before, when he was hit in the face during a school hockey match.

Then there was Jack Breene, an accountant, who was unexpectedly posted up-country from Calcutta and needed a reliable horse. He wrote to an Australian horse-coper of his acquaintance in Calcutta, enclosing a check for 500 rupees, and asked him to send the best available horse for that price by rail, as soon as possible.

The horse-coper decided that this was an unexpected opportunity to be rid of an ailing animal, for Breene was so far away it seemed unlikely they would ever meet again. The horse had convulsions and died as the coper's men pushed it into a horse box at Howrah Station in Calcutta. The coper cashed Breene's check and quickly put the matter from his mind.

Next spring, he unexpectedly ran into Breene in the bar of Calcutta Racecourse, and after some small talk, asked casually how Breene had found the horse.

"It was dead on arrival," Breene told him. The horse-coper looked sympathetic.

"Very nasty loss for you," he said.

"Matter of fact, it wasn't. I raffled the horse in the club for 10 rupees a ticket. Actually made 750 rupees on it."

"But what about the fellow who won a dead horse?"

"Oh, he was all right. *I gave him back his 10 rupees.*"

Mrs. Grice came into the room.

"Has Lewis gone?" she asked. "I didn't hear him leave."

"He had a taxi waiting."

She sat down and began work again on her embroidery.

"I was just thinking about some of the fellows in the Calcutta Light Horse," said her husband. "Seeing Lewis again brought back some memories."

"Harry Squire's the one who always made me smile," said his wife. "How he got the zoo out of debt."

Squire was a merchant with an interest in nature and had devised a most successful means of raising money for Calcutta zoo, when it was in financial trouble. Many Bengali men in middle-age believed that rhino urine possessed unique aphrodisiac qualities. A considerable trade was done in this commodity between East Africa and Calcutta before the war, and the retail rate was one rupee for a small bottle.

But some potential Bengali customers questioned the purity of the African product, so Squire persuaded the zoo keepers to train their rhinos, through the judicious use of carrots and bits of sugar cane, to urinate at the strike of a gong, and in a bucket rather than haphazardly in their pool. He then provided a metal rail near the rhino enclosure, where clients

41

could lean while they satisfied themselves that no adulteration took place between production and its bottling.

So popular was this aphrodisiac in Calcutta that it was soon producing an annual income of thousands of rupees, which helped to rescue the zoo from its debts.

Squire was a character; his wife was right.

But then all the Light Horsemen were characters, individuals, originals—and all volunteers, as they had been from 1759 when Robert Clive, the first British Governor-General, formed the Volunteer Cavalry from which the Light Horse claim descent.

Clive had hurriedly enlisted local merchants and other Europeans in Calcutta to help repel an invasion by 700 Dutch troops with 800 Malayan mercenaries on the then new settlement. The Dutch and Malays sailed up the Hooghly in seven large ships, landed by sheer weight of numbers, and began to advance steadily on Calcutta.

Clive concealed his men behind a ravine, a *nullah,* and as the invaders paused, wondering how best to cross this, the Volunteer Cavalry charged them on their horses. Dutch and Malays fled in surprise and confusion.

The Calcutta merchants had greatly relished this taste of the military life, and kept the association alive through successive units—The Mounted Company of the Calcutta Volunteer Rifle Corps, the Calcutta Volunteer Guards, the Calcutta Volunteer Lancers, and finally, the Calcutta Light Horse.

Clive, so Grice recalled, described that first action laconically in a report to his superiors in London as "short, bloody and decisive." Now, in Grice's opinion, this war was long, bloody and indecisive, and he longed to take a fighting part.

On the Sunday war had been declared, the whole regiment had gathered in the clubhouse in what for many would be their last full parade. Grice remembered the general feeling that the gaiety and the fun and the often schoolboy humor of the thirties were now all passing. No one quite knew what the future held, except that it would be—must be—different.

To recall that parade was like looking through the wrong end of a telescope, to see good times diminished, along with unnumbered companions whose names you did not mention any more, for they had also gone, along with the sound of laughter, and the warmth of friendship.

Every man in the Light Horse had volunteered for active service, and many had left Calcutta within weeks. Now they were scattered in units of all kinds across Burma and North Africa, in Iraq and India. Only those too old or too important to their firms, or considered unfit by their doctors, remained in Calcutta.

"You're very quiet, dear," his wife said. "Is everything all right?"

"Yes, thank you. It's only . . ."

"It's only what, dear?"

She had not been married to him for so long not to recognize the wistful tone in her husband's voice.

"Oh, nothing, really. Nothing at all. Shall we go in to dinner?"

But it was not nothing; it was everything. It was feeling unwanted, being thought too old for action. (How ironic now to recall that, in the First World War, they had said he was too young!) It was feeling that the real mainstream of events was passing him by, passing them all by. They were spectating, and not taking part. But he could not dress these thoughts with words. He had been prepared to offer all he could—and what had been asked of him was to put a name on a letter of lies!

In silence, Grice followed his wife into the dining room.

FOUR

Pugh and Stewart were driving in a second-hand Ford V8 station wagon along the dusty road that led to the frontier between India and Goa.

They had met at the Taj as agreed, bought the car that same afternoon, and immediately had it resprayed beige. This was a neutral color, much used by civilian Indian army contractors, who supplied police and army units with food and tents, and so was unlikely to attract attention.

They drove from Bombay to Belgaum, the nearest town in India of any size on the road to Goa, and stopped there for the night. Belgaum was like most other small towns in India with a considerable military and official community, who lived in what was known as the cantonment; an area of rambling bungalows with large gardens and well-kept lawns. Near this lay the city, a welter of narrow streets lined with open-fronted shops.

Belgaum was also the headquarters of a distinguished Indian Army regiment, the Fifth Mahrattas, and a more recently established Officers' Training School. Many towns the size of Belgaum had one hotel, with permanent and elderly European guests who regulated their lives with manners and customs long outdated in Europe. These hotels were often called Brown's or White's or Pink's, or in the case of Belgaum, Green's. Pugh had often thought it odd that so many seemed to be named after colors—or were these the names of their original owners?

Pugh knew the Belgaum superintendent of police from pre-war days and so paid him a courtesy call to explain that he and Stewart were on their way to Goa on a secret mission. He thought it advisable to do this

44

in case anything went wrong and they needed police help urgently. Pugh also asked the superintendent whether he could provide a cell or some other safe place where they might hold a prisoner from public view, until he could be transported to Bombay for interrogation.

The superintendent had no wish to involve himself in military matters. He had enough trouble already dealing with sympathizers of the Congress Party who were strongly against helping the Allies in any way unless India was guaranteed immediate independence. He referred Pugh to the local military army commander, a colonel who had only recently been brought out of retirement.

"What can I do for you?" this colonel asked them crossly, with the air of one who intended to do as little as he possibly could.

Pugh produced two civilian identity cards bearing the false names under which they were traveling.

"My colleague and I are actually in the army, sir," he explained. "We are attached to the Ministry of Economic Warfare in Meerut. My real name is Lewis Pugh, and this is Gavin Stewart. I am a lieutenant colonel and my colleague is a captain. We would like your help on a most delicate matter."

"What is it? Why are you here on forged identity cards if you are in the army?"

"We are on a secret mission, sir. I regret I can tell you no more than that. We need a room where we can hold a prisoner for a day or maybe two until we can move him to Bombay for interrogation."

"What sort of prisoner?"

"I cannot be specific, sir. But I can say he is a very important person, and a dangerous man, who has been actively working against the Allies. He is not British, of course."

"Hmm!"

The colonel had spent a quarter of a century in India without ever seeing any active service, and to him the words "not British" meant only one thing. The man must be an Indian.

Now the only Indians who seemed dangerous to

him, and who had been actively working against the Allies were politicians—Congress wallahs, as he called them contemptuously. He had had some experience already of involving troops in what the Army manual quaintly called "assisting the civil power," and he wanted no more of it.

This meant riots, Europeans being stoned, thousands of screaming hysterical youths, rampaging about, tearing up paving stones and smashing windows, while others lay down in the roads to impede the traffic. The colonel felt he could live without any more of this kind of behavior.

"What's wrong with the guardroom?" he asked. This was where soldiers, awaiting sentence for minor charges of being drunk or absent for a day without leave, would await a hearing.

"Too public, sir."

"Who is this prisoner who must be kept out of sight?"

"I cannot reveal his identity, sir."

The colonel considered this reply.

Mahatma Gandhi, the Indian Congress leader, was conducting one of his regular and well-publicized fasts against cooperating with the British authorities. Gandhi was fasting in the Aga Khan's palace outside Poona, about 180 miles to the north. Every morning, newspapers carried long bulletins about his condition, with medical and political estimates of his chances of success—and even of his survival.

What if this prisoner was Gandhi? This would provoke riots and disturbances on a prodigious scale, and the colonel would be in the center of it all, with no hope of anything but criticism, perhaps even disgrace. This prospect was totally without attraction to him, and he considered its implications for some time before he replied.

"I will inform you of my decision," he said at last. "Where are you staying?"

"Green's Hotel, sir."

The colonel nodded to show that the interview was over, and Pugh and Stewart returned to their hotel.

As soon as they were out of the colonel's office he telephoned, not the local police superintendent or SOE in Bombay, but Lieutenant General Sir Noel Monson de la Poer Beresford-Peirse, the General Officer Commanding-in-Chief, Southern Army, at his headquarters, to ask whether he had ever heard of a Lieutenant Colonel Pugh.

Beresford-Peirse, known by the nickname "BI," had also only recently assumed command and so was equally unwilling to become embroiled in a political situation which looked potentially disastrous.

"Of course, I know *an* officer named Pugh," Beresford-Peirse told the brigadier. "We both went to Wellington and Woolwich—although not at the same time. And he served under me when I commanded 15 Corps. But how the devil do I know if *this* fellow's Pugh or not? What's he look like?"

"Medium height, sir. Very fit, quietly spoken. With a very tall man. Name of Stewart. Captain Stewart. They say they are attached to the Ministry of Economic Warfare in Meerut, but they have forged civilian cards in other names."

"Sounds fishy to me. Forged cards. False names. Important prisoner."

The possibility that this might be Gandhi also crossed the General's mind. The whole thing seemed like an attempt on the part of the political people to involve the military by back door means. Well, he could play at that game, too.

"Arrest the buggers until you can check their stories," ordered Beresford-Peirse shortly. "We can't take any political risk, not with the state India's in at the moment."

The colonel in Belgaum therefore telephoned to the local superintendent of police, and asked for Pugh and Stewart to be arrested at Green's Hotel as discreetly as possible.

At midnight, they were awakened by a subdued tapping on their bedroom door. An Indian police inspector in plain clothes was standing in the corridor. He apologized for calling at such a late hour, and explained that the superintendent could delay the

47

arrests until about three o'clock in the morning because he required a magistrate's signature on the warrant.

"So you are really giving us three hours' start?" asked Pugh.

"That is an interpretation the superintendent hoped you might put on the situation," the inspector agreed gravely.

They packed hastily, ordered hard-boiled eggs to eat on the way, paid their bill, and by three o'clock were 100 miles nearer to Goa. The road was empty except for a few unlit bullock carts, drivers crouched asleep over the shafts. Once, near the border, they overtook a country bus, one of the regular service from Belgaum to Goa.

At the border, they showed the letter from the Midnapore Zemindary Company to a yawning immigration official and without even leaving his hut he ordered the guard to lift the barrier. A few miles inside Goa, they stopped in a clearing in the palm forest for a wash before they entered Panjim, the capital. Like most motorists on a long journey in India, they carried a canvas *chagal* of water tied to one door of the car. This container was in the shape of a hot water bottle, and since canvas is slightly porous, the water inside kept cool.

They each drank a glass of water, washed and shaved in a canvas bucket, ate their hard-boiled eggs and then walked about the dusty patch to stretch their legs. Then they placed the egg shells on the ground to mark the walls of an imaginary room with a door, and rehearsed what they would do when they entered Trompeta's house. Some other people might be with him and there could be a struggle, so they wanted to be sure that their movements were coordinated.

They had brought hypodermic syringes with them and glass phials of pentothal to keep Trompeta drowsy during the drive back, and also two small incendiary devices of the sort that SOE supplied to Resistance Groups in France. These were no larger than

48

fountain pens, but could be set with a timing device to erupt with phosphorescent fury. If things went wrong at Trompeta's house, this diversion should give them the chance to escape.

As they climbed back into their car to set off on the last stage of their journey, the Indian country bus they had overtaken on the Belgaum road turned into the clearing, and stopped.

It had a locally built wooden body on an old Chevrolet chassis, painted bright red with green and yellow designs of peacocks and tigers' heads. The roof rack was crammed with black tin trunks secured by ropes, and big wicker baskets that contained live hens clucking indignantly. The passengers, all men, some in *dhotis*, others in crumpled cotton shirts and trousers, filed out of the rear door and walked stiff-legged towards the trees.

Ram das Gupta, conscious that he must be the only passenger in the bus who had been to a university, alone remained in his seat. As a university man, he preferred to wait until he had reached the privacy of his hotel in Panjim before he relieved himself. He had not, in fact, actually taken a degree at the university, but at least he had completed the course, and this he commemorated by having visiting cards printed: Ram das Gupta, B.A. "Plucked" Aligarh University. After all, what did three hours of missed examinations matter against three years of study?

He sat on the hard wooden seat, with chickens clucking inches above his head, beyond the thin metal of the roof. Flies buzzed in the still morning air, warming their wings for a hot day ahead. Ram das Gupta, at 24 years old, a thin-faced man with a disappointed downward curve to his mouth, and a cultivated sense of his own importance, was also ready for what the day might bring.

He was a Hindu, and had left university in disgrace after a Moslem invigilator, whose old father had recently been badly injured in a Hindu riot, reported him for copying another candidate's answers in an examination. Ram das Gupta had not helped his chances by accusing the invigilator of religious bias, and after further acrimonious exchanges, he had been asked to leave the university.

Ram das Gupta's parents had both been humiliated at this, because to have a son at Aligarh was something of which they were extremely proud. To save them (and himself) further shame, Ram das Gupta left Aligarh, a large town 40 miles from Agra, and went as far away as a train would carry him, to Bombay. Here, a relation grudgingly helped him to find a post as a clerk in a hotel, and then he heard of a vacancy as a clerk in a shipping firm, with the promise of prospects. Somehow the promise did not become performance, and as these prospects refused to materialize, his own inner discontent grew.

The work was boring and repetitive, and Ram das Gupta felt convinced that many of his superiors only owned their positions to the fact that they were British. He also resented Indians giving him instructions simply because they were graduates, and he was not. His talents and abilities were unrecognized and ignored, and gradually he found some comfort and an expression of his bitterness in political activity and agitation, and especially in civil disobedience marches and demonstrations.

At Aligarh, Ram das Gupta had admired many of his student contemporaries who had thrown stones at tram cars and refused to speak English or wear European clothes as a gesture of protest at British involvement in India.

One of their heroes had been Subhas Chandra Bose, a former mayor of Calcutta, educated at Cambridge, who proclaimed himself to be the deliverer of the Bengali nation from European bondage. The authorities imprisoned Bose for his anti-war activities, and the strikes and demonstrations he organized, but then had released him on parole in 1941.

Bose immediately broke his parole and, although he was, of course, Hindu, he disguised himself as a Moslem holy man and fled to Kabul in Afghanistan. Communist agents contacted him and arranged for him to travel to Moscow, but the Russians were not then in the war, and Bose traveled on to Rome and Berlin. Mussolini and Hitler both received him, and Hitler ordered that he should have every assistance to form what Bose called an Indian Legion, from Indian Army soldiers captured in North Africa.

Bose declared that he would lead this legion alongside German forces as they advanced into Russia, and then branch south through Afghanistan and into India. Bose made regular radio broadcasts from Germany to India about his intentions, and greatly impressed Ram das Gupta, along with many others of his age and background.

About this time, Ram das Gupta was also impressed by a middle-aged Indian woman he met who allowed him to listen to Bose's broadcasts on her own radio, which could pick up short wave transmissions, and who also had a great deal of literature—pamphlets, books, papers—about Bose and his work for India and against the British. More, she claimed she actually knew Netaji, the leader, as she called him, and spoke so much about him that Ram das Gupta soon felt a great wish to help the aims of such a noble patriot, who, like himself, had suffered unfair discrimination in his youth.

Unexpected Russian resistance to the German invasion then caused Bose to change his plans, and this woman told Gupta he was traveling out to Singapore in a German U-boat. With an Indian National Army raised from other Indian prisoners of war captured when Singapore fell, Bose would then march on Delhi from Burma, and lead his country to freedom. Would Ram das Gupta not like to help Netaji—and so India—in any way he could?

Of course, replied Ram das Gupta instantly, for freedom was the most emotive word in any language in India, with as many different meanings as mouths to utter it.

To Ram das Gupta, freedom meant release from a dull and depressing job and the chance to face his parents, not as a failure but a success. The woman assured him that those who helped Netaji in his struggle would be well rewarded—once the struggle was over. And she explained that Ram das Gupta could best help Netaji (and India) by supplying details he learned in his work about ships, their ports of arrival and departure, their crews and speeds and cargoes.

He accepted this task willingly enough—for was he not helping his country?—and he was paid for each item he supplied. Soon, he was meeting others who supplied information from docks, the customs, and rival shipping offices. With each assignment, his payments grew, and so did his self-esteem.

Then one morning, when he went, as usual, to the room the woman rented near Victoria Station in Bombay, an Indian man he had never met was there, very agitated and nervous, lighting one cigarette from the stub of another. This man's forehead shone with fright, and in seeing his terror, Ram das Gupta also felt fingers of fear tighten around his own heart.

"They've got her," the man told him brusquely.

"Who?"

"The police."

"Do they know about us?"

"I don't think so—yet. But some of us are going to lie low for a bit. You will have to do more. You will collect material as before, but now you will also take it to this address. Café Pescadores, Panjim, Goa, Don't write it down, remember it. Someone will make himself known to you there."

For the first time since he had become involved, Ram das Gupta felt reluctant to continue. It had been exciting to work with the woman, to feel he was a cog in a gear train working for his country's freedom, but not if this meant the loss of his own freedom. Yet this was no time to back out. He must go on, to be worthy of the woman's sacrifice, of Netaji, of India. He did not think of asking this stranger why he should do more if others felt it safer to do less.

"Tell your firm you are ill," the man went on. "Then meet your contact at six o'clock tonight at the Hindu crematorium, and catch the evening bus to Goa."

The crematorium was near the sea, surrounded by a concrete wall. A strong smell of burning and scented wood hung for a hundred yards around it. On the left of the wide entrance was a store packed with logs five feet long, and a giant set of scales. Every body to be burned was first balanced against logs to discover how many would be required to consume it.

The place of burning lay to the right, in the open, with green metal benches where mourners could watch and beggars could sleep. The bodies were wrapped in rush mats and laid on metal grids, made from lengths of railway line, bolted together. Attendants piled logs on them. They burned until only ash remained.

Ram das Gupta joined a crowd of people waiting and weeping by several slowly burning bodies. An older man put his arm sympathetically round his shoulders.

"Very sad, he died so young," he said. "But he left these for you."

The man handed an envelope to him—and then was gone up a side alley between stalls of silversmiths and woodcarvers. Gupta buttoned the envelope in an inside pocket, and took a tonga to the bus station.

He had made the journey to Panjim 11 times since then, and the shipping office, after complaining of his continual absences, and inexplicable illnesses, had finally dismissed him. Gupta did not feel greatly concerned; this other work was far more important, and routine had dulled his sense of danger. He would travel to Panjim, stay in an Indian hotel near the river, and at nine o'clock in the morning go to the Café Pescadores for tea and Indian sweetmeats. A European, who spoke English, but who was obviously not English, would sometimes join him. At other times this man would walk past the café, and Gupta would get up and follow him. An envelope changed hands and Gupta would catch the evening bus back to Bombay. The routine, accomplished so frequently, seemed completely safe and secure.

And so it would be this morning and every morning until his country was free and independent. Until the British, the Americans and all the other imperialists who now swarmed over it, fighting their own war on its frontiers, would be driven back over the seas. Until, indeed, Ram das Gupta, and millions like him, would come into their rightful place as the rulers, and not the ruled.

The British consul in Goa, a retired Indian Army colonel, had an office near the Burmah Shell oil storage plant in Marmagoa docks. He was of military appearance (he had won the Military Cross in the First World War) and gray-haired, with a neatly trimmed moustache. He stood up behind his desk to receive Pugh and Stewart. Beyond his office window loomed huge circular oil tanks painted silver against the heat. Some Goanese workmen in blue overalls and pith solar topees were tightening a valve on an oil pipe, thick as a man's thigh, that led down to the docks. A tanker was due to discharge.

"What can I do for you, gentlemen?" the Consul asked in his quiet voice. Pugh showed him Grice's letter about the Midnapore Zemindary Company. The consul handed it back without comment and looked at them enquiringly.

Pugh mentioned Trompeta's real name.

"We would like to know where he lives."

The consul looked at Pugh sharply.

"He has nothing to do with the Midnapore Zemindary Company, surely?" he asked drily.

"No. Our business with him is of a more—ah—personal nature."

"I see."

The consul did not ask any more questions in case one of his clerks, who he knew eavesdropped on most of his visitors, heard what he said. He put a finger to his lips and inclined his head towards the door. Pugh understood the gesture, one widely used in India when dealing with confidential matters that could interest others not officially concerned. The consul wrote down an address and directions for finding it on a sheet of paper. Pugh put this in his pocket.

"Do you anticipate any difficulty, gentlemen?"

"You will not be involved if there is," Pugh assured him.

"Can I help in any other way?" the consul went on hopefully, in the same tones Grice had used in Calcutta.

"We'll be in touch if you can," replied Pugh, and they shook hands. Pugh and Stewart went out into the heat of the day. A strong smell of oil lay heavy on the air and all shadows had shrunk, for the sun blazed directly overhead. They had lunch and then strolled along the waterfront, and looked at the four ships anchored in the harbor.

It was dusk when they returned to their hotel in Panjim. After dinner, they sat on the verandah watching small boats go busily up and down the river. A gramophone was playing in the next bedroom. The record slowed as the clockwork motor ran down. Then it was quickly wound up, and the song came through their wall clearly: "South of the border, down Mexico way."

Pugh and Stewart raised their glasses of Portuguese brandy in a silent toast. Each hoped that by the same time on the following evening, they would be safely north of the border with their prisoner.

FIVE

Trompeta was a tough, broad-shouldered, stockily built man in his early forties, with the sort of build that can easily put on weight. He had kept his figure, despite years in a hot climate, by taking regular exercises and long walks. Trompeta's clear blue eyes showed that he did not drink or smoke, and he wore his straw-colored hair very short because, in an alien land, he was proud of his nationality, and had no wish to be taken for a renegade American or an Englishman.

He stepped smartly out of the primitive shower in the stone-flagged bathroom of his bungalow in Panjim. A lizard moved a little distance down the wall and watched him. Trompeta flicked his towel at it, as the reptile's tongue flickered insolently at him in its tiny dragon head.

Every morning he saw that lizard. Or was it a different one? Captain Röfer had told him how some of the cooks aboard *Ehrenfels* had painted cockroaches red and green and blue to resolve an argument about whether the same ones kept appearing every evening in the galley. Perhaps he should paint this lizard? He toweled himself vigorously, dressed, and walked into the front room. This overlooked the narrow street outside and was small and overfurnished. Four cane chairs crowded around a table covered by a square of vivid blue patterned oilcloth. A cactus poked rubbery leaves from an earthenware pot on a wooden stand. Brightly colored prints of saints with fuzzy haloes hung on the walls, with a portrait of the 15th-century Portuguese national hero, Dom Henrique O Navegador, Henry the Navigator, who had devoted his life to fostering maritime expeditions and the art of accurate navigation.

Trompeta's wife was already sitting at the table. She was slightly older than Trompeta, and her skin was sallow and greasy after too many years in the East. She was crumbling a roll nervously in her left hand, a sign she felt uneasy about something.

"The bearer says Captain Röfer sent a messenger to see you last night," she told her husband as he sat down. "He is most eager to talk with you."

"I will see him this morning," Trompeta promised. Then he remembered he had an appointment with an Indian courier from Bombay at the Café Pescadores. Well, the Indian would have to wait; Röfer was the more important.

Trompeta had no telephone in the bungalow, and he and Röfer therefore always conducted their business face to face, *unter vier Augen*—four eyes only —in the German expression, and usually in Röfer's cabin.

Röfer was a dedicated sea captain, a disciplinarian who had disliked but unquestioningly obeyed the unexpected orders that had forced him to rush from Calcutta and seek shelter in a hot and humid harbor, although he was personally convinced that his ship's speed could have guaranteed her safe passage to a friendly port.

Although Röfer guessed that Trompeta was engaged in intelligence work, he did not know how successful and important this was. Trompeta was, in fact, one of Germany's two most important and successful spy masters in the East. The other was Richard Sorge, in Tokyo, where he was ostensibly a correspondent for the influential German newspapers, *Frankfurter Zeitung*. Both men had worked there together before Trompeta had orders to leave for Batavia and Calcutta, and finally, Goa.

When war had been declared, several other German citizens had raced across India to Goa by train and car, eager to escape internment. They had brought Indian currency and diamonds with them, which could in extremity be exchanged for cash. Trompeta had sufficient funds to live in Panjim indefinitely, and other amounts arrived regularly from Lisbon, addressed to a Portuguese trader in the town.

Only one other man in Goa knew Trompeta's real importance. This was Fritz Pöller, who appeared on *Ehrenfels'* manifest as first officer. He was actually rather more important to Trompeta's activities, for while all German seagoing naval officers were trained radio operators, Pöller was also a skilled radio engineer. In addition, he decoded radio messages for Trompeta, and was proud of the fact that he spoke seven languages. He had learned Portuguese since he had been in Marmagoa.

Trompeta poured himself a cup of coffee and glanced out at the street, bright in the early sunshine. A queue of people had already gathered outside the Portuguese merceria, the grocery shop nearby. On the far side of the road, the Goanese owner of the Photo Art Studio was taking down metal shutters from his shop front. Advertisements in his window for Agfa film always reminded Trompeta of home.

Fifty yards away down the hill, over a crossroads, stood the gray and white church of Mary of the Immaculate Conception. The silver bell on the roof was already booming the hour. Or was it being rung to mark the death of another believer from typhoid or cholera? The colony's slothful administration offended Trompeta's neat and tidy mind. Carcasses of dead cows and pigs would be left to lie in the streets until they exploded with putrefaction. Disease was accepted as a necessary scourge of the Almighty, and Goa still had no adequate water supply for washing or drinking. In the hot weather, a mug of water could cost two annas—a vast price, for with 16 annas making up each rupee, a Goanese laborer might only earn 35 rupees for a whole month's work. But when the monsoon came, and rain lashed down, streets became roaring rivers. Last year, rain had actually washed away the roof of another church.

At the crossroads, a Goanese traffic policeman

stood beneath a square metal sunshade which incongruously bore the exhortation in English: *Life is short. Don't make it shorter.* Trompeta, as a professional spy, was in full agreement with this advice. He had carefully chosen his bungalow because it was in the safest place he could find—near this crossroads, where a policeman was on duty during daylight, close to shops which stayed open until after dark, and within sight of Panjim's finest church.

Trompeta calculated that any enemy attempt to kill him or kidnap him would be too dangerous to make in daylight because of so many possible witnesses. And after dark he always closed thick wooden shutters across each window and padlocked them. The bungalow was built into the side of a hill, so attack from the rear was virtually impossible.

After breakfast, Trompeta took out his little car from the garage he rented and drove down to the ferry. Tonga ponies stood, heads down, eating hay piled on the ground near a whitewashed balustrade on the river bank. Several balusters were broken and had never been replaced; these gaps seemed like teeth missing from an old man's smile.

A cannon barrel upended in the pavement served as a mooring bollard. The smells of petrol, exhaust fumes and salty river mud made him wrinkle his nose in distaste. The cries of sweetmeat sellers and the honking horns of country buses followed him as the ferry put out into the oily river. Trompeta's was the only car it carried.

On the far bank, Trompeta drove past paddy fields, where pools of water blazed like mirrors. The road was built up with a ditch on either side, and then palm forests stretched into a green infinity. Houses with verandahs and elaborate staircases stood defiantly in small clearings with crosses beside them as though daring the jungle to overgrow them. Rust had eaten away corrugated iron roofs, and time mellowed and muted the violent colors the Goanese liked; green walls, vermilion doors, bright yellow gates.

Trompeta parked near the harbor, where local fishing boats with two masts bent forward at a sharp angle towards the bows, instead of leaning back to the stern, lay anchored in pairs. Stinking strips of fish dried in the sun on a patch of waste ground. Stray dogs snapped and snarled at each other, and hogs rooted for food among piles of rubbish.

The lookout aboard *Ehrenfels* had seen Trompeta's car, and two sailors were already rowing ashore to pick him up. The four ships were anchored about 150 yards apart at the mouth of the Zuari River, their bows pointing out to sea. *Drachenfels* lay closest to the land. Her commander, Captain Schmidt, had spent several months in various hospitals in Goa suffering from chronic dysentery, and it was convenient for him to be near the shore, since he was still being treated by a Portuguese doctor in the port. This physician had recommended a new course of drugs and injections, which had produced the unfortunate side effect of paralyzing the captain's left leg.

Behind *Drachenfels*, farther up the river, lay the Italian *Anfora*. Next to her was *Ehrenfels*, with *Braunfels* in midstream. As they rowed past *Anfora*, Trompeta heard the grunt and squeal of pigs aboard her. The Italians had cleared one of her decks and had laid out a garden, with small trees and shrubs in wooden boxes, and a lattice for creepers. They were rearing pigs on swill from the galley.

Part of this deck was shaded by slatted bamboo screens, and an Italian officer, stripped to the waist, sat at a table, glass in his hand, a bottle of Chianti already open in front of him. This was part of the ship's cargo, which the crew had broached on the excuse that the wine would not keep in the excessive heat and should be drunk, rather than be allowed to go sour. The officer raised his glass in a silent salute as Trompeta's boat went past.

Ehrenfels' hull loomed ahead like a solid tarred wall, scored and streaked with rust. One of the bilge pumps was working. Frothy seawater spewed from a hole in her side. The crew had painted out the German red and white and black markings on her funnel, but the paintwork on her white decks and superstructure was kept in good condition. Trompeta heard the scrape and rasp of chisels as sailors in ragged shorts, with sweat rags tied around their necks, scratched at rusty patches, to prepare them for re-painting. Captain Röfer ran a tidy ship, and believed that constant maintenance was necessary in the hot, humid climate, and an essential discipline for crews cooped up indefinitely.

Röfer was in his cabin, examining a stamp collection which he had started years ago. He knew that the British consul also collected stamps and would have liked to discuss the subject with him, but of course that was out of the question. Röfer was proud of his albums. At different ports of call during his career it had been his habit to address envelopes to himself at his home in Germany, for the sake of the stamps.

Since he had been in Marmagoa, he had only received three letters from home, all through Lisbon. Some of his crew had not even received one. A framed photograph of Hitler in uniform looked down from the white wall of the cabin, as he greeted Trompeta.

"I am glad you have come to see me so quickly," Röfer began. "I have to report something important. The British have sent an envoy here to offer me money to slip anchor and surrender to them outside the three-mile limit. Twenty thousand pounds sterling."

"You refused, of course?"

"Of course. So the man increased it. Thirty thousand pounds sterling. Just like that. And I had the strong impression he would go even higher."

"Was he English?"

"No. Indian. But he spoke good German."

"Did he say why they wanted the ship?"

"He admitted they are very short of merchant ships."

Trompeta nodded, but he guessed the real reason why the enemy wanted *Ehrenfels*, and the thought was like a stone in his stomach.

"I would like to see this go-between if he ever comes back, Captain."

61

"The difficulty is contacting you quickly in Panjim. Could you not move aboard here for a few days? We have a spare cabin."

"I would like to, Captain. But if I did, I might miss appointments with other people I have arranged to meet in Panjim."

"Well, if you do change your mind, just arrive."

"Thank you."

Trompeta went below decks, through the engine room, with its peculiar smell of warm oil and polished metal, and tapped a rat-tat-rat-tat on a gray painted steel door. On the outside was painted a red skull and crossbones with the information: "Danger of Death. High Voltage." This was to discourage curiosity from the crew as to what might be beyond the door which Pöller opened from inside and closed it quickly behind Trompeta.

Down here in the heart of the ship the only ventilation came from an electric fan drawing air through louvers cut in the metal, and Pöller was sweating heavily. Red pimples of heat rash prickled his damp, pale shoulders. He was a large, plump man wearing a singlet and faded cotton trousers. On a shelf under the radio controls were stacked code books with heavy lead covers, so they would sink instantly if thrown overboard in an emergency. The lead shone like pewter, through almost constant handling.

Pöller handed two decoded signals to Trompeta. They reported four successful sinkings. Two were on November 28, and two more on November 30. Trompeta checked the signals he had sent regarding the movements of certain ships, and calculated that these casualties must be the British *Nova Scotia* and *Llandaff Castle* of 6,796 tons and 10,799 tons, and two small Greek freighters, *Evanthia* and *Cleanthis*.

"I should have more for you to send tomorrow or the next day," Trompeta promised Pöller, thinking about his meeting with Ram das Gupta. Pöller nodded; he was a man of few words. Trompeta went up on deck, thankful to be out in the open air. Röfer followed him to the boarding ladder.

"If you change your mind . . ." he said.

"Thank you."

Trompeta and his wife had built a small hut on the beach near Marmagoa, from pieces of packing cases, with a long bench seat inside. Now Trompeta drove to this hut before he returned to Panjim. He undressed and swam in the warm sea. Then he ate the cold lunch of two hard-boiled eggs, slices of bread and an apple he had brought with him and lay on the bench, thinking about this Indian and wondering how much the British knew. It might be a good idea to move aboard *Ehrenfels* for a while; he would be safer than he was in his bungalow if the British did attempt anything. Soon, he felt sleepy and he dozed. When he awoke, it was late afternoon, and heat was draining from the day. On the drive back to Panjim, rain began to fall. The green forests steamed in the brief dusk, and once a long, silver snake writhed across the shining road. Some of the crosses and shrines by the roadside had candles lit in glass jars beside them.

When Trompeta reached the ferry, the rain stopped. Panjim was a glittering mass of lights on the far bank, reflected like stars in the rushing river. Out by the medical college, beyond the barracks for the Portuguese garrison on the edge of the town, a carnival was in progress. The boom-boom of drums, the bray of trumpets, and excited shouts and screams and whistles carried over the water to him.

When the ferry tied up, he drove off quickly. The church of Mary of the Immaculate Conception was floodlit, and a service of some kind was in progress. He heard chanting as he passed. He garaged his car and walked down the hill to his bungalow, savoring the cool night air. To the left, beyond a slope of trees, the river ran silver to the sea. He stood for a moment, watching it, and listening to the familiar sounds of darkness; the clockwork whirr of cicadas, the gruff croak of bullfrogs, the maddening whine of mosquitoes.

Then Trompeta unlocked his front door and let

63

himself into the hallway. Four ships in two days, he thought. And probably as many more by the end of the week.

Henry the Navigator watched him from the far wall.

Early next morning, Pugh paid his bill in the reception hall of his hotel, under the portrait of another Portuguese hero, Vasco da Gama, who, in the 15th century, had been the first European voyager to reach India. Stewart was already waiting in the car with their luggage behind him. They had discovered that Trompeta rarely received visitors before nine o'clock in the morning, and so had decided to call on him at eight. Panjim would not be very busy then, and it was likely that Trompeta would still be on his own.

They drove in silence past the church, up the Rua Pe Agnelo, past Trompeta's bungalow, to the top of the hill. Here the road widened into the suburb of Altino. Pugh turned the car and coasted downhill, and stopped outside Trompeta's front door. At the crossroads, the traffic policeman was climbing up into his kiosk. A few barefoot Indians, coolies or bearers, going to work at the bigger houses in Altino, trudged slowly up the hill, carrying bundles of washing wrapped in white cloth on their heads.

Pugh and Stewart climbed the red brick steps to Trompeta's bungalow, and crossed the narrow verandah to the front door. Too many hot summers had blistered and faded its green paint. Creepers trailed long fronds from hanging baskets. They smelled the early morning bitterness of newly watered geraniums.

The rattle of a bolt and a restraining chain, and the door opened a cautious three inches. Trompeta looked out enquiringly. He was wearing a short-sleeved check shirt and cotton trousers. It seemed unlikely he was carrying a gun.

"Who are you?" he asked in German. "What do you want?"

"We have an urgent message for you," Pugh replied in German. "Let us in quickly."

Trompeta closed the door to release the chain and then opened it and beckoned them inside. As he shut the door behind them, Pugh took out his Colt .32 automatic, and prodded the muzzle into Trompeta's ribs.

"Hands on top of your head," he told him. "Don't shout or try anything, and you'll be all right. But do exactly as we tell you."

Stewart went on into the front room. The table was laid for breakfast. He saw a glass coffee percolator, cups and saucers, a loaf of bread. An ant sluggishly explored sugar in a blue china bowl.

"I have been half expecting something like this," Trompeta said in English, as though speaking to himself. "But not so soon."

Footsteps creaked on the wooden floor of the hall. Stewart drew his automatic. A woman entered the room. She had fair hair drawn back in a bun, and wore a loose cotton dress.

"Who are you?" Pugh asked her.

"My wife," answered Trompeta for her.

"My God," said Stewart. He had never thought to ask the consul if Trompeta had a wife or family.

"Stand against that wall," Pugh told her. "Put your hands on top of your head, like your husband."

While Stewart kept them both covered, Pugh made a hasty search of the bungalow. It contained two bedrooms, a kitchen with a tap dripping into the sink, a small room for the bearer who had not yet arrived.

Pugh came back into the front room. A country bus, a bullock cart and two private cars made the road outside seem crowded. They had no time to lose. He gave a quick nod to Stewart to hit Trompeta as had been agreed, but Stewart felt suddenly too embarrassed to do so. It seemed unfair and demeaning to hit an unarmed man in front of his wife. Instead, Stewart jerked his revolver towards the door, and told Trompeta, "Go out in front of me. Get into the back of the car, both of you, and sit quietly."

Trompeta and his wife walked slowly across the

65

verandah and down the steps. As they reached the street, Trompeta suddenly shouted in English to the Indians going up the hill, "Help! We're being kidnapped! Help us!"

The Indians looked at each other in surprise. One spat red betelnut juice onto the pavement. Then they walked on, averting their eyes. This was a matter for the sahibs; this was no concern of theirs.

"Help!" yelled Trompeta again, now frantic. He made a leap to one side, hoping to run to the traffic policeman, who was also staring at them. Stewart seized the back of Trompeta's shirt and bundled him into the car. Trompeta's wife began to scream hysterically, hammering the roof with her fists. Pugh pulled her away and threw her in beside Trompeta. Stewart jumped in and jabbed his revolver into Trompeta's side.

"If you don't shut up, I'll shoot you both—*now!*"

The policeman began to walk towards the car. Pugh started his engine and released the handbrake. He had hoped to search the bungalow thoroughly, but that was now clearly impossible. He had not even time to shut the front door. The policeman began to run, blowing his whistle, waving to Pugh to stop. Pugh waved back to him, but did not stop.

Two hundred yards away, traffic lights turned red. Pugh could not jump them because a crowd of Indians on bicycles, and bullock carts heavy with sugar cane and mangoes, were crossing slowly in front of him. He glanced at his mirror. The policeman had been joined by several other men. They were pointing to the station wagon. As the lights changed, Pugh accelerated away and drove out of the town towards the border. He pulled up in the clearing where they had stopped on the way from Belgaum. Stewart opened the glove compartment and took out the hypodermic.

"Are you going to kill us?" asked Trompeta.

"No. It's just to make you feel drowsy for a bit."

Stewart jabbed Trompeta and his wife in their arms with the pentothal needle. Slowly, their eyelids

66

drooped and they sagged back against the seat. Stewart pulled a blanket over them. Pugh took a pair of pliers from the car's tool kit, slipped them into his pocket and began to climb the nearest telegraph pole to cut the wires. He was concerned in case the traffic policeman had reported the kidnapping to the local police station and someone there had telephoned ahead to close the border post into India.

The pole was unexpectedly smooth and difficult to climb. Finally, he managed it by standing on Stewart's shoulders and then on his head. By stretching up, he could take some of his weight on one of the cross bars that carried the wires. Holding on with one hand, praying the bar would not break, he sawed through the wires with his pliers. The wire was unexpectedly thick, and the Indian-made pliers unusually blunt. For what seemed like an age he hung there, sawing away frantically, greatly concerned in case someone passed by and saw him. But the road stayed empty, and soon the wires were down. They drove on to the border.

Here, Pugh waited in the car, a bag of rupees in his lap, while Stewart walked across to the immigration official's hut. Pugh's plan was to throw the bag out into the road if there was any attempt to detain them, and while the officials ran to see what it contained, they would drive right through the horizontal pole that marked the border.

A Goanese officer returned with Stewart to the car and stuck his head into the driver's window. Pugh inhaled odors of garlic and sweat and jasmine scented hair oil.

"I trust you have completed your business to your full satisfaction?" the officer asked him in English.

"I hope so," replied Pugh truthfully.

"Bom dia," said the officer cordially, and waved them across the frontier.

Pugh threw the bag of rupees out into the road.

"A present for you," he said as he let in the clutch.

He did not stop the car until they had reached Green's Hotel in Belgaum.

The Café Pescadores in Panjim was near the river, where ferryboats and barges bumped against the bank. Across the road, country buses waited in line, old vehicles with locally made bodies, many without glass in their windows or treads on their tires. Drivers poured buckets of river water into ancient, steaming, leaking radiators. Passengers, reluctant to endure the ovenlike heat of these buses until the last moment, walked up and down on the pavement or in the shade of the buildings, or supervised the safe strapping of their luggage on the bus roof.

The owner of the Café Pescadores was naturally eager to catch as much as possible of this passing trade, and especially British and American soldiers on leave from India, for they had foreign currency to spend, worth three or four times its equivalent in local money.

Knowing the language difficulties, he had commissioned a giant painting above his establishment, to illustrate the extent of his menu. He had not been able to make his requirements fully clear to the local artist, who had therefore painted a picture of a huge plate, flanked by a knife and fork. On this plate, apples, fish (with heads and tails intact), two fried eggs, oranges, a slice of fruit cake, jam, bread, a squid with eyes and tentacles, and a chicken, complete with feathers and feet, were piled with Lucullan prodigality.

Ram das Gupta sat beneath this representation, facing the activity around the ferry and the buses, and yet not really seeing it. He had waited in the café for one hour on the previous morning, and when the European had still not appeared, he had walked from the ferry to the medical college and back again, in the hope of meeting him.

Today he had also waited in vain, and now he felt uneasy. Had something gone wrong—or was the man merely ill? Since Ram das Gupta did not know his name or where he lived, he could not visit him at his home to find out. He did not care to ask the café owner about him, because that would mean admitting he did not know his name and might make the owner suspicious about their relationship—and the last thing he wished was to draw attention to himself. Yet he had a thick envelope to hand over, and he was reluctant to return to Bombay without doing so, for then the Indian who gave him his instructions would wonder whether he was losing enthusiasm for his work, and whether he could still be trusted.

He waited for half an hour more; then for an hour, then an hour and a half, drinking cups of very sweet tea, thickened by condensed milk, and brushing flies away from his face. The café was hot, and the moving windshields of cars flashed like heliographs in the burning sun. Finally, Ram das Gupta made up his mind. He would stay on for a third day, and if his contact still did not appear, he would have to return to Bombay and explain what had happened.

The road from the border to Belgaum had no roadside telephones or village telephone booths where Pugh and Stewart could ring their Bombay office and explain that they had not one but two captives. The only telephone was in the manager's office at Green's Hotel. Pugh used it to make a guarded telephone call to Colonel Freddie Hutson, a friend of his in army headquarters in Bombay. He asked Hutson to arrange secure accommodation for two visitors he was bringing to Bombay within the next few hours.

The effects of the drug had worn off and Trompeta and his wife were both now awake. Pugh and Stewart therefore invited them into the hotel lounge. There, under photogravure likenesses of the four Allied leaders, Churchill, Roosevelt, Stalin and Chiang Kai-shek, with elderly permanent residents staring at their party curiously from time to time, captors and captives took tea and buttered toast.

After tea, Pugh led them out to the car where Stewart explained he would not handcuff them if they would give him their word they would not attempt to escape. He added that if they did try to escape he might be forced to shoot them. Trompeta and his wife accepted this situation philosophically and sat together quietly in the back of the car while Pugh drove north. By early evening they were in Bombay.

At the next meeting of SOE in the bungalow in Meerut, Pugh and Stewart reported what had seemed to be a successful operation. But for the meeting on the following week the radio monitors produced more transcripts of decoded German messages from the Marmagoa transmitter. As before, these contained details of ships and cargoes and destinations.

"Anything happened to any of these vessels?" asked Pugh.

Fletcher nodded gloomily.

"I'm sorry to say, it has. Five have gone down. The Panamanian *Amaryllis,* the Norwegian tanker *Belita,* the Greek cargo ship *Saronikos,* the British *Empire Gull* and the Dutch *Sawahloento.*"

"So Trompeta must have a stand-in carrying on his work?"

"It would appear so. He gave the interrogation chappies in Bombay a description of an Indian courier, and they picked this fellow up as he came off the bus from Goa. Usual disaffected failed student type. Ram das Gupta, formerly of Aligarh University. Offered no resistance, and actually was still carrying a wad of information he'd been unable to pass on to Trompeta. He's led us on to someone else who's also telling what he knows."

"We'll never catch them all—but we *can* scotch the whole operation if we destroy that transmitter."

"That's absolutely out of the question," said Mackenzie firmly. "The Foreign Office has already reported that the German Embassy in Lisbon has protested most strongly to the Portuguese Foreign Minister over the way two German subjects, for whom they claim diplomatic status, have been forcibly abducted from Goa. They accuse the British of violating Portuguese neutrality.

"The Foreign Office has also warned our Minister once more of the dangers of allowing anything further to happen that might prejudice the Allies' relationship with Portugal."

"So what do we do?" asked Stewart. "Nothing?"

"We have offered Röfer more money. But he's still not interested," added Fletcher. "Must say, I rather admire the fellow."

"Gentlemen," said Pugh. "Let me put a question to you. If the professionals—like us—can't act, then who would you say can?"

"The amateurs, I suppose," replied Fletcher. "But what exactly have you in mind, Pugh?"

"A proposal to stop these broadcasts. Even if we discover the identity of Trompeta's number two and deal with him, there is bound to be a third. And then a fourth, and so on. So let us concentrate on their transmitter. What would the Foreign Office say if I could persuade a group of dedicated amateurs—civilians—to seize that ship and either sail her out or blow her up at anchor—and either way put her radio out of action for ever?"

"They'd say what I'd say. You were mad—or they were," retorted Fletcher bluntly.

"Let them say," said Pugh philosophically. "But if nothing whatever linked these men with any of the Allied forces—what would the local Portuguese authorities say then—*if* the attempt failed?"

"A great deal, I should imagine," said Mackenzie. "But probably not as much as if we'd attempted the job with a Naval boarding party or Commandos —and failed."

"And if we made certain payments to certain local officials in Goa?"

"Then no doubt they might say a whole lot less."

"And that, gentlemen, would be our worst possible case—with everything going wrong. My own feeling, knowing the men concerned, is that nothing at all would go wrong. They'd go in, deal with the ship, and out again."

"But who are these people, Pugh?"

"Mostly a lot older than we are," replied Pugh, enjoying himself. "Company directors, insurance agents, solicitors, accountants, jute merchants."

"I didn't ask *what* they are, but *who* they are."

"They're all members of a part-time territorial regiment you've probably never even heard of. The Calcutta Light Horse."

SIX

"I've heard of them all right," said Fletcher. "Been to some of their parties, too. Used to be called the Calcutta *Tight* Horse then. But what makes you think they could do a job like this? They're all *burra sahibs* and *boxwallahs* who like a ceremonial parade once a year, and only belong to the unit because they're keen on polo or gymkhanas or paperchases, and rather fancy themselves in mess-kit at a dance."

Fletcher deliberately called them *box-wallahs* and *burra sahibs* to show his opinion of them. Originally, a *box-wallah* was a traveling Indian pedlar, who would carry a wooden or metal box of his wares on his head, and tout it round European bungalows. He would seek an audience with the *memsahib*, the mistress of the house, and open his box on the verandah to show her the goods he hoped to sell.

In Fletcher's meaning, the term was applied to British businessmen in India, who were sometimes considered to be lower in the delicate European social scale than, say, members of the Indian Civil Service, or officers in British or Indian regiments. And the British and Indian armies again contained even more subtle but rigid social subdivisions of their own.

The word *burra sahib* simply meant a big man, an important person. Fletcher's implication was that, as successful business or professional men, they were perhaps more important in their own estimation than in other people's—and hence too accustomed to a soft life with servants to be able to adapt easily to the rigours of active service.

"Most are a pretty sound lot," replied Pugh. "And they are eager to do something—*anything*—for the war, either because they are too old or too important to their firms to join up."

"But how can they possibly deal with *Ehrenfels* from Calcutta?" asked Mackenzie. "They are about 1,400 miles away for a start. Do you propose they cross into Goa as tourists, and then swim out to the ship? It is just not feasible, Pugh. And we'd still be in a hell of a mess if anything went wrong. All these middle-aged businessmen, accountants and whatever, rounded up by the Portuguese, carrying arms, and trying to board a German ship in a neutral harbor! Be serious, please!"

"That's the strength of the whole thing, sir," replied Pugh. "If it all went wrong—and I repeat I don't think it would—we could explain it away by saying that they went to Goa for an annual holiday celebration of some kind. Then, unfortunately, they celebrated too well, and on the spur of the moment someone suggested they board the German ship.

"The Government of India could deny all knowledge of the whole thing—and quite truthfully, too. The Portuguese would huff and puff a bit, but I don't believe they would do much more, because they would realize that this explanation could just possibly be true."

"I see. And how many men do you think you could enlist for such a scheme?" asked Fletcher.

"There are probably about 120 Germans and Italians altogether, although I would hope they wouldn't all be aboard *Ehrenfels*. I suggest we could finance some diversion on shore—a carnival, a party for seamen, that sort of thing—to try and whittle down the numbers a bit.

"There can't be all that many active Light Horsemen left in Calcutta. I'd say we could probably get between 15 and 20."

"A hell of an undertaking, for 15 middle-aged men to tackle, say, eight times their number of fit young German and Italian sailors, then destroy a transmitter and either seize or sink a damn great ship. Not the sort of odds I'd bet on."

"It is just possible they could do it," said Peterson.

"Eighteen months ago, when I was still in London, we put a special party aboard a German ship in the Azores and sailed her out of harbor without any fuss."

"That was before Japan was in the war, and before our relationship with Portugal was so important," pointed out Mackenzie. "Circumstances here are totally different."

"It is one thing using trained soldiers or sailors, and quite another using men who have been sitting behind office desks for 10 or 20 years, apart from a few evening parades, and most of those spent propping up the bar," added Fletcher.

"I don't think there is any other way," said Stewart. "We cannot use regular forces for obvious reasons. Yet it is imperative we silence that transmitter. Our only hope is to use these civilians who have had some basic military training."

"I would suggest accompanyng them," said Pugh.

"So would I," added Stewart.

Mackenzie smiled rather wanly.

"I don't like it any more than I liked your idea of kidnapping Trompeta," he said. "But that worked and so could this—I suppose. And, as you say, we really have no alternative."

He turned to Pugh.

"Find out whether they will agree in principle. But on no account tell any of them more than you have to, and only divulge the actual destination to the C.O."

Grice went up in the lift to his flat. His wife opened the door before he could fit his key into the lock.

"We have a visitor," she announced. "Lewis Pugh."

Grice showed surprise. He came into the room and poured himself a drink. Pugh stood up to meet him, a glass of whiskey already in his hand.

"Thought you were in Goa," said Grice. "What happened? Trip canceled?"

"No. Went off perfectly, and that letter was most valuable."

"Glad to hear it. So what brings you back here so soon? Leave?"

Pugh paused before replying. Doris Grice guessed he had something to tell her husband that was for his ears only.

"I'll go and tell the bearer to lay another place for dinner," she said tactfully, and left them alone.

"Well?" asked Grice. "What is it this time? Another letter?"

Pugh swirled his drink in his glass, wondering how best to broach the subject. What had seemed so simple to propose in Meerut was unexpectedly difficult now he was facing the man who would have to lead the raid.

Pugh knew he was expecting Grice and the others to accept almost suicidal risks—at their own expense, in their own time, and with no hope of any official backing, recognition or help if anything went wrong.

If it did, at best they could be interned. At worse, they would be killed in a fight with men half their age, who far outnumbered them. These were risks Pugh could accept, even if reluctantly, as a professional soldier. But it was another thing altogether to expect civilians without his training and experience to volunteer for such a mission.

"I don't quite know how to begin," Pugh said simply. "But you have repeatedly told me how keen you and other Light Horsemen were to get into action. Are you still of the same mind?"

"Of course," replied Grice immediately. "What can you offer?"

"Nothing much more attractive than Churchill's blood, sweat and tears. But it is a task I have suggested to my people that you might conceivably feel like carrying out, although I must point out that the odds against success could be high.

"And even if you do succeed, you will not be able to tell anyone not involved where you have been or what you have done. I'm being blunt about it, Bill, for we've known each other for ten years, and I don't want to bull you."

76

"Why ask us especially for this job, then, whatever it is?"

"Because it's a damned delicate operation. We can't afford to involve any regular forces for political reasons. But you are all civilians with some military training, which could be a way round it."

"And so if things went wrong we could cause no embarrassment to you?"

"Well, that did come into our considerations," admitted Pugh rather shamefacedly. "Let me tell you the proposition, then you can decide for yourself. But this is strictly between ourselves. After I've spoken, forget what I've said, whatever you decide to do. Right?"

"Right."

"As you know, I have been to Goa. As you may also know, four Axis merchant ships are anchored in Marmagoa harbor. We want one of them, the fastest and the newest, *Ehrenfels*, either sunk at anchor there or towed out. If we can get the other three, that's a bonus, but no more. The main thing is to deal effectively with *Ehrenfels*—and quickly."

"Why, exactly?"

"One reason is that if she made a break for Singapore, the Japs could fit her with guns from our naval dockyard, and she'd be a most dangerous merchant cruiser."

"And the other reason?"

"For your ears only, the Germans have a transmitter aboard *Ehrenfels* the Portuguese authorities in Goa know nothing about. An Axis spy net in India is channeling information about shipping through that radio direct to U-boats in the Indian Ocean. We *have* to silence it—somehow. We are losing ships there more quickly than we can replace them. The job's as important as that."

"I see." Grice thought for a moment.

"How many men would you want?" he asked.

"Fifteen to twenty."

"I'll appeal for volunteers, bachelors if possible. I can also ask our friends in the Calcutta Scottish."

CALCUTTA LIGHT HORSE, A. F. (I),
HEADQUARTERS, 24, PARK STREET,
CALCUTTA, 20 FEBRUARY, 1943.

KIT REQUIRED BY MEMBERS PROCEEDING TO RANCHI ON SPECIAL COURSE.

1. **CLOTHING & EQUIPMENT.**

   Members will travel in CIVILIAN CLOTHES.
   In addition they will take :-

   (a) Khaki dungarees.
   Gaiters.
   Ankle Boots with leather soles (NOT rubber) NO nails.
   Steel Helmets.
   C.L.H. Topee or bush hat.
   Jersey (one regulation, other pullovers (woollen) should
   be taken).
   Greatcoats.
   One complete change of service dress (slacks or shorts,
   shoes etc.).
   Muffler.

   (b) Bedding and mosquito net. Take plenty of blankets.
   Camp beds may be taken.

   (c) Knife, fork, spoon, mug, plate, tin-opener.

   (d) Toilet requisites.

   (e) Stores for train journey. Cigarettes. Alcohol limited
   to one bottle per head.

2. **Medical.** - First Field Dressings will be carried.

3. **Arms & Amn.** - Pistols and 18 rounds will be carried.

Sd/- W. H. Grice,
Lt.-Colonel,
Commanding, Calcutta Light Horse,A.F.(I).

MWB.

This was another Auxiliary Force regiment, with whom considerable good-natured rivalry existed. The Light Horse purported to think the Calcutta Scottish rather small beer. The Calcutta Scottish, for their part, considered that the Light Horse gave themselves too many social airs and graces. Members of both regiments met annually in dignified competition on the cricket field, and, more aggressively, played rugby. At the Calcutta Cricket Club and Football Club, teams and spectators would afterwards mingle amicably over gin and limes or chota pegs, but fraternization had not so far extended to their military duties.

"I'll call a parade for tomorrow, 18:30 hours, at the clubhouse. When would we need to leave?"

"Ask them to be ready to go in about 10 days from now. I'll fix up some training for you first. Tell your people they'll be away from Calcutta for 10 or 12 days, but give them no inkling whatever as to their destination or the task in case anything leaks out. They can tell their families and offices they are going to Ranchi for a special course."

Ranchi was the site of a large army weapon training school about 200 miles north west of Calcutta. It would be a believable reason for several days' absence from homes and offices.

"What you're saying, Lewis, is that I can't tell my people a damn' thing worth knowing about this outing? You expect them to volunteer without any idea what they are volunteering for?"

Pugh nodded.

"That's about it, Bill," he agreed. "It's very risky and very important and top secret. So—no credit."

"No pay, either?"

"No—and not much chance of pensions for anyone killed or wounded if anything goes wrong."

"How attractive you make the conditions sound, Lewis. And no medals either, just supposing things go right?"

"No medals, Bill. No medals whatever."

High above the dockside buildings in Marmagoa, beyond the crooked fingers of cranes and the busy shunting engines, morning kite hawks turned and dived and rose again like dark parentheses in a burning sky.

Through the brass-rimmed circle of his cabin porthole, Captain Röfer saw them wheel and soar, and he grimaced with distaste. They symbolized so much that Röfer hated in Goa; heat, dirt, the almost overwhelming inertia of the climate. He glanced at the other three captains around his table. None of them seemed to have noticed, or perhaps they had grown so accustomed to the sight that they accepted as commonplace the kite hawks and the vultures and the bloated carcasses of dogs and pigs at street corners.

Röfer mopped his neck and forehead with a handkerchief. He had ordered two electric fans to be brought into the cabin, but they could not cool the air; they only circulated a damp warm breeze. The Italian captain of *Anfora* sat nearest to the cabin door, his blue shirt already dark with sweat. He was a burly man with thick black curly hair worn long like an operatic tenor he admired. The other captains could not pronounce his name and so nick-named him Garibaldi.

Next to him sat Schmidt, captain of *Drachenfels*, and the oldest of them all. His face was pale and gaunt and he sat with his chair pushed back from the table because he could not bend his paralyzed leg. Schmidt was sure that the physician had injected him with far too many drugs in the hope that twice as much would do double the good in half the time.

Johann Biet, the captain of *Braunfels*, was a dapper man with a thin narrow face lined with the frustration he felt at being incarcerated in this stinking backwater when other members of his family were fighting in North Africa, on the Eastern front, and at sea. Usually, these four captains met once a week to discuss problems of discipline among their crews, pilfering from cargoes and the bartering rate of so many razor blades, torch batteries, or tubes of toothpaste for fresh fruit, such as mangoes and pawpaw.

The captains and their crews relied for fresh food on Indian and Goanese traders who ran small, open-fronted shops near the docks. These men knew that the Germans and Italians were short of money, because their wages came by way of Lisbon, and so were frequently months in arrears. They were therefore willing to allow them credit, and even more ready to barter food for goods otherwise only obtainable in Goa on the black market. Thus a single bottle of German beer or Italian wine could command as much as a crate would fetch in a less restricted market.

Röfer had called this meeting to discuss something far more important than living conditions or the going rate for items of cargo; he wished to discuss their own security, perhaps their ultimate survival.

"Gentlemen," he began. "I have to inform you we have still had no news whatever about our friends abducted by the British in Panjim. I have personally protested to the Portuguese governor here at this conduct in a neutral colony. Our foreign office in Berlin has also made similar representations to the Portuguese government in Lisbon."

"All very admirable, captain, I agree," said Biet in his dry, thin voice, "but it does not release our friends. Nor does it help us—for if the enemy can seize two people in a supposedly neutral capital, what intentions have they towards us?"

"That is why I have called you here together," said Röfer. "Shortly before the kidnapping, an Indian came to see me on British instructions and offered me a large sum of money if I would sail my ship out beyond the three-mile limit and surrender."

"You would never get your money," said Garibaldi shortly.

"Probably not," agreed Röfer. "I refused, of course, but the man admitted the British are extremely short of merchant ships—due to the brilliant work of our U-boats—and to see four merchant vessels right under their noses must be a great temptation. I fear they may now attempt to capture us."

"I cannot agree," said Schmidt sharply. The thought was so appalling to him in his frail condition that he simply could not bear to entertain it.

"They would never risk that. The Allies get far more from Portugal's so-called neutrality than we do. And they know the Portuguese would never forgive them. Such an action could put Portugal into our camp, like Spain."

"That would entirely depend how it's done," declared Biet. "The Portuguese need know nothing about it. The British could send in boarding parties

81

by night in submarines and overwhelm us by sheer weight of numbers. By morning, our ships would be gone, and they'd say *we* sailed them out, and so *we* violated Portuguese neutrality."

"I still don't believe they'd take the risk," maintained Schmidt stubbornly.

"Well, whether they do or not, what do you propose?" Garibaldi asked Röfer. "We already keep a day and night watch. Do you want to double the number of men on guard duty?"

"Possibly. But primarily I suggest we prepare to repel any assault. It is pointless to have our lookouts report enemy ships approaching if we cannot deal with them when they arrive."

"It would be impossible for us to repel a naval attack," said Schmidt petulantly. "How could we fight off warships?"

"They wouldn't come with warships," replied Röfer patiently, mentally making excuses for his colleague's ill health. "Obviously, they could not attempt an assault by air or from the land. But they could easily send in a submarine or several motor launches on a moonlight night. A naval boarding party."

"Just possible," allowed Schmidt. "But very risky for them. For we could just as easily thwart such an attempt."

"Precisely," said Röfer. "Which is why I called this meeting. For a start, I believe you have in your holds 2,000 bags of explosive each weighing about 50 kilos?"

Schmidt nodded.

These explosives had been intended for use in local iron ore quarries, and had never been unloaded.

"Then I suggest we share out a number of these bags between us, and place them on companionways, against hatchways, at the entrances to holds and around the decks.

"You, Garibaldi, carry a cargo of tin and aluminum sheets and marble slabs, and sacks of flour. So. We pile these up on top of the explosives. And every

82

time our crews go ashore they bring back bits of scrap metal and logs of wood, to put on top of the flour bags."

"But how to set off the explosives?" asked Schmidt uneasily.

"I think Captain Biet has the answer," replied Röfer.

Biet showed surprise.

"Yes," Röfer continued. "I believe you have several hundred car batteries in your holds?"

Biet nodded.

"We also share these out between us and charge them up. Our electricians wire them into a circuit with detonators so that at the touch of a switch we can set off controlled explosions all around each ship —wherever the enemy sets foot on our decks."

The others nodded more enthusiastically. This made good sense. A direct short circuit across several fully charged 12-volt batteries wired together could provide a spark strong enough to ignite a length of fuse. Because the charges would be on the open decks they would do little damage to their ships, but could annihilate any boarding party. And, unlike using firearms, such a means of defense should not in any way violate the neutrality of their hosts.

"I agree with that," said Biet approvingly. "I would also propose a second line of defense. We ask our crews to fill every empty oil drum they can find on shore with kerosene. Then we place these drums at strategic points on deck, and fit them with hand pumps and hoses. If intruders arrive, we can spray the decks with kerosene, fire a round from a signaling pistol, and—wham—all the decks are aflame."

The others nodded agreement.

"There is one point I would like to make," said Schmidt, still not enthusiastic about the scheme. "The Admiralty have given us orders that if it seems likely our ships will fall into enemy hands, we should scuttle them. I suggest we see that all Kingston valves are well greased so they can be opened quickly."

These valves were set deep below decks and could be opened to allow seawater to flood the holds in case of fire with an inflammable cargo. Marmagoa harbor was shallow, so the ships would not sink completely, but simply rest on the sea bed with much of their superstructure above the surface of the water.

"So we are agreed, gentlemen?" asked Röfer. The others nodded.

"I suppose we have no option," said Schmidt with a sigh. His leg was paining him. "I hope they do not attack us, but by God, if they do, let us make them wish they had never left home. Would you advise our friends among the Portuguese that we expect a visit?"

Röfer shook his head.

"The British also have friends among the Portuguese. Tell no one of our fears or our plans. If anyone asks why our crews are collecting kerosene it is to clean the engine and to stop rust. If anyone wonders why we are moving cargo, it is to clear the holds for necessary routine inspections. Any other questions, gentlemen?"

"You believe that this attack may be imminent?" asked Garibaldi.

"In view of what has already happened, I would say, sooner rather than later."

"Then if any lookout sees any unfamiliar vessel approaching the harbor, however innocent she may appear, I propose he inform his captain who stands to his ship's company and warns the others."

"Agreed."

"And I propose that one officer aboard each ship has the responsibility for sounding the siren immediately to alert the others in case of any isolated attack," said Biet. "Then we all take what action we feel necessary."

"Agreed," repeated Röfer.

"The moon is full now," continued Garibaldi. "If I were planning an attack, I would arrive when the moon was down."

"So would I," replied Röfer. "But these swine may attack at any time. So from now on, until further notice, let us post double watches. And remember, gentlemen, we will be fighting for our ships, our freedom, our lives and our Fatherland. No mercy. No quarter. And, above all, no surrender."

SEVEN

Bill Grice stood on an improvised dais in the Light Horse Clubhouse in Calcutta. It was just after half past six in the evening, and the room was full.

"Gentlemen," he began. "I have asked you all here for a special purpose. As you know, the Light Horse has not been in action as a unit since the Boer War in 1900. Then it operated as part of Lumsden's Horse—after Colonel Lumsden, a well-known planter, had called for volunteers.

"Tonight, *I* am asking for volunteers. Eighteen men for a special and secret job against Germans.

"I can tell you nothing about it except that the operation should take about a fortnight and will involve a short sea voyage. There it is, gentlemen. I leave it to you. Is anyone willing to volunteer?"

Facing him on the old-fashioned upright chairs sat every member of the Light Horse the two Army staff sergeant instructors had been able to contact that day. Every man immediately raised his right hand.

"What name do we take this time, sir?" asked Breene. "The Light Sea Horse?"

The question caused some laughter, and at once tension eased, for until Bill Grice had spoken, no one knew the reason for this hurriedly called meeting.

So urgent had the summons sounded that they immediately postponed out-of-town visits to tea estates and jute mills, and put off social engagements and evening rides. Men who had not attended parades over the last few weeks, or who had excused themselves the rigors of the previous month's camp owing to business commitments, wondered whether this could be the reason for such a summary invitation to appear before their colonel. They had all been re-lieved and even more mystified to discover that so many of their colleagues had also been asked to at-tend. Now that they knew the reason, they felt a surge of excitement. Training with blank cartridges was one thing; action, another.

"Any unarmed combat, sir?" asked Breene.

"There could be," replied Grice.

"Then I propose Charlie Wilton as the man to lead it."

The others laughed and looked at Wilton, a tall, mild, humorless merchant, who was frequently the butt of many of Breene's jokes. Wilton had rarely been known to smile, except once, so it was said, when he found a mistake in a column of figures about jute shipments that a Bengali clerk had added up wrongly.

When Wilton had first arrived in Calcutta, Breene, sensing a natural victim, had abstracted a piece of headed notepaper from Wilton's office and, forging Wilton's signature, wrote to the Bengal Boxing Fed-eration. He explained he was a fanatically keen amateur middleweight boxer, and would be extreme-ly grateful if they could fix him up with a five or ten round fight with a middle- or light-heavyweight.

To Wilton's amazement, he received a letter from Bengal Boxing Federation thanking him for his en-quiry and saying that they were pleased to report they had arranged a match for him to fight heavy-weight Seaman Jones over ten rounds.

Now Melborne had a question.

"When do we report, sir?" he asked.

"Very soon," replied Grice. "I see there are about 30 of us here, but I'm afraid I won't be able to take you all."

He glanced at several men whose health he knew was not robust. It would be foolhardy to involve them. They could too easily become a liability to the others. As he looked at them individually, he gave a slight shake of his head. They realized without being told directly that they would not be required, and they sat crest-fallen, while their friends pressed forward to give their names to Cren Sandys-Lumsdaine, the only other officer present.

Lumsdaine was a lieutenant in the Light Horse, a tall, cheerful man who wore horn-rimmed spectacles. His eyesight had kept him out of the services despite many attempts to join, and even learning by heart the letters on the eye test card in the medical officers surgery. He was in his mid-thirties and worked for a large tea company. Lumsdaine was also extremely keen on cars, and had persuaded the unit to buy several second-hand Ford and Austin car chassis, which they had fitted with homemade bodies of sheet steel for use as armored cars to help the police control riots and in case the Japanese army ever reached Calcutta.

He was renowned for racy and topical lyrics he could write to popular songs which were sung at Light Horse parties. Around Calcutta he was frequently accompanied by a sort of bull terrier he named Catto "as he was a liberal peer." Now he noted the name of each volunteer with telephone numbers where they could be found at office or at home.

"What about me?" Manners asked Grice. "You know I've only got one eye."

"That was good enough for Nelson," replied Grice drily. "Why shouldn't it be all right for you? Put your name down."

Manners, much relieved, gave his name and number to Lumsdaine.

When Lumsdaine had 15 names with several possible candidates in reserve, Grice nodded a dismissal to those who would be left behind. Slowly, with infinite reluctance, they filed out of the lecture room to the bar. Grice closed the door behind them. One older man, whom he had not selected, Trooper Jock Cartwright, a *box-wallah* with a jute company, gripped his arm.

"You haven't chosen me, Bill," he said. "But I'd like to ask one question before I bow out. You're certain this operation isn't really against the Japs?"

Cartwright's eldest son, Timothy, had worked in a Calcutta bank, and after being commissioned in The Border Regiment, had been missing since the previous year's retreat from Rangoon. Time and again, Cartwright had tried to volunteer for the army in the faint hope that he might be posted to Burma and so could somehow discover whether his son still lived, or, if not, how he had died. But always Cartwright's age, and the importance to India's economy of his civilian job, had been against him.

"No, Cartwright," replied Grice gently. "I told you. It's against the Germans."

"Where the hell are you going then? Europe? The Second Front? North Africa?"

"I can't tell you," said Grice.

"Well, I can tell you, Cartwright, there are positively no Germans in India," said Manners. "All the Germans I used to know who worked here for Opel and Agfa and Zeiss and so on, were interned the day war broke out."

"It's no good guessing, gentlemen," said Grice. "I can tell you no more.'

"I'd still like to have a go," Cartwright told him. "I can speak a bit of German.'

"I know how you feel," said Grice. "I don't want to rub it in, but you have a dicey heart, and we just can't risk it."

"Well, it's your show, Bill. But if you find anything I *can* do—remember me."

Then Cartwright went sadly out of the room and closed the door quietly behind him.

At six o'clock on the following moring, white mist drifted like shredded lint across the grass of Bally-gunge *maidan*. In the chill of half-light, the boating lake steamed. The ornamental bridge across the river that fed it looked like something from a willow pattern plate. Already, early morning *dhobi* men were out, hawking in their throats and slapping clothes they had to wash against the rocks to drive out the dirt. In the British Army camp 200 yards away, ration trucks were being started up with a great backfiring of engines.

Two civilian cars drove through the thinning mist and stopped near the bridge. Four Light Horsemen climbed out of each one and fell into step. They wore khaki drill shirts and trousers, and bush hats or solar topees. One corporal had no hat, and his hair seemed thin on top for a serving soldier. The others looked plump to be privates but marched smartly enough. They carried revolvers in webbing holsters on their belts.

Two regular Army sergeants stood beneath a banyan tree, whose branches hung down and burrowed into the earth like roots. They exchanged glances. One raised his eyes to heaven as though beseeching an unknown Almighty to relieve him of the task of drilling such a squad. He was smoking in the old-soldier fashion, holding a cigarette curled inside the palm of his right hand so that its glow would not be seen by any superior. Now he took one enormous drag on the damp stub, trod the butt into the grass and blew smoke out of his nostrils like a war horse.

"Here they are, then," he said to his companion. "All I can say is, if these are the *Light* Horse, what must the heavy mob be like?"

He marched smartly towards the new arrivals.

"You four gentlemen follow me," he told them in a strange mixture of obsequiousness and command.

"The second group will please follow Sarn't Browne. He will endeavour to instruct you in all matters pertaining to the officers' personal arm—otherwise known as the Smith & Wesson Thirty-Eight, the Thompson sub-machine gun or the Chicago Piano as it is known, and the Sten. Now, let's be having you. Smartly, gentlemen, if you please. Left, right, left, right, left . . ."

They marched along, feet scuffing dust under glittering beads of dew on the ground. Sacred white cows veered away hastily from their path; bells tinkled around the necks of grazing goats. The mist was thinning rapidly now and ahead of them the

Light Horsemen could see a line of rifle butts and tents, and soldiers with mess tins moving in twos and threes. Smoke climbed vertically from the cookhouse chimney, and somewhere out of sight, a bugle blew. The sergeant halted his team by the bus. He pulled smartly on a rope, and a few yards away a cut-out plywood target of a grinning Japanese soldier with large tombstone teeth and huge round spectacles jerked along against an earth bank.

"You, sir," said the sergeant to the nearest Light Horseman. "I would like to see you fire four rounds rapid. I take it you are conversant with the use of the arm?"

"I am," replied Alastair MacFarlane. He was a well-built bearded man, just starting to run to fat. He had a red face on account of which his friends had given him the nickname of Red Mac. He spoke with a strong Scottish accent, and usually carried a hip flask of strong Scotch whiskey. When that was unobtainable, he filled the flask with locally brewed whiskey, which was sometimes even stronger. His eyes now were slightly bloodshot, which was why the sergeant had picked on him. The sergeant realized that if he could make him appear foolish before his colleagues, then they should all be easier to control. He had heard they were important civilians, *burra-sahibs* in their own right, who could doubtless have bought and sold him a dozen times, but now he was their superior with three stripes on his arm, and he had to show who was boss.

"Stand back then, gentlemen. Give him a fair try."

The other men in the squad moved a pace backwards as the sergeant pulled the rope. The target began to shake and shudder across the butts.

"Fire!"

For half a second, Red Mac paused. The target fuzzed as he forced his eyes to focus on it. His pistol trembled as he gripped it with both hands.

Then he fired. The shots sounded like whips cracking.

"Right, gentlemen," said the sergeant. "Stand at ease. Stand easy."

He marched towards the target. To his amazement all four shots had hit within a circle of three inches. He swallowed his irritation.

"Very good indeed, sir, if I may say so. But you would have done better if you had had a good night's sleep."

"If I'd had a good night's sleep, sergeant, I wouldn't be here. I always fire best on the swing."

Red Mac's hand went towards his hip pocket.

"No, sir, if you please. No drink on parade. Now the next gentleman. Let us see if you can beat that. Four rounds. When you're ready, sir. *Fire!*"

Other cars and taxis containing the rest of the Light Horse contingent had meanwhile arrived and for half an hour the men fired their postols at moving targets. Then they were issued with Sten guns, crudely made weapons, mass produced in a hurry because any sub-machine gun was obviously better than none.

The Sten's tolerances were so wide and the general workmanship so rough that the barrel would accept British and German ammunition, although the cartridges were not the same size. This was claimed as a deliberate part of the design so that, in any Allied invasion of Europe, captured German ammunition might be used. But this optimistic advantage was balanced by the fact that a smart slap on the butt of a Sten could sometimes cause it to fire.

The Light Horsemen now learned of this weapon's other peculiarities; how it could jam easily, and how it could be freed. They tied handkerchiefs around their eyes and tried to dismantle and reassemble the gun blindfold. They fired and fired again, and when the sun was up, they handed in their arms and climbed back into their cars.

The traffic was thickening now. Hundreds of Indian clerks, known as babus, wearing white shirtlike *dhotis* and long sleeved white shirts, cycled to work, clogging every crossroads.

Within half an hour, the Light Horsemen were at their office desks, under slowly turning fans. Some were sipping *nimbu pani*, fresh lemon juice and iced water as they read their office mail; others were already dictating to Bengali male secretaries. The only signs that they had called elsewhere on their way to work were some split fingernails and scraped knuckles grazed by a revolver hammer or a rough-headed bolt on the Sten.

At six o'clock each morning for a week, these volunteers, now joined by four from the Calcutta Scottish, reported on Ballygunge *maidan.*

The *dhobi* men grew accustomed to them running over an assault course, intended for soldiers as young as their sons. Middle-aged hearts hammered as the men stretched middle-aged muscles. They swung Tarzan-like from ropes and jumped trustingly from the tops of walls. They learned how to overcome a larger and fitter enemy. How to strangle a man, having first disarmed him; how to fall in a fight and roll with their opponent, using his impetus to make them come out on top; how to kill silently; how to fend off several attackers at one time.

The *dhobis* shook their heads at this madness in sahibs of their age and importance. But others remarked that it was well known how all sahibs from over the sea were mad in one way or another. And others expressed their opinion of the proceedings in the washerman's song, with each beat of sodden sheets on the rocks: "Black man, *good* man, white man, *bas*tard."

"What's all this in aid of exactly?" the sergeant asked his colleague on the fifth morning as they waited beneath the tree.

"Don't really know. Suppose they are training in case there are riots with Congress wallahs and VCs." This was service slang for Fifth Columnists.

"Well, it's certainly getting their weight down. That's for sure."

Wives became resigned to husbands setting bedside alarm clocks for five o'clock or even four-thirty, if they lived some distance from Calcutta. And then, after a quick shower, a cup of tea and a peeled orange, they would hasten off to Ballygunge.

"But what can you *do* on the maidan at this

hour?" Mrs. Breene asked sleepily. If her husband had claimed he was attending a Light Horse parade each evening, then she would have been suspicious that perhaps he was meeting some other woman. But not at half-past four in the morning; not Jack. They had been married for 15 years and he was definitely not an early morning man.

"We drill, darling. With a bit of weapon training and unarmed combat thrown in."

"But surely not you, Jack? You've been in the Light Horse for 10 years, and you are still only a trooper. By now you must know all the drill there is."

"Always new tricks to learn—even for old dogs," replied Breene cheerfully.

"Well, don't overdo it, that's all I say," replied his wife as she drifted back to sleep.

Other wives and girl friends in Calcutta were surprised to discover that only 14 or 15 Light Horsemen were attending these parades. Usually they were all involved, as at camp—so why this sudden discrimination?

"Matter of fact, darling," Hilliard told his fiancée, "I may have to go off for 10 days or a fortnight. A special weapon training course at Ranchi."

"But we were going to Darjeeling. To stay with my mother. You promised."

"I know, darling, and I'm very, very sorry. We'll go as soon as I come back."

"But it's not convenient then. She probably won't still be there."

"Well, in that case, we'll just have to manage as best we can on our own, won't we?"

Melborne regularly telephoned his wife on their out-station to find out how she was coping, and to dictate replies to letters she read over the phone to him.

"I can't understand it," she said, perplexed. "You almost never go to Calcutta—say you can't stand the place. Yet you've stood it well enough for nearly 10 days, and now you tell me you are going off somewhere else for two weeks. And you won't tell me where or why."

"It's business," Melborne answered her brusquely. "Delhi."

His company had a branch office there, and it was the first name that came to his mind.

"Anyway, you know everything there is to know about tea. And you've got a good manager."

"I am amazed you allow me to stay here alone," she replied bitterly. "But if I can cope on my own, then I'm not going to be kept here all the time when you come back. I'd like to visit Calcutta more often, too. Understood?"

"Understood," replied Melborne less brusquely. His wife's voice had a sharp edge to it he had not heard before.

"I can't say what's happening," he went on, "but believe me, it's important. And listen. If anything should happen, see Sandy. You know Sandy, the bank manager?"

"Of course I know Sandy. What do you mean, if anything should happen?"

"Oh, anything. I might get bitten by a snake."

"No snake would be so foolish," his wife told him with the certainty of a long marriage. "Be honest about it. Is there anyone else?"

"A number of us."

"No, no. I don't mean the Light Horse. I mean a woman. Are you in Calcutta because of her?"

"Good Lord, no."

The thought that his wife might actually be concerned about him had never really entered Melborne's head. Now he experienced a strange feeling of surprise and gratification that his wife should care. Maybe he had underestimated her, treated her as an inferior, almost as a possession for too long? But before he could express these thoughts in words, the Indian operator disconnected their line. He was left with only a buzzing in his ear and a strange feeling in his heart.

On the outskirts of Calcutta, near Bally Bridge, where the River Hooghly ran smooth and wide, the color of mulligatawny soup and nearly its consistency, stood Tagore Villa, one of the strangest houses in the city. This had originally been the bungalow of an indigo planter—and locally it was still called *Nil Kothi,* the blue house.

Later generations had elaborated this homely building with curved verandahs, reached by two flights of steps, an ornamental Chinese tea house, a lily pond with synchronized fountains, rose gardens and lawns hemmed in by formal hedges. Now all bore the scars of neglect. Radio aerials stood higher than its roof. Washing was strung between trees, and cars were parked haphazardly around it.

Force 136 had taken over Tagore Villa for purposes of their own. In rooms with stained glass windows, under French chandeliers, men of various nationalities—Indians, Malays, Chinese, Burmese and British—learned the dangerous arts of the secret agent's lonely trade; how to kill quickly without weapons and without a sound; how to fix a plastic explosive charge; how to manipulate tiny radio transmitters with batteries charged by turning an adapted bicycle pedal. Pugh and Stewart had their own room in this house, which they used on visits to Calcutta, and here they studied Grice's list of volunteers.

"They seem all right," said Pugh at last. "And the training camp people tell me they are doing well."

"But how the devil are we going to get 'em to Goa?" asked Stewart. He spread a map on the table, and picked up a pair of dividers and a ruler to calculate distances quickly.

In theory, the Light Horse and Calcutta Scottish could travel by train to Goa and then make their own arrangements to reach *Ehrenfels* in harbor. Alternatively, they could sail all the way from Calcutta, a voyage of more than 2,400 miles.

In practice, they could do neither. It would be impossible for so many men to board *Ehrenfels* from the shore without special boats to ferry them out. And it was also proving impossible to find any vessel that could transport them from Calcutta; there simply was not a suitable ship in the port.

"I've been on to all the naval people here and in Delhi and they've absolutely nothing," said Pugh.

"There's not one naval tug left in Calcutta, and only one in Bombay, which is in use all around the clock. Everything else here has been moved south to Colombo in case the Japs invade."

"What if we go by train to some port well south of Goa, on the same coast, say Calicut or Cochin? Then hire or buy a boat there?"

"They're mainly fishing ports. We'd not be able to find the right sort of craft without everyone knowing. We might as well send Röfer a telegram saying we're going to call."

"What do you suggest, then?" asked Pugh.

"I am having lunch with Jock Cartwright at the club," said Stewart. "He has a friend who works for the Port Commissioners here. Maybe he can help us."

"While you're doing that, I'll get hold of Yogi Crossley, for we'll need him with us."

"A good idea. I saw him in the mess at breakfast. He's probably in his room.'

Yogi Crossley was one of that rare breed of Englishmen who had identified himself so closely with India as the country of his adoption that he spoke several dialects perfectly, and for years had made a comparative study of the country's religions. As his nickname implied, he was also a believer in the benefits of yoga.

During the first war, John Crossley was commissioned from Sandhurst, and then served in India with one of the Indian Army's finest cavalry regiments. During the recession of the 1920s, British and Indian armies were both drastically reduced, and young officers were offered what appeared to be extremely generous terms—£1,200 gratuity, with a further annuity of £300 a year for three years—if they would resign voluntarily. Crossley did so and traveled to East Africa, where, with other officers, he started a coffee plantation. But crops failed, unexpected problems multiplied, and soon what had seemed a lot of money in Calcutta had melted away completely.

He returned to India, where he had many friends, and built up a timber business in Calcutta producing boxes—from tea chests to coffins—and exporting rare woods from the forests of Burma to be used for veneers in Britain and the United States.

From boyhood, Crossley had dabbled in explosives as others interest themselves in stamps or old coins. He rejoined the army in England on the outbreak of war and was eventually posted to India. Another officer in his troopship learned of his interest in explosives, and arranged for him to join Force 136 where his hobby would have a special value.

His room was on the next floor of the Villa Tagore, and his response—"Come in"—to Pugh's knock sounded strained. Pugh discovered why as he opened the door. Crossley was standing on his head, in the far corner, reading the Calcutta daily newspaper, *The Statesman.*

Pugh always found it awkward to conduct a conversation with Crossley in this position; it was difficult to know whether he had heard what was said. Pugh had to turn his own head upside down in order to find out. Crossley folded the newspaper neatly and put it on one side.

"Are you in a fit state to speak?" Pugh asked him.

"Depends what you want to say."

"We've a job for you, Yogi. To blow up a ship in a neutral harbor."

"No problem in that," replied Crossley at once. "Give me a couple of days' notice so I can get my gear together."

"Do you want to know where it is?"

"What difference does that make? So long as you can get me where I have to be, I'll carry out my orders."

"Don't be too confident," Pugh warned him. "You won't have a second chance at this target."

"Have I ever needed one yet?" replied Crossley quietly. He swung himself down on his feet and stood up. He was a man of medium height with a lean ascetic face and a strange serenity in his eyes. He is born out of his century, thought Pugh, part

98

dreamer and part man of action, in the mould of Sir Francis Walsingham, the Elizabethan statesman and founder of Britain's secret service, or his contemporary, Christopher Marlowe, who could wield a sword as effectively as he could write a sonnet.

"Who's coming with me?" asked Crossley. Pugh told him.

"Some of them may look a bit old for this sort of thing," he added. "But I know they'll do their best."

"I'm probably as old as any of them," replied Crossley. "The difference is that yoga keeps me feeling so much younger."

"Damned if I can see how standing upside down on your head can help you."

"It's very simple, really, Lewis. When you're young you always want to be up and about. But as you grow older, gravity pulls you down slowly—your shoulders, your stomach. Middle-aged people try to compromise by sitting down or lying down whenever they can. They say they're taking the weight off their legs.

"This exercise goes a bit farther. It turns the tables on gravity. In the Sanskrit, it's called Sarvangasana, meaning something that benefits all parts of the body. Arterial blood flows to the brain and not the feet. You relieve pressure on the spinal column, and so on."

"You certainly look fit on it, Yogi. Especially for a man your age."

"I'll give anyone 10 years younger a fair run for their money. Remember, Lewis, a man only counts his years, when he has nothing else to count."

"What do you count, Yogi?"

"My blessings," replied Crossley quietly. "And my friends."

As Gavin Stewart came into the Light Horse bar, Red Mac gave him a mock salute.

"Whiskey?" he asked. "To drink to deeds of daring —and the men who'll have to do 'em."

"Bit early for me," said Stewart doubtfully.

99

"Early? Would be a bit late if we were in America —10 hours back. Think about that now."

Stewart thought about it. The Indian barman poured two pink gins.

"Lunching with anyone?" asked Red Mac.

"Yes. Cartwright."

"Pity he's not in this. He's terribly cut up about his son. If we were going against the Japs instead of Germans I'm sure he would have squeezed in somehow."

Stewart frowned and shook his head warningly. Red Mac had a chattering tongue.

"Forget it," Stewart told him. "Let's talk of something else."

"I see you are one drink ahead of me," said someone over their shoulders. They turned. Cartwright stood behind them. The barman pushed a gin and lime across the counter towards him, and the three men sat down at a table by the window overlooking the garden. In the 18th century, the whole area had been a private zoo park owned by the British Chief Justice of Bengal, Sir Elijah Impey. Now all that remained was this patch of garden and the name, Park Street, on the road jammed with traffic in both directions.

"Any news of your son?" asked Red Mac.

"None," said Cartwright shortly. "I've been on to the army and the Red Cross. But—nothing."

He shrugged his shoulders. They made small talk, and then Red Mac drifted away. Stewart and Cartwright went into the dining room for lunch. After they had ordered, Stewart said, "I'm hoping you can help me. I need to hire or even buy a ship capable of the voyage to Bombay. We've tried everyone we can think of—the navy, civilian shipping lines—but no luck."

"I've a friend in the Port Commissioners' office," replied Cartwright. "Let's pay him a visit after lunch."

At half past two, Cartwright's car dropped them outside a red brick building on the corner of Hare Street and Strand Road, near the river. An ornamental cannon pointed its barrel boldly through the

100

front door. They walked up a brass-edged staircase to the coolness of a corridor on the second floor. Indian messengers, known as *chuprassis*, wearing neat khaki uniforms, sat on benches outside offices. They stood up to salaam the two men. Cartwright knocked on a door near a seven-foot model in a glass case of the twin-screw suction hopper-dredger *Gunga*, built by William Simons & Co., Ltd., in Renfrew, Scotland, in 1921. Gunga was the local name for the Hooghly River.

Inside the room, a plump, middle-aged man in shirt sleeves sat mopping his brow behind a vast desk. Screens outside the windows kept out the early afternoon glare. The blades of a ceiling fan were reflected in the polished marble floor. A large-scale map of the Hooghly River and wooden sections of model hulls decorated the walls.

"Hallo, there," he said cheerfully, gripping Cartwright by the hand.

"Let me introduce Gavin Stewart," said Cartwright. "One of my oldest friends, Doug Lomax."

"We've not met, but I know your company, Stewarts and Lloyds," said Lomax. "We've done business together in the past. What can I do for you now? There must be something. Old Jock here never comes to see me unless he wants something—if it is only a case of booze."

"Not as difficult as that this time, Doug," Cartwright assured him. "But for your ears only, Gavin wants a boat capable of sailing to Bombay and back, with 20 men aboard, excluding crew."

"Five thousand two fifty miles give or take a few," said Lomax, making a face. "You'll need quite a craft for that, especially at this time of year. Quite a risk, too. Cargo ships are taking a hell of a hammering from submarines. Much worse than ever appears in the papers. Why the devil do you want to go to Bombay by sea? It's quicker by rail!"

Stewart and Cartwright exchanged glances.

"Oh, something secret, is it?" asked Lomax. "Well, let me tell you, I was in the first war in the trenches for three years, and as Jock knows I was also in the

Light Horse until I married and my lady wife took exception to all those evening parades. If you want a little help, give a little help. What's all this about?"

He motioned them to two cane armchairs. They sat down.

"I am in the army, helping with a secret job," Stewart began carefully. "I can't be more specific. I have to transport 20 men from Calcutta to do a special job somewhere in the Indian Ocean, and then on to Bombay. Not just men, Lomax. Light Horsemen. You follow me?"

"I am beginning to. And you can't get any official help for one reason or another, so you come around the back way to see what you can scrounge from us?"

"To put it crudely, yes."

"Let me ask you a question now? If we lend you a ship, and you lose it, who pays?"

"I can give you a letter this afternoon accepting responsibility at an agreed value," said Stewart.

"Fair enough," said Lomax. "Well, let's see what we've got. We're not a ship-hiring agency, you know. You will have to have a tug or a barge or some god awful thing that isn't supposed to be seaworthy beyond the Hooghly River. But that's up to you. You've got to make the journey, not me, thank God!"

Lomax glanced at a blackboard on one wall on which were chalked details of ships involved with the Port Commissioners' activities on the Hooghly River. He patted his forehead again with his handkerchief, then took a looseleaf book from the drawer and began to look at the pages.

"This is what we can do for you," he announced at last. "*Phoebe*. Otherwise Hopper Barge No. 5. Rather like the model of the *Gunga* outside my office, but older. Built in Glasgow in 1912 by Ferguson Bros. Good, sound makers. Overall length, 206 feet. Breadth, 38 feet. Indicated horsepower, 677. Original operating speed, nine knots an hour. Present operating speed, probably a bit less."

"Can she make the distance?" asked Stewart.

Lomax shrugged.

"She's basically just a hull, a bloody great floating iron bath with an engine. We use her up against a river dredger which has buckets on an endless chain scooping up mud from the river bed. We fill *Phoebe's* hull, then she steams out to sea. The captain opens two doors under her belly, the mud drops out, and back she comes to begin again.

"But you'll need a crew of 20 at least, and there's just no room for another 20 men. They can't sleep in the hold. It stinks like a sewer, and anyway you'll need it to carry the coal to keep the boiler going."

"Where do the crew sleep?"

"Wherever they can. There are a couple of bunks for officers. No need for any more for *Phoebe* doesn't usually operate at night. And, remember, this trip will take 10 days to a fortnight each way from here—if you're lucky."

This meant that for reasons of time and space it would be impossible to embark the Light Horse contingent in Calcutta and sail around India as Stewart had hoped. They would have to travel by train to some other port and join *Phoebe* there. But the main thing was that at least they had a ship—of a kind. Lomax was already scribbling figures on a sheet of notepad. He tore this off and handed it to Stewart.

"That is what she'll cost to rent for three weeks minimum. You will be responsible for all wages, salaries, mooring fees, pilotage charges, fuel, rations and insurance against act of war, collision, storm, malpractice, mutiny, foundering, and so on."

"You will have a letter this afternoon confirming everything," said Stewart, putting the paper in his pocket. He stood up to leave.

"One last thing," said Lomax. "What about a captain and crew?"

"You mean you can't supply them, too?"

"Sorry. No can do. Most of our British staff are away in the services. Those left like me are too old or too busy.'

"So where can we find a crew?" asked Stewart. "Can you help us?"

"Well, there are always some men between trips. Maybe they have jumped ship for one reason or another, or the ship they were due to join has been sunk. You'll have to find them yourself, but I can give you the name of someone who might help you."

Stewart warmed to Lomax and his helpful approach. The discussion was typical of others in which he had taken part during years in India before the war; and each time the feeling of comradeship, even kinship, far from home touched his heart anew.

Perhaps, he thought, this sequence of events was not confined to India? Perhaps it also obtained all round the Empire, where so many of the men in control of companies and districts, or in the services seemed to share the same background, the same outlook, the same aims? Even though they had never met each other before, within an hour it was as though they belonged to the same family.

Lomax wrote a name and address on a piece of paper.

"Commander Bernard Davies," he said. "He is a regular naval officer who joined us after he retired before the war. Then he went back in the Navy. Now he is going to rejoin us. So he's physically free and might be willing to help."

"You trust him, Doug?" asked Cartwright.

"Anywhere. Even round the Horn in a Force Ten."

"Even in *Phoebe?*" asked Stewart.

"Especially in *Phoebe*," said Lomax with a grin. "He'd like the challenge of it."

He pressed the bell for a *chuprassi* to call a bearer to bring afternoon tea and biscuits for the three of them.

Bernard Davies was a trim, middle-aged Welshman of medium height who had a flat in the center of Calcutta. After 20 years' service, mostly in aircraft carriers and destroyers, he had retired. He was married, with two young children, and in England during the late nineteen thirties, a suitable job where his experience could be utilized had been difficult to find. Then he met someone on leave from Calcutta who told him that the Port Commissioners there had a vacancy. Davies applied for it and was appointed Assistant Conservator, in charge of a 200-mile stretch of the Hooghly River inland from the coast.

The Hooghly is an extremely treacherous river to navigate, because twice a year it rises in full and dangerous floods. In March and April, snow melts in the hills and sweeps down, shifting sandbanks and flooding hundreds of miles on either side of its banks.

The second crucial season comes when the big sea tides force their way upriver and push these sands in another direction. One of Bernard Davies' duties was to utilize a fleet of hopper barges, like *Phoebe* and *Gunga,* to keep tracks open between these shifting sandbanks so that ships could pass freely up and down the river.

He opened the door to Gavin Stewart, and looked at him enquiringly.

"I have just come from Doug Lomax," Stewart explained. "I am with the Ministry of Economic Warfare. I wonder if I could discuss something important with you?"

Davies examined Stewart's identity card and invited him inside.

"What I have to say is for your ears only."

"Understood," said Davies.

"I am hiring *Phoebe* to go to Goa. We have to carry out a secret task there, and then go on to Bombay."

"Who's we?"

"The Calcutta Light Horse."

Davies raised his eyebrows.

"Some of those chaps are getting on a bit for that sort of job, aren't they?"

"There are reasons for using them."

"How many men are going?"

"Roughly, twenty."

"Impossible with a full crew," replied Davies immediately. "*Phoebe's* far too small."

"So Lomax tells me. But she's the only boat available. And we have to get there by sea. Have you any suggestions?"

"I suppose I could take her round the coast—at a pinch—and pick up your people some place south of Goa. Say, Calicut or Cochin. You'd have to get your fellows there by train."

"You think *Phoebe* can carry so many people the four or five hundred miles from one of those ports to Goa?"

"If we have reasonable weather, yes. A very cramped and uncomfortable voyage, though. And it means starting as soon as possible in case the monsoon's early. I wouldn't put her nose a mile out of the Hooghly in the monsoon. She was never designed for open sea work, you know. Purely a river boat, and like the fellows you're taking, a bit old for rough stuff. And we couldn't possibly carry enough life rafts for the crew and your people, plus coal and rations."

"Do I take it, then, you would be her captain?"

"So long as I can check with the Port Commissioners and they agree, yes. There is only one difficulty. I haven't a Master's Ticket."

"Is that important?" asked Stewart.

"I qualified as a master mariner when I was in the navy, but not for civilian ships. We'll be flying the Red Ensign for the journey round India, so if anything goes wrong I need someone who can say he's the master. Then, when we go into action, I'll take over.

"I have a friend, William Harrison, who I think will agree to take on this job. And I'd also like to bring along a chief engineer who knows *Phoebe*'s engine, and a retired petty officer who can make himself generally useful."

"That's fine. What about the rest of the crew?"

"I can find enough lascars to man the barge, but I daren't tell them how far from Calcutta we are going, for they're only used to working around the coast."

"Pay them what you have to," Stewart told him.

"I'll need to give them double wages for a start. And then I'll keep largely in sight of land, because they are not deep sea sailors."

106

"I'll be responsible for any expenses you have."

"That's something. First, I think we should alter her appearance a bit in case anyone wonders why a Hooghly River barge is so far from home. How much time have I got?"

"Days, only. Less than a week."

"Hmm. Doesn't give us a chance to do much in the camouflage line. I'll lengthen the funnel so from a distance she'll look like a small oiler or a waterboat."

"Do what you like. I'll leave all arrangements to you."

Davies smiled.

"Thanks," he said. "I've commanded many ships in peace and war, but this is the first time I—or probably anyone else—has taken a hopper barge into action."

As Bill Grice's bearer opened the door of the flat to Cartwright, Grice came into the hall.

"I wanted to see you, Bill," Cartwright explained. "Privately."

The two men went into the sitting room. In one corner a gramophone was playing "The Blue Danube." Grice lifted the arm. Violins squealed protestingly and died.

"Well?"

"I hear you are calling a meeting for the others," began Cartwright.

"That's right. And I am sorry you will not be coming."

"I am sorry, too," replied Cartwright. "But surely there's *something* I could do? Your children are still small, Bill. My only son is grown up, and I don't even know whether he is alive or dead. It is the waiting and hoping and not knowing that is so awful—for my wife and me. Whatever it is, I don't mind, so long as it's useful. I was in the navy in the last war, like you, remember."

"I'd forgotten that," said Grice slowly. "Well, there *is* something, but I don't know whether it's up your

107

street. Pugh said he would arrange for his people to handle it. But if you could, then this would be a Calcutta Light Horse show all through."

"What has to be done?" asked Cartwright simply.

"I must make it clear that no one else knows where they are going or what they have to do."

"I can keep a still tongue."

"We are heading for Goa. A German ship is in Marmagoa harbor. We have to sink her or seize her. It doesn't matter which, so long as we put her out of action. Three other Axis ships are also in that harbor, each with a full crew, so someone has to go ahead and organize a diversion on shore to get as many of them off their ships on a certain night next month."

"Can you give me the night?"

"If you will undertake this job."

"I'll do it,' said Cartwright at once.

"Then it's the ninth of March. Pugh says his people will supply any money you need. You can either take it with you, or see the local rep of Cox and King's."

"Good old Pricks and Princes," said Cartwright, using the irreverent nickname by which this most distinguished firm was known to some Light Horsemen. "What have you in mind for a diversion?"

"That's largely up to you. There may be a saint's day or a public holiday which could be the excuse for a fiesta or carnival. Or bribe all the brothel keepers in Marmagoa to give sailors free bangs during that week. Organize an official party. Invite all seagoing officers, with officers of the local police, the harbor guards and so on. Anyone—and everyone. Spend what you like. Do what you like. But always remember that less than 20 of us will be taking on the crews of four big ships. So every man you can somehow persuade to go ashore that night helps our chances."

"Understood. So what would you say is the first thing I should do, Bill?"

"The first thing," replied Grice gravely, "is to get to Goa And the next thing is to visit all those brothels."

108

street, Pugh said he would arrange for his people to
handle it. But if you could free that this would be a
Calcutta Light Horse showing all

EIGHT

The Light Horse bearer placed a tray with a pot
of early morning tea, an apple and a biscuit at the
side of Dick Melborne's bed, and then expertly rolled
up the mosquito net and shook his master gently by
the shoulder.

"Morning time, sahib," he said. "And there is just
now this letter."

Melborne sat up, rubbing sleep from his eyes and
glanced at the alarm clock. Ten past five. Time for
a shower, a shave and off to Ballygunge *maidan* for
a session of unarmed combat. He slit open the brown
envelope with the apple knife and read the single
typed sheet, headed 24 Park Street, Calcutta.

"Kit required by members proceeding to Ranchi
on special course."

Melborne read on, puzzled and not realizing until
he was half-way down the page that there was no
special course at Ranchi. These were his marching
orders.

All members, he read, would travel in civilian
clothes, but they should take with them khaki dungarees, webbing gaiters and ankle boots. These should
have leather soles but no nails or studs or metal
heels. In addition, every member should gum half an
inch thickness of felt to the soles of his boots. They
should also take a topee or a bush hat, and a bedding roll. A mosquito net was required, and a change
of shorts or slacks, and a great-coat and, of course,
a knife, fork, spoon, mug and a plate.

They should carry first field dressings (little packets
containing cotton wool pads and gauze bandages that
fitted in a special pocket in the dungarees), a razor,
a toothbrush and a supply of cigarettes if they were

smokers, and not more than one bottle of alcohol apiece if they were drinkers.

They should draw from the stores their pistols and 18 rounds of ammunition each, with a knife S.K.— for Silent Killing—a cosh and a pair of handcuffs.

Melborne laid the letter aside and poured himself a cup of tea. Felt on his boots, a cosh and handcuffs? What the hell was in store for them? Was this only a police job after all, to arrest some malcontents? Grice had specifically mentioned Germans, but where would they find Germans to knife or handcuff in India, or wherever they were going on a short sea voyage? He got up and went into the next room, where Harry Squire was sitting on the edge of his bed, reading his instructions.

"What do you make of it?" Melborne asked him. Squire shrugged.

"Mine not to reason why," he said. "Doesn't make much sense to me at this time of day. But I see there's a meeting called for tonight at 18:30."

"Didn't read that far," admitted Melborne, and went back to his room to finish his tea.

All the others had received similar letters, but apart from raising eyebrows and shrugging shoulders, they did not discuss them that morning in front of the staff sergeant at Ballygunge. But seeing, in a typed official letter, their orders to draw knives, coshes and pistols, and inexplicable instructions to gum thick felt to their boot soles, made them realize that this might not be quite the light-hearted romp they had imagined; a wartime extension of pre-war annual camps, with sing-songs to Cren Lumsdaine's witty words, apple pie beds and plenty to drink.

That evening, 18 silent men crowded into headquarters to hear what news Grice had to tell them.

"Gentlemen," he began. "You have all received your instructions, and I can answer no questions about them. Just make sure they are all carried out and you have all the items required. Once we leave here, it will be impossible to make up any deficiencies. We are going initially to Madras, by train, in three separate parties."

The Last Action of the Calcutta Light Horse

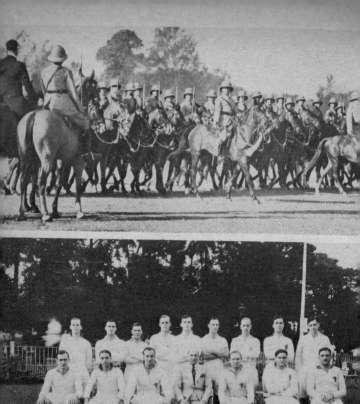

Top: Proclamation Parade, January 1, 1936.
The Calcutta Light Horse marching past the Honorary
Colonel, Lord Linlithgow, then Viceroy.

Bottom: The Calcutta Light Horse rugger team
1939, winners of the Bethell Trophy. All 15 saw
commissioned service in the forces 1939–45.
Some were killed, some never returned from POW
camps. Lt. Col. W. H. Grice, ADC, in center.

Top: A paperchase 1939—the first fence.

Middle: Annual camp exercises.

Bottom: Another time the Calcutta
Light Horse took to the water.

Top: Col. W. H. Grice, ADC, ED.

Bottom: The traffic policeman on duty
here saw the kidnapping of Trompeta and his wife
from their house on the left of the road.

Top: Ferguson Brothers of
Port Glasgow built seven of
these Hopper Barges between
1911 and 1912 but only
Phoebe was used as an
"assault craft" in the Far East.

Bottom: The Calcutta Light
Horse club house as it is today.

Top: *Ehrenfels*.
Middle: *Drachenfels*
Bottom: *Braunfels*

Top: *Ehrenfels* and *Braunfels* in Marmagoa
harbor before the raid. (ILLUSTRATED LONDON NEWS)

Middle: The Axis ships burning in Marmagoa
harbor, March 9, 1943.

Bottom: Settling into the water.

INDIAN NEWSFRONT

NAZIS SET OWN
SHIPS ON FIRE

Trouble Among Crews In Goa

After three years' incarceration in Marmagoa, considerable dissension is understood to have become rife amongst the crews of the German cargo ships. It is believed that the Nazi element on board favoured the plan of making a dash for the open seas with a view to joining the Japanese in Singapore. The remainder, whose morale had been lowered by the heavy toll of disease levied by the past hot weather, the cramped accommodation on board, coupled with monotony, favoured the plan of taking up residence on shore for the duration of the war.

This led to a violent struggle on one of the ships. Finally the malcontents appear to have fired their vessels rather than face the desperate voyage.

Top: *Drachenfels* after the raid.

Middle: "Mutinous Axis crews burn their ships in Goa." Headline in *Illustrated Weekly of India*, March 21, 1943.

Bottom: As reported in *The Times of India*.

After Calcutta and Bombay, Madras was India's most important port, 1,000 miles south of Calcutta on the east coast. Surely this must mean that they were to embark there in naval craft, and cross the Bay of Bengal for some desperate action on the Arakan coast of Burma?

"Lieutenant Cren Lumsdaine and Trooper Dick Melborne will leave tomorrow from Howrah Station on the Madras mail. On the day after, Corporal Manners and Troopers Harry Squire, Mike Crofter and Mark Hilliard will catch the same train. The rest I will take on Sunday afternoon. We will be joined by some others not in the Regiment or the Calcutta Scottish. First, there is Lewis Pugh, who I need hardly introduce to any of you because of his family connections with the Light Horse. Next is Gavin Stewart, who's never been a member, but has often been our guest in this club. And then there's Yogi Crossley, who most of you also know either socially or through business connections. He is going to deal with some—ah—explosive matters.

"I want to impress one fact on you all. This is not an exercise, this is real. The other day I saw on an army notice board this information: 'Good health—keep your bowels open. Good security—keep your mouth shut.' Remember, careless talk costs lives. And on this operation, the lives it costs can be our own."

The British Consul in Marmagoa sat in the ante-room to his office, one sheet of foolscap in the old upright Oliver typewriter usually used by his Goanese secretary. It was long after hours, and beyond the silver cylindrical shapes of the oil tanks, dockyard floodlights were shining. He typed slowly, pecking at the keys, his brow furrowed in concentration. This was a report he felt he should produce himself with no copies for the file.

A short time before, he had forwarded his report about the disappearance of a German subject and his wife from Panjim. He had not mentioned the fact that two of his own countrymen had previously called to ascertain the man's address, for he did not know who read all these reports or how secure they really were. He was an old soldier, and knew from his own experience how little, apparently isolated happenings, when viewed against other equally unimportant and seemingly unconnected incidents, could sometimes produce clues to a problem which had previously seemed insoluble.

There was no obvious link in his mind between these events and sudden activity aboard the four Axis ships, but then he only saw a part of the picture. Others might instantly see the significance of items of cargo being shifted from ship to ship. Sailors had also moved a quantity of car batteries from the *Braunfels*, and marble slabs and sheets of metal and heavy sacks of flour from the *Anfora*, and distributed them among all the vessels.

In addition, when German and Italian sailors came ashore, they searched for logs and scrap metal—the rear axle of an abandoned car, a pair of rusty wheels, a part from an ancient mangle—and carried these unlikely items aboard. Others were buying drums of kerosene, far in excess of any use that the consul could imagine, and through his binoculars, he had watched fatigue parties stacking the sacks and slabs of marble and scrap metal in little piles around the decks.

What if the sacks contained some of the explosives he knew the *Drachenfels* was carrying, and these pyramids of junk were to be blown up in some way—possibly using the batteries? But—why?

Perhaps the two men who had claimed to belong to the Midnapore Zemindary Company also planned an attack on the ships? If so, they could not realize the defensive preparations they would face unless he warned them.

The consul had thought long before committing these tiny items of news to paper, because he guessed that his superiors might smile at them, but he was here to report what was happening in Marmagoa, and he felt it his duty to record this activity.

As he typed, he heard the doorbell ring. It was late

for any official caller, so he carefully removed the paper from the typewriter and placed it upside down in the desk drawer before he opened the office door. A strong smell of oil, overlaid with the scent of jasmine and night-blooming flowers rushed in, thick and sickly. A peon from the local post office handed him a telegram. The consul tipped him, locked the door and opened the yellow envelope.

"Please report Bombay March 6 for special consultation. Accommodation reserved for one week Taj hotel for you and your wife."

The consul replaced the sheet in his machine and finished typing. He would take it with him to Bombay and hand it to his superior there. Then he locked up his office and went home to tell his wife the good news of an unexpected week's leave.

Mark Hilliard smoothed his hair nervously, and pulled down his alpaca jacket. Then he knocked gently on the door of his superior's office. He was an accountant, and rather younger than his Light Horse contemporaries. Flat feet had kept him out of the services, and in an attempt to keep up with the exploits of a brother in the Navy and a sister in the WAAF, he volunteered for every regimental duty he could. In addition, he loyally worked longer hours at his office than his colleagues, and found that this decication was very soon taken for granted.

"Well?" the chief accountant asked him. "Having trouble with that tobacco audit? We need it as soon as possible, you know. Head Office is crying out for the figures."

"Actually, it wasn't about that, sir."

"Well, what was it about?"

His superior was a short irascible man, thin on top and given to indigestion.

"It was about that fortnight's leave I asked for last month, sir."

"Leave?" repeated the chief accountant, as though he had never heard the word before.

"That course at Ranchi with the Light Horse."

113

"Good God! I'd forgotten all about that. Well, what about it?"

"I hadn't a date then, sir, when I needed to take it, but I have just been given one. I would like to leave this Saturday."

"But, dammit, you won't be through with the audit until next Wednesday at the earliest."

"I am sorry, sir, but this is important."

"Do you think this audit isn't, then? Who else can do it? I'm doing three men's jobs here as it is, and now you want to take a fortnight off to go shooting at targets.

"I saw Bill Grice in the Bengal Club the other day and gave him a piece of my mind. Told him I thought it was disgraceful taking fellows off work to go target shooting in Ranchi."

Hilliard said nothing, and the older man continued in a more conciliatory tone.

"Well, I suppose I can't stop you taking leave when it's due. But I hope this is the last time you want time off for this sort of thing."

"You can be sure of that, sir. It will be the last time."

Mike Crofter, another accountant, sat in his room in his chummery in Tollygunge. The bedroom was impersonally furnished with hired furniture, and owed any individuality to its occupant's taste and sporting inclinations. Three framed photographs stood on a chest of drawers. One was of Crofter's mother, the widow of a Hertfordshire clergyman; the second showed his school second eleven cricket team when he was captain, and his younger brother, now missing at Singapore, had been twelfth man. The third was of his fiancée, Marion, the daughter of a Calcutta surgeon.

Two tennis racquets lay in presses in the corner, with a bag of golf clubs and a stack of unread copies of *The Accountant*. Crofter sat at the bedside table, with the reading light lit and a pile of note-paper and envelopes in front of him. He was writing eight letters to his fiancée, numbering each one carefully in sequence on the first page. They were the supposed account of a visit he was making to a tea estate to do a snap internal audit. He wrote to her regularly twice a week, and knew she would be concerned if there was any lapse in his letters. He intended to post them to a friend on the estate, and ask him to forward them to her at intervals. Crofter was a careful and religious man, the same age as his friend Hilliard, and still a civilian because of severe short sight. He wore spectacles, and as he wrote he would remove them, polish the lenses between finger and thumb and replace them. This was strictly a nervous gesture because he found the deception on which he was engaged distasteful, although, in his view, necessary.

How much more difficult it was to express something in words instead of in columns of figures! He had to invent meetings with people—and what if his fiancée should meet any of them before he returned? What would she think if they said they had not seen him on the estate? The words of Sir Walter Scott, which his father had drummed into him in many a sermon, came back now with their full meaning: "O, what a tangled web we weave, when first we practice to deceive."

With a sigh, Crofter pulled another sheet of paper towards him.

"My dearest Marion," he began for the sixth time.

Jack Breene stood alone in the study of his large house in Alipore, one of Calcutta's smarter and more expensive suburbs. A tumbler of whiskey and water stood on his desk. A cigar grew a gray head of ash in a silver ashtray.

Breene was a cheerful man with a loud laugh and the habit of slapping an acquaintance on the back in the Light Horse bar, and then turning him around by the palm of his hand to hear the latest joke he had to tell.

He was a senior member of a large insurance company and friends ascribed his considerable success in this profession to his outgoing character. Others, less charitable, said clients took out policies they did not really want in order to be rid of him, so they would not have to bear his funny stories or, worse, become the victims of one of his practical jokes. Over the years, this fate had befallen a number of his friends.

Now, Breene looked like the victim of someone else's prank, for he stood, incongruously dressed in traveling clothes of khaki shirt and shorts, with a revolver tied tightly by its lanyard around his waist.

Carefully, he unbuttoned his fly and lowered his shorts, then pulled them up over the revolver. He took a sip of whiskey, and drew on his cigar. Then he walked a few paces around the room, and jumped up and down, grimacing with discomfort. The tip of the revolver's blued barrel still pointed down at the floor from the right leg of his shorts.

Damn the thing he thought irritably. The lanyard was so tight it nearly cut him in two, and still that bloody revolver wasn't completely concealed. Breene dropped his shorts again to make a further adjustment, and his wife walked into the study.

"Jack," she said in astonishment. "Whatever are you doing?"

"Trying to hide this revolver."

"But why? I've never seen you with a gun before. Is there some trouble?"

"Heavens no. Well, not yet, that is. But I need to take this on the course at Ranchi."

"Oh, that. But why conceal that in your shorts? Can't you carry it in a holster like soldiers do?"

"I don't want anyone to see it."

"But why ever not?"

"I'm not meant to be carrying it, that's why."

"Are you sure you are all right? I mean, every morning for the last week you have been up at an ungodly hour and out on some exercise on the *maidan*. Now, you are off to Ranchi with a revolver you say you shouldn't have, hidden in your shorts."

"There *is* something special on," admitted Breene.

116

"I can't tell you what, so please don't ask me. But if you really want to help I'd like your suggestions as to where I can keep this confounded weapon out of sight on a rail journey?"

Years of being the unwilling butt of her husband's jokes rose before her. As she had so often heard him lead on others, she repeated his question.

"You really want me to tell you where to put it so no one will see it?"

Breene nodded irritably. So she told him.

Melborne sat well back on the hot cracked leather seat of his open taxi as it waited in a queue to cross Howrah Bridge to reach the station. The bridge, a mass of gray painted iron girders, looking as though it had been made by a giant Meccano set, was jammed solid in both directions.

Cren Lumsdaine sat next to Melborne, now and then glancing at his watch, worried in case they should miss their train. Cars, army trucks, single decker silver buses had been waiting for so long, with trams and *gharries*, that many drivers had switched off their engines, for petrol was rationed and expensive. Coolies trotted past, balancing enormous loads on their heads. Underneath the bridge, the Hooghly River swept sluggishly to the sea.

Both men wore khaki bush shirts and trousers, the usual wear for Europeans making a tour of some outstation or tea garden or a business visit to another city. They sat with their feet up on their bedding rolls. These resembled huge Swiss rolls bound by two leather straps with a leather carrying handle. Their clothes and equipment were inside the rolls. Every now and then, Lumsdaine and Melborne shifted position because their revolvers, under the waistbands of their trousers, dug uncomfortably into their flesh. Slowly, their taxi moved forward to Howrah Station, a red brick reminder of the solidity of Victorian architecture. Outside it, rickshaws waited in neat lines, shafts on the ground; tonga ponies

117

munched piles of hay, and beggar women holding children on their hips ran alongside their taxi, hands held out for alms.

Lumsdaine paid the driver and called two coolies to carry the bedding rolls into the station. The booking hall roof soared upward like a cathedral, on pale green girders. Birds flew in and out, and perched on the hands of the clock, decorated with wings to show the speed at which time could pass. The Howrah-Madras Mail waited, engine steaming, on platform 12, all doors open. They already had bought tickets individually and so walked straight to their reserved compartment. Here they would spend that night, the following day and night, and reach Madras on the morning of the third day.

A guard locked their door and saluted. He blew his whistle and waved a green flag. The train jerked forward. The first two volunteers from the Light Horse were on their way to war.

Fourteen hundred miles to the west, as Melborne and Lumsdaine began their journey, Cartwright was ending his. He sat behind the wheel of a second-hand Ford V8 touring car he had bought cheaply in Belgaum, and would sell there on his return. It was impossible to hire a car, and to engage a taxi and driver would be impractical if he needed to leave Goa in a hurry.

The canvas hood flapped like a loose drumskin above his head as he bumped down the road into Vasco da Gama, the residential suburb of Marmagoa. For a second before rickety shabby houses hid the view, he saw the blue crescent of the harbor. A British tanker was anchored near the Burmah-Shell oil tanks. Behind this lay the four Axis ships, *Ehrenfels* standing out because of her size and modern lines.

Then rooftops cut off the view and he was down near the docks, passing cafés and hotels with splendid names; the Ritz, the Diana Bar, the Marcel. In some cafés, gramophones blared harsh music as he passed. Behind balcony rails, near hand-painted signs advertizing X-Ray specialists and dentists and doctors with names like Da Leppo and Diaz, sharp-eyed Goanese children watched the crowded streets, missing nothing. On a strip of land near the docks, two vultures dug curved and bloodied beaks into the stinking carcass of a pig blown up with putrefaction and decay. Cartwright wrinkled his nose at the smell and drew up outside the Gran Palacio Hotel. This stood on a crossroads about 100 yards from the docks and was the best hotel in town.

Now that Cartwright was actively engaged in something he considered worthwhile, he had eaten better, slept more peacefully, and had at last resigned himself to the fact that perhaps his son was dead. Well, he should be thankful they had known so many good times together before the war. He felt sorry for fathers who had not been so fortunate.

He signed the register in his wife's maiden name, which he could remember easily enough and which also began with the same initial "C". This might be useful if anyone grew suspicious of his identity and checked the initials on his handkerchiefs or shirts.

He had told his wife he was going on tour for about a fortnight.

"But you were away only last month," she replied.

"I know," he had said. "But this is something different."

"Are you going up-country again?"

"No such luck. Bombay this time. Some special business."

"But what kind of special business? You haven't even an office in Bombay. And you promised me we'd have a break by the sea before it hots up."

"I know," he agreed. "I can't tell you exactly what I am going to do. But its something to do with the Light Horse."

"Can I contact you if there's any news of Tim?"

"I will ring you," he promised. "But please be careful what you say on the line, my dear. And whatever you do, don't mention the Light Horse."

She looked at him, trusting him, not seeing him as he was, growing bald and running to fat, tired after

119

too many years, too many worries, in a cruel climate, but as he had been when Tim was small. Just as sometimes, looking at Tim, she had seen her husband in his eyes, in his bearing and his manner. Now Tim had gone and Jock was going, and she felt lonely and tired and out of things. She could not put her thoughts into words, and if she had tried then her husband would not have understood. She wished, not for the first time, that they'd had a daughter; a daughter would understand.

"I'll be in most evenings," she told him.

This was always the best time to telephone long distance in India because when the sun went down, atmospherics decreased, and with luck it was actually possible to hear fairly clearly across hundreds of miles what the person at the other end of the line was saying.

Cartwright's thoughts were interrupted by the arrival of a bearer in a white uniform. Cartwright followed him to a room facing the harbor, and unpacked his bag. He carried no passport, no driving license, no letters addressed to himself, no means of identification whatever. He had some high denomination rupee banknotes in a waterproof oilskin pouch on a canvas body belt. A further large sum had been deposited in an account opened in his wife's maiden name in the Marmagoa branch of the Banco Agricultura.

It was possible that the Portuguese political police would examine his belongings, since he was a foreigner, but they would discover nothing about him he did not mind them knowing. The only item that might surprise them he had placed in a padlocked metal box which a Belgaum blacksmith had welded under the floor of his car. He kept the only key of this padlock on a fine gold chain around his neck.

Pugh and Grice had given Cartwright certain addresses, which he had memorized. Now he left the hotel, climbed into his car again, and drove back along the road by which he had entered Vasco da Gama. A couple of miles out in the empty countryside, he stopped, lifted the carpet and opened the box. He removed a small parcel wrapped in brown paper which he put in the dashboard cubby-hole. Then he drove on.

Water buffaloes cooled their dusty hides in muddy pools; a wayside cross wore a garland of withered flowers. Some miles nearer Panjim he turned into a gateway marked by concrete posts and drove up to a house built in the Portuguese eastern colonial style with a pagoda-shaped roof.

The walls were whitewashed; plants sprouted from terracotta pots on the verandah. A Goanese servant in white livery showed him into a sitting room. Silk shades drawn across the windows gave the room a dim, greenish aspect as though they were under water. A Goanese man of early middle-age came into the room and looked at him enquiringly. Because of the sallow color of his skin, the number of carved ivory ornaments on side tables, and Chinese cabinets bright with red and black lacquer, Cartwright guessed that he had served most of his life as a government official overseas in such outposts as Mozambique and Macao. He hoped he would have no trouble in coming to a satisfactory accommodation with him.

Cartwright shook this man's hand and introduced himself in his wife's name.

"I believe an Indian colleague told you I would be calling?"

The Goanese official bowed his head in affirmation. The Indian SOE operator who had unsuccessfully tried to bribe Captain Röfer had also paid him a visit.

"He intimated that a friend might wish to discuss a private business matter," he replied carefully in English.

"I would suggest we discuss it outside by the river. It is cooler there."

This was not altogether so, but it would certainly be safer; no one could easily overhear their conversation in the open air.

121

They walked down wooden steps, across the dusty dried-up grass to the edge of the Zuari. Motor launches chugged gamely against the running tide.

"Now," said Cartright. "I hate to come to business abruptly when we have hardly met, but my time is short and the need urgent."

"Please continue," said the other man impassively. His eyes were two dark olives watching Cartwright's face.

"You have two sons at school in Dehra Dun in India?"

Surprise showed briefly in the official's face.

"That is so," he agreed. "And their fees are ruinously expensive. We have serious inflation here in Goa. In India, our currency only fetches a quarter of its face value. So it is as though I were paying fees for eight sons and not just two."

"I have heard as much," replied Cartwright. "It might be possible for me to alleviate your expenses—to pay all your fees—if we could reach an accommodation."

"On what matter do you seek such an arrangement, senhor?"

It was not the first time he had been offered a bribe. He hoped it would not be the last, because his salary was meagre, and took little account of rising costs. But first there was a delicate area of negotiation in which a rigid protocol must be observed.

"I need your help," said Cartwright simply. "I want to ask you to use your great influence to persuade the Governor-General here, or some other senior official, to organize a reception. I want every officer concerned with the port of Marmagoa to be invited, and all officers of every ship anchored in the harbor. As a neutral country, this is diplomatically quite in order. I also wish for a carnival or fiesta to be arranged which will attract the crews of all these vessels."

"The fiesta is no problem, senhor. But I must tell you that the Governor-General does not entertain a great deal. He is a very busy man. Also, he is due to leave tomorrow on a tour of the colony. What you have in mind would therefore be very difficult and expensive to arrange."

"The difficulties I leave to you to overcome," replied Cartwright shortly. "I will deal with the expense. How much?"

"I could not give any sum without consulting others. I would have to arrange food and wine and servants, and other details. But our countries are old allies, senhor, and I will certainly give your request my best attention."

"I must have something firm before I leave," said Cartwright. "If you cannot help me, then I will make other arrangements."

"You mentioned my sons and their school fees, senhor?"

"So I did. I could arrange for all their fees to be paid into a bank in India. No money would come here. There would be no risk of any discovery in Goa."

The other man stood for a moment, fear of consequences fighting with greed.

Cartwright glanced ostentatiously at his watch.

"I have unfortunately little time," he said. "I must press you for a decision. Is it yes or no?"

The official swallowed.

"It is yes, senhor."

"Right. I have already printed some cards. You can fill in the name of whoever will actually be the host."

They walked back towards his car. He undid the little parcel he had taken from the metal box. It contained beautifully engraved invitation cards, dye-stamped with the crest of Goa and the green and red colors of Portugal. This had caused Fletcher some headaches in Meerut, but through his contacts he had managed a perfect translation of the text.

"These are beautiful," said the official, turning them over thoughtfully in his hands.

"Please ensure that it is also a beautiful reception," said Cartwright. "The time, as you see, is 22:00 hours on the evening of March the ninth."

"What is your reason for this?" the man asked him.

"That I cannot tell you," said Cartwright. "And I

think it would be unprofitable and unwise to ponder too deeply upon it."

A puzzled frown furrowed the other man's forehead.

"Others may also enquire as to the reason for this reception," Cartwright continued. "It is important—vital—that they have no suspicion it is anything other than an expression of your country's hospitality and neutrality. If this condition is not met, then I would feel free to renegotiate my side of our arrangement. That would mean, regrettably, but inevitably, your sons would—ah—suffer."

"I understand."

"Good. And to reimburse your immediate and personal expenses, I have brought you some money."

He handed him an envelope.

"I am at the Gran Palacio hotel, if you wish to contact me."

The official did not follow Cartwright as he walked to his car but stood, holding the envelope. He was remembering the inexplicable disappearance of the two Germans from Panjim, and rumors that the British had organized it.

He thought about his sons and his visitor's use of the word "suffer." He felt uneasy. Then he folded the envelope and the banknotes inside crackled reassuringly, and he felt more cheerful.

Cartwright was half a mile along the road towards Marmagoa when he realized that he had not been offered the glass of Madeira which was usual for callers at that hour. Not to worry, Cartwright decided cheerfully. He would make up for it with a large brandy in the Gran Palacio bar.

The Madras Mail steamed into Madras station at a slow and stately pace. All third class carriages were crammed with Indians. Hundreds more clung outside the doors. Others lay full length on the roof, or crouched around the buffers between each carriage. They had traveled without tickets, and as the train slowed to a standstill they leapt down and scuttled away into sidings.

Bill Grice led the final contingent of the Light Horse through the crowds that crammed the arrival platform waiting for friends, past squads of British troops with scrubbed topees and starched khaki drill uniforms, waiting for other trains, and out into the station yard.

They hailed two taxis and drove to the Connemara Hotel, where the men who had traveled ahead of them were sitting in the main lounge, waiting for them. The air was thick with cigarette smoke, through which fan blades in the ceiling paddled dimly.

Red Mac raised his glass.

"To our colonel, and all who ride or sail with him," he said.

"Order drinks for the new arrivals," Grice told him. "And then I'll tell you what our next move is."

A bearer carried in a tray of gins and tonics, and bottles of Murree beer, and withdrew. Breene closed the folding doors and drew curtains across them so no one outside could hear what was being said.

"Well, gentlemen," said Grice. "So far, so good. Now for the second stage of our journey. We will leave in two groups. Cren Lumsdaine will again take the first party, and I'll take the same men who've traveled with me from Calcutta."

He unlocked a small traveling case and took out a number of railway tickets which he handed round.

"Our destination, as you will see, is Cochin."

"Cochin? To hell with that," said Red Mac. "That's sleepy hollow, a one-horse town, where even the horse left years ago. What kind of target are we going to find in Cochin?"

"You will find yourself back in Calcutta on the next train unless you keep better security," said Grice sharply.

"Sorry, sir," said Red Mac, abashed.

"At Cochin, we will split up between two hotels, The Malabar and the Harbour House. They should have room at this time of year. But if they haven't,

125

any of you with branches of your firms there should use their bungalows. The RAF station usually has a few spare places in their mess, if all else fails.

"If anyone asks what so many people who obviously know each other are doing in Cochin, it's either a few days' leave or seeing local conditions, or making a survey. But nothing whatever about the Light Horse. Understood?"

The others nodded.

Grice glanced at his watch and then turned to Lumsdaine.

"The Cochin train leaves in two hours," he said. "We'll follow you tomorrow."

Breene turned to Wilton and nudged him.

"Well, at least you'll be leaving Madras without any trouble this time, Charlie," he said.

The others laughed, for they knew the background to Breene's remark.

Before the war, Wilton had been due to sail from Madras to Rangoon on business. In his usual pedantic fashion he had taken pains to inform everyone of the full importance of this trip, and how essential it was that nothing should go wrong.

Breene had his own ideas about the value of Wilton's mission, and sent an urgent telegram to the shipping office.

"My ticket and passport stolen. Please delay any impostor attempting to use them. Signed—Charles Wilton." This, the wretched Wilton had found difficult to explain away.

Now, for all of them, tomorrow held another journey across a vast parched land, baking in the South Indian heat. It meant another long session in a railway compartment the size of a small room, playing cards, smoking, and ordering drinks and meals at one stop to be collected at the next; another opportunity for seemingly endless theories about their possible destination. Burma seemed now out of the question since they were going across to the west coast of India. So where could their target be? North Africa? Italy? Questions chased elusive answers among both

126

groups. Out of a mist of conjecture only one fact remained constant. Soon they must be told where they were going—and why.

Bernard Davies stood on *Phoebe*'s narrow bridge, his legs braced against the long slow dip and roll of the little barge. Before he had sailed from Calcutta he had fitted the long extension to the funnel, as he had told Stewart, but had not realized how this addition would change *Phoebe*'s handling characteristics. As soon as she reached open sea, she began to roll and pitch in an alarming fashion. He hoped his expected passengers had good sea legs, otherwise he doubted whether they would be capable of going into action after such a rough voyage.

In Calcutta, Davies had visited the Senior Naval Officer to explain he was taking a hopper barge to sea on a secret mission. This officer asked no questions, but immediately supplied him with certain papers to show to the captain of any Allied warship that might halt them and wish to know their reason for being so far from their home port. He explained that his jurisdiction only extended south along the East coast of India, and if Davies intended to sail beyond this coast he advised him to have his papers counter-signed and stamped by a colleague in Trincomalee or Colombo in Ceylon. Davies decided to call at the first of these naval bases, for it was the smaller of the two, and he guessed there might be fewer awkward questions to parry about the reason for his voyage.

He did not take *Phoebe* right into Trincomalee harbor, but anchored some way out, and lowered a small boat in which two of his crew rowed him ashore. He did this for two reasons. First, the arrival of such an unlikely craft as *Phoebe* would be less likely to cause interest if he did not dock, and he felt he would minimize the risk of any of his crew jumping ship.

He had previously explained to them that they were going south from Calcutta on a special salvage and towing job, and for this reason had taken aboard

127

sandbags and railway sleepers to keep the barge low in the water. Actually, Pugh had suggested these to provide protection against any shooting.

Several times on the voyage, Harrison had told Davies that some of the lascars were growing increasingly uneasy, since they had still not reached their destination after nearly a week at sea. Davies could not risk any desertions because replacements would be impossible to find.

He explained to the naval officer in Trincomalee that he required papers and provisions for a voyage to Bombay. Again, no questions were asked. By dusk, the stores had been ferried out, and *Phoebe* was on her way.

As the coastline of Ceylon sank down into the sea, Davies walked around the ship's small deck and noticed with concern signs of discontent among the crew. A mooring rope had not been coiled abaft the hold; the freshwater tap in the galley was leaking, and coaldust, which the wind had blown from the hold, had not been sluiced away. He asked Harrison for an explanation.

"The men wanted to go ashore in Trinco, sir," Harrison explained. "They're growing more concerned because they are so far from home."

"They're going to be a damned sight farther before they get any nearer," retorted Davies.

"I know, sir. But I must point out there are nearly 30 of them to three of us."

"You mean they are intending to mutiny or something?"

"I would not say that exactly, but we are out of radio contact with land, and absolutely on our own. They are not deepwater sailors and believed we were just sailing down the coast. Instead, we have already been at sea for nearly a week. And they know the course we are on obviously isn't set for home."

"Right," said Davies. "You speak Hindustani?"

"I have been out here for nearly 20 years," Harrison told him tartly. "I can make myself understood."

"Good. Call them all on deck."

One by one the crewmen appeared, some in faded

trousers and shirts, others barechested, wearing shorts or with *dhotis* wrapped around them like sarongs.

"Say I am pleased with their seamanship and I intend to give them each a further bonus," Davies told Harrison. "A hundred rupees will be paid to every man—once we dock in Calcutta."

Davies stood, hands clasped behind his back as Harrison related the message. One man asked a question.

"What does he say?" asked Davies.

"When will we reach Calcutta?"

"I wish I knew myself. Tell him it should be within a week, but for every day still at sea over one week from today, I'll pay them each a further bonus of 10 chips. And for that I expect hard work and discipline. For a start I want this damned deck swabbed and the ropes coiled and the tap attended to *and* the brasswork polished. Otherwise, no one gets any extra money at all."

Harrison translated. The men nodded.

"So that's all right then, is it?"

"For a moment, sir," replied Harrison. "But they're a rough lot, and I'll sleep a lot more easy once we're back in the Hooghly."

"What makes you think you're the only one?" retorted Davies, and returned to the bridge.

Squire's bunk rocked and heaved like a fairground dipper. The sudden jerk carried his body forward and rammed his head against the bunkhead.

He had been dreaming of his early attempts to raise funds for the zoo. He would feed crows to his snakes and the smaller carnivores, and he trapped the birds in a wire cage with a one-way door designed on the principle of the lobster pot. Indian crows are very inquisitive, and as soon as one was inside, others crowded around, eager to be inside as well.

"It's like marriage," Breene had remarked to him one day. "Those inside want out, and those outside want in."

The sight of so many crows in a cage soon attracted spectators—and Squire charged for this as an added attraction. But in his dream there was commotion in the cage. Someone hit him over the head with a stick and all the crows began to screech deafeningly.

He started up from sleep, and hit his head again on the low roof of the compartment. He muttered a curse and fumbled for the light switch. He flicked this down, but the light was not working. Gradually, he realized where he was, on the train from Madras to Cochin, somewhere in the middle of India. The screeching of the crows became the scream of brakes. Then he noted that while he had gone to sleep lying flat, his bunk was now inexplicably at an angle, and he was jammed up against the wall. He must have hit his head when this happened.

Across from him, in the other upper bunk, Squire could hear Melborne cursing, and down somewhere on the sloping floor Crofter and Hilliard had been flung out of their lower bunks and were crawling about on their hands and knees in the darkness.

"Anyone got a torch?" asked Melborne.

Squire searched under his pillow until he found his flashlight. The carriage was at such a steep angle that their luggage had slid across the floor.

"Must have been an accident," he said. "We've gone off the rails."

"Open the window, someone," shouted Melborne. "Lets see what's happening."

Crofter was the nearest, and lowered the mosquito screen, then the wood frame of ventilation louvres, and stuck his head out into the darkness.

They could all hear the roar of escaping steam from the engine, and men shouting in Hindustani and English. Little stabs of light shone from torches. In the next coach, other Light Horsemen were also awake and peering out of the windows, and farther down the train a detachment of British troops were already out of their carriage and forming up with their rifles.

Squire joined Crofter at the window. The carriage ahead of them was at a crazy angle and farther up still, the engine had left the rails and plowed down the embankment. The firebox still glowed red hot, and above the boiler hung a great white cone of escaping steam. A guard came running down the length of the train carrying an oil lamp in one hand and a red flag in the other.

"What's the matter? What's happened?"

"Much trouble, sahib," replied the guard. "I think stones were on the line."

"Bloody Congress wallahs," said Melborne bitterly. They pulled on their trousers and shirts and boots and removed their pistols from the bedding rolls in case they should need them.

The guard had meanwhile found the master switch and turned on the emergency lights. A dim blue bulb glowed in the ceiling of their compartment. Squire switched off his torch.

They had all read frequently of riots and demonstrations intended to force the British into granting immediate independence to India. They had also heard from friends who had been involved, when cars were stoned and office windows smashed and telephone lines torn down. But all those things had happened to others; this was the first time they had been personally involved.

"You don't think . . ." began Crofter.

"We don't think what?" asked Squire.

"Well, that the enemy has wind of what we are about—and know we are on this train?"

"How could they, if we don't know ourselves?" replied Melborne.

"Just because we don't know, it doesn't mean to say *they* don't know," retorted Hilliard.

"Probably a genuine accident, not even sabotage," declared Squire hopefully.

No one agreed or disagreed, but the seed of doubt had been planted, and the four men now looked at each other with a new awareness. Perhaps this unknown task, for which they had volunteered so lightheartedly, might be more sinister and dangerous than they had imagined in the familiar atmosphere of the Light Horse headquarters in Calcutta?

The train, hauled by a reserve engine, was several hours late in reaching Cochin Harbor station, and so when it finally did arrive, a tense and weary body of men, with dirty, smudged clothes and unshaven faces (because all the water in the rooftop storage tanks had leaked away), climbed thankfully down from their carriage.

They went at once to their hotels. Cochin, even before the war, only possessed a small British community, and this was further reduced with so many men away in the services. The arrival of about 20 Europeans in a group would therefore cause some comment, which Grice was anxious to prevent. He ordered all the contingent to keep out of sight as much as possible during their stay, which, he warned them, would be for at least a day and a night.

Some remained in their rooms, playing crap or cards. Others found a private swimming pool, and a few of the more athletic hired bicycles and toured the surrounding countryside.

In different circumstances, most of the visitors would have found Cochin an interesting port. It was the earliest European settlement in India, for the Portuguese voyager Cabral had first landed there in 1500. The district of Mattancheri was known locally as Jewtown, for around 2,500 Jews lived here, more than in any other part of India. They were divided into two groups, the so-called Black Jews, who claimed descent from traders who had reached Cochin in the third century, and White Jews, whose ancestors had come from Spain and Germany in the 16th century.

The fishermen of Cochin had a strange way of catching fish, which usually caused visitors to pause and watch them. They suspended a net between two long wooden poles, pivoted and balanced by weights at one end. They would then lower the net into the sea on these poles. As the rushing current poured in, they would jump on the poles so that they swung up and out of the water, with fish leaping in the net.

But now the Light Horsemen and Calcutta Scottish

had other matters on their minds, and time passed slowly.

All shared a feeling of anticlimax, which they found difficult to conceal. They had left homes and jobx at a few hours' notice, to travel secretly and in haste—only to arrive here with indefinite time to spare, and still no inkling of their eventual destination.

Tension increased as one day stretched to a second, and the second to a third. Wilton lost a pair of tortoise-shell spectacles, and since he was sharing a room with Breene and Hilliard, accused Breene of hiding them in a misguided attempt at practical joking. Breene retorted angrily that he wouldn't touch Wilton's tortoise-shell *spectacles or* his tortoise-shell *testicles.* He proclaimed it as his opinion that Wilton had stuffed them up his *gonga.* Hilliard interposed with the remark that this was unparliamentary language between colleagues. Breene retorted that Hilliard was an accountant and everyone knew that as regards doing anything useful, accountants were much like eunuchs; they knew how it was done, but they couldn't do it themselves.

Crossley was the calmest. He would spend hours in meditation, sitting crosslegged in his underpants on his sheepskin rug, but even he was not immune to the mood of irritation. His habit of refusing hotel food and eating bananas and raisins and nuts from a huge bag he had brought with him found no favor with Melborne, who shared a room with him.

Relations reached breaking point on the morning of the third day when Crossley, who slept on his rug on the floor instead of in the hotel bed, complained he had been badly bitten by fleas during the night.

"It's that damned filthy rug you lie on," Melborne told him grumpily.

"Rubbish," Crossley retorted sharply. "I've slept on it for years."

"That's what I mean. You're not only being bitten by young fleas but by their fathers and grandfathers, too."

133

Crossley also spent a lot of time in the swimming pool, covering length after length with long, easy strokes, and apparently never short of breath.

Crofter and Hilliard, who could not swim, watched his effortless progress with envy. The thought of even a short sea voyage, with the strong risk of enemy action, was unattractive to non-swimmers.

"Afraid of drowning, are you?" Crossley asked Crofter.

"Aren't you?"

"It's very difficult to drown unless you're ill or injured," Crossley assured him from the deep end. He stopped swimming and let his legs drop. He took a deep breath and folded his arms, drew up his legs, and crossed them in the Lotus position. Then he floated, head above water.

"Keep breathing steadily and deeply and you can stay afloat indefinitely. Try it.'

Crofter shook his head in disbelief.

"Well, I will if you won't," said Red Mac, who had arrived wearing swimming trunks at the side of the pool.

"Come on," he called to Manners. They both jumped into the water. As they surfaced, they carefully copied Crossley's position, and floated.

"Come on in and try it," Red Mac called to Crofter —and promptly sank. He came up, spitting out water.

"The secret is breathing, not bellowing," Crossley told him caustically.

Late in the morning of their third day in Cochin, Melborne buttonholed Grice and Pugh as they were leaving the hotel.

"Any idea when we're off?" he asked them belligerently. "I can't see the point of hurrying to leave Calcutta at a few hours' notice if we're to be stuck here in this hole for days. What was all the rush about?"

"We're still waiting for the ship to arrive for us," Grice explained. "Come and see if there's any sign of it."

They walked in silence, past fishermen with their nets on poles, to the harbor. Several freighters were discharging cargo, and three hundred yards out a small shabby craft with an absurdly long funnel was letting down her anchors. The tip of a black pyramid of coal showed above the line of her deck.

Grice and Pugh exchanged glances.

"See anything?" Grice asked Melborne.

"Nothing I've not seen too often already. Except for that ridiculous ship with the Puffing Billy funnel."

"That's what we mean."

"What are you talking about?"

"She's going to take us where we are going."

"Where can we go in that? Doesn't look seaworthy enough to trust out of the harbor."

"Well, we will now be able to put that to the test," replied Grice. He glanced at his watch.

"High tide is at 17:00 hours today. Come back to the hotel and I'll give everyone their orders."

He led the way with a new springiness in his step. The last lap of their journey was about to begin.

Melborne went through the corridors of the Malabar Hotel beating on the doors of his friends' rooms. Breene and Squire did the same thing in Harbor House, with the same message:

"Meeting of all visitors in the Harbor House lounge —now."

They crowded into the room and sat in the easy chairs, on the arms of the chairs and on tables. Outside the windows, the sea shimmered under a vertical noon sun.

"What do you see?" Grice asked them, nodding towards the harbor.

"Damn' all."

"A lot of sun and sea."

"A funny little boat with a long funnel."

"Gentlemen, you are looking at the ship that's come to take us on to our assignment."

The men crowded to the window, disbelief and disappointment on their faces.

"That little tiddler?"

"We thought we were going to have a destroyer, or at least a proper landing craft."

135

"Are you serious, sir?"

"Absolutely," Grice assured them. "The first two out will be Mr. Lumsdaine and Trooper Hilliard, and you will leave your hotel in half an hour.

"The next two are Corporal Manners and Trooper Breene. Pay your own bills, but tear them up afterwards," he went on. "And no one must carry any letters written to them with their Light Horse rank or any document that could identify them or associate them with the Light Horse. Understood?"

They nodded.

"Right. I'll see you aboard, gentlemen, and give you full details of the operation when we are at sea."

"Some of us have drunk the bottle of liquor each brought from Calcutta," Red Mac pointed out.

"Buy another one, then, but only one. If you find a friend who's teetotal, then you can bring a second bottle in his name.

"Any other questions?"

"No, sir."

Grice nodded dismissal. Some men returned to their rooms to pack. Others walked down to the bazaar to buy a bottle of local rum or Portuguese brandy.

Then, their gear packed in their bedding rolls, they sat down in the lounge or in their rooms and played vingt-et-un and poker. But in their minds they were already out at sea. The games seemed to have neither beginning nor end; no winners and no losers.

Four thirty in the afternoon, out in Cochin harbor, Harrison approached Davies on *Phoebe's* bridge.

"First of our passengers coming aboard, sir," he reported. Davies raised his glasses. Two heavily built men with bedding rolls beside them were sitting awkwardly in a small rowing boat, which the boatman was maneuvering alongside, against the current.

Their combined weight brought the gunwales down almost to water level. Her bows bumped and scraped *Phoebe's* side, and Davies winced at the rasping noise. He bit back years of naval pride in paintwork, remembering he was no longer commanding a destroyer but a dredger's barge.

Two lascars lowered a rope ladder. Cren Lumsdaine and Mark Hilliard climbed aboard, and the boatman handed up their bedding rolls after them.

A few minutes later, it was the turn of Lewis Pugh and Bill Manners. Pugh leaned over *Phoebe's* stern rail, looking at the little armada of small boats, known locally as *kishtis,* each carrying two or three members of the Light Horse or Calcutta Scottish. Of them all, Yogi Crossley was the only man to sit alone. The space taken by a companion in the other boats was filled in his by an enormous bunch of bananas, and supplies of dried raisins for his special vegetarian diet.

"Look a bit old to me, some of these fellows, for a job like this," Harrison remarked to Davies.

"That's what I said when I heard about it first of all. But you know what they say. Good tunes are played on old fiddles."

"With respect, it depends who calls the tune."

Davies shrugged his shoulders and went down to meet Bill Grice on deck. They shook hands.

"I'm sorry, but you'll have to spread everyone out round the edge of the hold—and warn any sleepwalkers about the dangers of falling in it, or overboard," he told Grice. "I've had bed spaces chalked out, but I fear you're in for a rough passage. We've tried to disguise *Phoebe* with a long funnel, but it makes her roll like an Irish washerwoman. Hope your fellows are good sailors?"

"If they're not now, they will be after this jaunt."

They exchanged a smile of understanding; two middle-aged bluewater sailors with years of sea time between them, surrounded by a lesser breed of landlubbers.

The Light Horsemen dumped their bedding rolls between the chalked lines. On one side of the narrow deck, the huge hold yawned like a pit, with coal steaming in the evening air. Feet away on the other side, the oily water of the harbor reflected the dying sun like a mirror of liquid glass.

137

"Not much of a warship, this," lamented Breene, shaking his head in disappointment at the flaked, chipped paint and the long scabs of rust on the decks.

From up near the bows a pungent smell of goats spread over the decks like a miasma. Live chickens clucked and fluttered in wicker baskets. The crew had brought them aboard in Calcutta. When the chickens stopped laying eggs, they would be killed and eaten. The same fate awaited the goats when they ceased to supply milk.

"What about the facilities, captain?" asked Red Mac sarcastically. "No bar or deck games?"

"This is a hopper *barge*, not a cruise liner," replied Bernard Davies severely.

"Unless you'd told me, I never would have guessed," said Melborne. "Surely there's a lavatory where we can relieve ourselves, or a tap where we can have a wash?"

"Heads are over the stern," Davies explained, and pointed towards a wooden box the size of a telephone booth. This had a slatted floor and was lashed by ropes to the deck rail. As the others looked, Crossley stepped from it. Breene gave him an ironic cheer.

"Glad to see you don't do that on your head as well," he called.

"Less noise there," said Lumsdaine.

"There's a tap in the galley for drinking water," Davies continued. "If you want to wash, lower a bucket over the side. Plenty of water in the sea. And I've a few spare bars of saltwater soap in case you haven't brought any."

"What about eating arrangements?" asked Crofter.

"We do bacon and eggs and curries in the galley. Bread and butter and jam. And loads of tea. But we've only one ship's cook, so if any of you can muck in, that would be much appreciated."

"And to think, only last week I was working on the accounts of a chain of restaurants," said Hilliard musingly.

"Right," replied Davies quickly. "I suggest you're ideal for this job. You'll find a couple of sacks of rice to be washed for this evening's meal, if you care to help."

"I don't greatly care, but I will," Hilliard told him. As he walked towards the little galley, smoky from its old oven, *Phoebe*'s anchor chains came up with a shriek of rusty links against the metal hull. The engine telegraph clanged. Beneath their feet, the engine began to thud. The deck trembled and shook as the propellers churned the harbor water into a yellowish scummy foam. *Phoebe* turned slowly and heavily, shuddering like an old sea beast against the stream of the evening tide.

Davies took her south for several miles until the coast fell away, and they were surrounded by sea and could no longer be seen by any watcher from the land. Dusk followed them down with tropical speed. The dying sun turned all the sea to blood, and then dipped below the far horizon. Davies deliberately lit no navigation lights. The risk of collision was far less than the risk of being seen by an enemy submarine that had surfaced to charge her batteries. Then he turned *Phoebe* through 180 degrees and headed north. When they were set on their way, he addressed his passengers.

"We are now steaming due north, gentlemen," he told them. "There will be a bit of moon later, but my advice is not to move far from your bed space in case you fall down into the hold or overboard. I must warn you it would be almost impossible for us to pick up anyone in the dark. The waves are much bigger out at sea than they might seem. And the last thing we can do is to shine a light to try and see you. Strike no matches and do not light any cigarettes. The glow can be seen for miles at sea. In a couple of hours, there'll be supper and a mug of hot tea each, courtesy of Mr. Hilliard and my cook."

The Light Horsemen looked at each other gloomily in the deepening dusk. At this hour, in more civilized surroundings, they would be reaching out for the first drink of the evening, the glass misted by the chill of chunks of ice. Ahead would be a leisurely bath, a change into clean clothes, laid out by their bearer, a car and driver waiting at the door to take them out for dinner or to visit friends. Instead of this, they faced a night on a bare metal deck, only feet above the swiftly running sea.

The initial enthusiasm with which they had all volunteered for an unknown task no one else could apparently undertake, waned as rapidly as the setting sun. A vast and increasing gulf of unease yawned between anticipation and reality. They had imagined a landing craft cruising crisply in to land on an enemy coast at dawn. Instead, they rolled in a wallowing iron tub, reeking of oil and coal and Hooghly River mud. And instead of dawn, lit by early sunshine and the promise of high adventure, darkness pressed down on them with the force of a physical weight.

NINE

Fritz Pöller came out from his radio room aboard *Ehrenfels*, locked the door carefully behind him and checked that the key was safely attached to a chain at his belt. Then he climbed the companionway to the deck. Dusk had dropped its thick dark curtain across the harbor. Dockyard lights were coming on, one by one, and strings of little colored bulbs—red, yellow, green and blue—began to shine from the verandahs of the cafés.

The evening smell of India, ancient as the East, a compound of spices, heat and oil, of scented dust from a million tombs, blew gently out to sea past the anchored ships.

As Pöller leaned on the rail, a searchlight blazed from the Portuguese army post high on the hill on the far side of the harbor. Slowly, it began to rake the bay. Its long white finger probed ships, the quayside, a tanker moored by the oil storage tanks, a motor bus on the coast road. Then the light went out.

Pöller checked his watch; 21:05 exactly. The Portuguese usually tested their searchlight at this time each evening, and then once later on at night. He was glad they did so, because Röfer's belief that they would be attacked had communicated itself to him.

For days, Pöller and other officers had supervised the charging of car batteries taken from *Braunfels'* holds and then had distributed these between the ships. Bags of explosive overlaid by sacks of flour now covered each hatchway, with slabs of marble and metal beams and wooden logs heaped on top of them.

Pöller had tacked electric wires along *Ehrenfels'* deck so the crew would not trip over them after

141

dark. These wires were connected to switches in the cabin of the officer of the watch.

Each evening, Pöller tested a different circuit in case it might have been accidentally damaged during the day, or to discover whether any of the batteries had lost its charge. Now two of the crew approached him for details of this task.

"We will try the one near the bows," Pöller told them. "You set it off. I'll check the spark is strong."

They synchronized their wrist watches.

"Five minutes from now," Pöller ordered.

The sailors went along the deck to knock on the door of the officer's cabin. Pöller walked alone towards the bows. The smell of rust and salt and oil was very strong. Pöller bent down with a flashlight to examine connections to two brass terminals with a spark gap between them on a small ebonite base. He had fitted a small length of fuse on this base which led to a detonator beneath the bags of explosive. He crouched, watching the minute hand of his watch. A blue spark suddenly leapt across the terminals, then died, and leapt again. The fuse flared and began to burn. Pöller pinched it out expertly between his fingers. Like all the others, this was working perfectly.

"You think we will need these tonight, sir?" asked one of the sailors as he returned.

"Maybe not tonight, but one night, yes," Pöller replied. "And the moment they set foot on deck we'll blow them all off into the sea."

Pöller went down to his cabin, drew the curtains across the porthole, took off his shoes, hung his jacket neatly on the back of a chair, and lay back on his bunk with a local newspaper.

He scanned the pages for items of war news, but there was nothing he had not already heard over his secret radio. He threw the paper on the floor and set his alarm for 23:30. He had to send a signal at precisely 19 minutes to midnight. Three Allied ships were on their way from Bombay to Durban, and two others were bound from Aden to Karachi. He lay for a moment, hands clasped behind his head, picturing the U-boat commanders preparing to surface, eager to

142

open hatches and be rid of stale air, to give their crews a brief chance of seeing the night sky, while generators pounded and the long radio antenna was wound out to receive Pöller's instructions.

Then he thought of the unsuspecting merchant ships on that same vast and heaving sea. Their crews trusted in their speed because they had nothing else in which to put their confidence, but still they were steaming to their doom. When Pöller touched his Morse key he also held the keys of life and death for crews and ships alike.

He raised his right hand to turn out the reading light. Propped up on the bunk-side table he saw the beautifully embossed card he had received that afternoon. In Portuguese it requested the pleasure of his company at a reception to be held at the home of an Assistant Commissioner of the Port of Marmagoa.

He would enjoy that. He must remember to have his number one uniform pressed for the occasion. Then Pöller turned out the light and composed himself for sleep.

Red Mac woke up suddenly.

He had been dreaming he was in the train when it went off the line and instinctively he threw out both hands to steady himself. His fingers touched cold steel decks, covered by a film of coal dust, damp with sea spray. He sat up, gasping for breath, wondering whether he was still in his nightmare.

The cool wind from the sea dried the sweat on his forehead, and slowly his tension eased and he remembered where he was—aboard a barge sailing north, without lights, up the west coast of India to goodness knows where, and heaven only knew why.

The moon had risen, and all around the gaping dark well of the hold, like a floating open grave, lay the sleeping bodies of his friends. Some slept on their backs, mouths open, others on their stomachs or their sides in the strange, twisted attitudes of slumber.

In Calcutta, these men controlled companies essential to India's economy. They managed jute mills

143

and vast tea estates, some the size of English counties. In air-conditioned offices they regularly handled sums of money larger than the budgets of many countries. But here they slept like schoolboys on a summer camp, in shorts or underpants, feet facing a pile of coal, heads barely a yard above the hissing, rushing sea. For a few days and nights, their other worries and concerns were put aside in face of a common danger. Red Mac poured himself a tot and drank to them all—and whatever it was they had been gathered together to do.

High above his head, the long funnel blew out puffs of smoke. The red glow of the furnace lit the engine room doorway. Against this, he could see someone behind the windows on the bridge. Then clouds shifted and the moon stretched a silver path across the sea. He watched it, the horror of his dream gradually receding. Suddenly, through that path, from left to right, a small object moved. He strained his eyes, for it did not appear to be floating. The object receded as he watched, and then advanced. He nudged the sleeping figure of the man next to him.

"What's the matter?" asked Hilliard grumpily.

"Something out at sea."

"What do you mean?"

Hilliard sat up now, wiping sleep from his eyes.

"Where?"

Red Mac pointed.

Hilliard was suddenly awake, alert.

"Do you think it's a sub?" he asked in a whisper.

"Hell! Never thought of that," said Red Mac, jumping up. "I'll warn them on the bridge."

He stepped carefully over other sleeping bodies, for a false step could fling him into the hold or the sea, and then he ran barefoot up the companionway to the bridge. Harrision turned to face him.

"What's up?" he asked.

"Something out there at sea," Red Mac explained breathlessly.

"Water, most like," replied Harrison solemnly. He turned his night glasses in the direction of Red Mac's pointing finger.

144

"What do you make of it?" asked Red Mac. "A sub's periscope?"

"I don't," replied Harrison. "Look for yourself through these.'

Red Mac focussed the glasses. In the dim red lenses, he saw what seemed to be a black stick turn to one side. Then it reappeared as a sharp triangular fin. He lowered the glasses.

"A shark, nothing worse," said Harrison. "But thanks for keeping your eyes open."

"I always sleep better that way," retorted Red Mac sheepishly.

Cartwright walked slowly along the main street of Marmagoa, his mind miles and years away. He was remembering an earlier visit to Goa before the war. He and Breene had been in Bombay on business and had decided to take a few days' holiday in a hotel near Calangute Beach on the north side of the harbor. When they arrived, they found that Charlie Wilton was also staying in the same small hotel, handling what he solemnly assured them was a most delicate and important contract for his company. They all had lunch together, and in their company Wilton drank far more than he usually did, so he took to his bed to sleep it off.

Cartwright and Breene meanwhile went for a stroll along the beach. They saw an Indian snake charmer at the edge of the sea preparing his snake for the afternoon performance. On the impulse, Breene bought the man's cobra for 10 rupees, tied a string around its neck, and led it along the beach—to the alarm and dismay of familes enjoying the afternoon sun. The snake suddenly made a bid for freedom, snapped the string, bit Cartwright in the buttocks—and took off.

Both men, now rather more sober, returned at speed to the hotel. Wilton had selected the only room with a telephone, because he said he needed this for business purposes. Breene now rang the local doctor from Wilton's bedroom, where Wilton was still asleep, and explained what had happened. The Goanese doctor understood English little better than he spoke it, but assured them there was no danger since, in his experience, all Indian snake charmers depoisoned snakes before employing them.

Much relieved at this information, Breene and Cartwright went down to the bar to take their own cure for snake bite—a bottle of Scotch between them.

The doctor, meanwhile, began to have doubts about the advice he had given so confidently. If anything went wrong, it would not help his medical reputation among other foreign visitors. He therefore decided to make a personal examination of the patient. The only address he had for his caller was Mr. Wilton's room in the hotel, so he went there with an assistant, and to his alarm found Wilton snoring fully clothed on his bed.

Wilton had all the signs of someone in a snake poison coma, so the two men hurriedly carried him out to their car and rushed him to the local hospital. Here, against Wilton's violent but still incoherent protests, they held him down and injected his buttocks with a strong serum against snake poison.

Cartwright smiled at the memory. How faraway those carefree days seemed now! He wondered whether they would ever return, or whether they had died in war with so many of the generation who had enjoyed them.

He pushed his topee to the back of his head and clasped his hands behind his back. As he walked, he glanced from side to side with the mild interest of a middle-aged Englishman on leave from a wartime Indian city, grateful to escape from the bustle of commerce to the sunshine of a neutral colony.

As Cartwright walked, eyes watched him from behind curtains in apparently empty rooms, through tiny cracks between closed and faded shutters. The houses on both sides of the street had verandas built on stone pillars, and in their welcome shade beggars and dogs slept in the dust, crawling with flies. Chickens pecked hopefully for food. Brown-eyed Goanese children paused at play, rolling old motorcar tires, in case this obviously wealthy stranger cared to throw them a few coins.

In one doorway stood a man about Cartwright's

146

age, screened from the street by a bead curtain. He had a huge paunch, a sallow yellowish face, and wore a dirty white shirt, cotton trousers and open-toed Indian sandals. He chewed on a matchstick, gauging Cartwright's potential as a customer.

Certainly the signs seemed favorable. Cartwright's bush shirt was well cut, he wore a gold wrist watch and a topee of the most expensive type. He was clearly English, a man of wealth, with time on his hands, just the sort of person with whom he might do business. The sallow-faced man threw away the match and gripped the beaded strings so that they rattled like a dead man's teeth. Cartwright paused, seeing him for the first time.

"You wish for something, senhor?" the man asked him in a voice a little above a whisper. His eyes were narrow, more Chinese than Goanese. He hissed in his speech. Like that cobra, if it could have talked, thought Cartwright.

"I do," he replied. "This is your house?"

The man nodded.

"You want quick jig-jig, clean girl, young boy?" he asked now in a matter-of-fact way. Contact had been made, so why waste more time with unnecessary preliminaries?

Cartwright shook his head.

"I'd rather have a talk with you," he told him. "Privately."

The man inclined his head towards the inside of his house. Cartwright followed him into the front room. It smelled of cheap scent, carbolic and hair oil.

"What is it then, senhor?"

"I have a strange request," Cartwright began.

"Ah!" said the man, and smiled with understanding. No request could be too strange, no desire too bizarre for him to accommodate; that was his profession and his pride.

"Years ago I was a sailor," Cartwright continued.

"So was I," said the other man. "And I know how it is with sailors of every nation. You like special thing, yes?"

"Yes," said Cartwright. "I would like to give all the sailors in every ship in this harbor a special party. And in every other place like yours as well.'

"How do you mean, a special party, senhor?"

"I want you to tell all sailors in port—no matter if they are British, German, Dutch, Americans, Portuguese, Italians or Indians, every nationality you can find—that every night for one week next month, Monday to Saturday, they can come here and go with girls—at no cost at all."

"But there will be cost to me," the man pointed out quickly. "I still have to pay my girls whether they work or not. We all must eat, senhor."

"Of course," agreed Cartwright. "But I will pay you all for every girl, for every night of that week."

"That will be expensive, senhor. All night, long time, twenty Indian rupees. Short time, five rupees. I have five girls. Across the road, there are seven, and next door, three. At the end of the road, there are two other houses with four each. Very expensive, senhor."

"Money," replied Cartwright, with the splendid magnanimity of someone not spending his own, "is only worth what it can buy. And here it will buy a little pleasure for these sailors far from home."

"You have a kind heart, senhor," said the man approvingly.

"I am honored that you should think so," allowed Cartwright. "Now. What is your price?"

The man stroked his chin, and then pressed a bell-push on the wall to summon a servant.

"We will work that out together, senhor," he said. "But first do me the honor of sharing a Portuguese brandy. It is not often that two old sailors like us meet."

"In these particular circumstances," replied Cartwright gravely, "I would agree, it must be extremely rare."

Bernard Davies stood on deck near *Phoebe's* hold, watching the Light Horsemen fold up their bedding rolls and stack them under the bridge, out of the way.

Barefooted lascars were already busy with seawater hoses, sluicing down the deck where they had slept, washing away the gritty film of coal dust with which the night wind had covered every flat surface.

"And how are you all after your first night at sea?" Davies asked the contingent in general.

"We've survived," Lumsdaine told him. "Pretty hard beds, though. And we've one fellow badly seasick." He nodded towards Crofter, who was leaning over the rail.

"He'll get over it," Davies said confidently.

Crofter held a handkerchief by one corner to test the direction of the wind. Then he retched and hung his head miserably towards the foaming speckled sea beneath.

"What you need is some food down you," Davies assured him, meaning well. "Had any breakfast?"

Crofter shook his head, unable to speak.

"Well, there's a mug of hot tea, porridge and a couple of fried eggs in the galley whenever you feel ready for them."

Crofter's face turned green at the horror of this prospect.

Davies called to a seaman.

"Bring me a fresh lime," he told him. When this arrived on a saucer, with a knife, he cut it in two and handed one piece to Crofter.

"That'll set your stomach right in double time," he said. Cautiously, Crofter put the slice of lime in his mouth.

"That's the best way of spending a rough voyage," said Breene, nodding towards Crossley, who had adopted his favorite upsidedown position of the headstand.

"Good God!" said Davies. "You really are a rum lot."

Shaking his head, he went on up to the bridge. And to think that all these men were very successful in their own careers! One man standing on his head, a second sick as a dog when the sea was still calm, and a third, with a revolver dangling out from under the right leg of his shorts.

Grice was up in the bows with Pugh and Stewart.

Pugh had been explaining to them how he wanted the operation to be carried out. Now they all came aft to join the rest of the party.

"I want to see everyone in the stern," Grice announced. Here the crew had rigged up a canvas canopy to give some shade from the burning sun. Without cabins or any sunshades *Phoebe* would be a floating iron grill by noon. The Light Horse and Calcutta Scottish crowded eagerly under the welcome shade of this green awning.

"Gentlemen," Grice began. "We are now on the final lap of our journey and so I can tell you our destination and our task. We are heading for the neutral port of Marmagoa, where a German ship *Ehrenfels* lies at anchor. She called in at Calcutta just before the war, where some of you may have seen her.

"*Ehrenfels* was specially designed so that, by removing some deck planks, guns can be fitted, and she could then become a most dangerous merchant cruiser. We have information that her captain may attempt a run for Singapore to do just this. Our task is to seize this ship for ourselves or to sink her at anchor."

Grice deliberately did not mention the silencing of the secret transmitter as the main object of the raid. Pugh had impressed on him that this was strictly a "need to know" situation, and so the less anyone knew about the real reason for the raid, the better, in case they were taken prisoner.

"Three other Axis ships have also holed up there, and if we can put them out of action, so much the better. But that is very much secondary to *Ehrenfels*. Now I am going to divide you into small groups. Each leader can then choose two or three men—probably friends, people he has already worked with—because everyone in each group will have to stick close together as ivy on the wall.

"First aboard will be Colonel Pugh and his group. They will seize the bridge and destroy radio equipment there and collect any code books.

"The second group, under Corporal Manners, will

150

go straight to the anchor chains and blow them apart with plastic explosive in the hope we can move the ship.

"I'll take the third group. We will destroy certain other radio equipment. Then we'll report to the bridge to reinforce Colonel Pugh.

"The next group, under Corporal Macfarlane, will deal with fire fighting aboard. You will have to carry fire extinguishers we have brought along, for the crew may attempt to set fire to the ship if they can't get rid of us in any other way.

"Next, Mr. Lumsdaine's group will stop the crew interfering with the rest of us in our tasks—that's where the handcuffs come in.

"If you take a prisoner, knock him out and tie him to the deck-rails so he can't get back into the fight.

"The rest of you will stay here to ward off any attack on *Phoebe*, either from the other ships or from the shore, or from *Ehrenfels* herself. We have machine-guns which we'll mount in the stern for this purpose.

"We also have some long bamboo poles in the hold, to make ladders for scaling *Ehrenfels*. We'll rearrange the sandbags and railway sleepers here to give us better protection as we pull alongside. Now—any questions?"

"Yes, sir," said Wilton. "What time are we due to arrive?"

"If we maintain our present speed, we should be off Marmagoa by one oclock on Tuesday morning. There will be no moon then and with a bit of luck we should be on our way again by three."

"How will we know who's who if it's pitch dark?" asked Manners.

"We've brought along circles of white cloth. You will sew these on the backs of your overalls so we can all recognize our own team.

"One point I must impress on everyone. We have to work quickly and quietly. That is why I have asked you to glue pieces of felt on the soles of your boots. This will also help to insulate your feet if there is

151

fire and the decks get hot, and stop you sliding about in the darkness."

"What happens if anything goes wrong, sir?" asked Crofter.

"Commander Davies will immediately give three blasts on *Phoebe's* siren. This is the withdrawal signal. Whatever you are doing, double back here at once. We can't wait for anyone."

"What happens if we are wounded, sir, and just can't make it?" asked Hilliard.

"Remember this cover story. You were in a party going to Bombay in a cargo ship. On the way, you persuaded her captain to cruise around Marmagoa harbor. He was reluctant to do so, but finally agreed. In the darkness, your ship bumped up against *Ehrenfels*. For a foolish drunken dare, a bet, you climbed aboard—and their crew attacked you.'

"You think they'll believe that?" asked Melborne.

"If you think of anything more convincing, then let us know. But whatever you do, on no account involve the Light Horse or Calcutta Scottish, and do not expect any help from the government of India, because they know nothing whatever about this. Our code word for this whole exercise is Operation Creek. And if anything goes wrong, we'll all be up that creek—without a paddle!"

"What if we are trapped aboard and can't get off quickly enough?" asked Manners.

"Dive in the sea and swim for it," Grice told him. "Aim for the Burmah Shell storage tanks. They are silver and floodlit at night. So even with your eyesight you can't possibly miss 'em."

"What do we do there?" asked Breene. "Apply for a job as nightwatchman?'

"You wouldn't get it if you did, Jack," said Melborne. "That job needs intelligence.'

"You will find Trooper Cartwright watching out for you," Grice went on, ignoring the interruption. "He has a car with him and money in notes. He'll do his best to get you over the border."

"Good old Jock," said Breene. "Remember that

boozy weekend we spent with him in Goa before the war, Charlie?"

Wilton grimaced; sometimes he still felt uncomfortable when he sat down suddenly on a hard seat.

"Well, let's hope you don't have to spend another weekend there, because if you do, you'll be interned until the end of the war," Grice warned them.

"But Cartwright isn't only there to pick any of us up. He should also have organized a diversion or two to encourage the enemy crews to go ashore that evening and so reduce the odds against us."

"What are the odds now, sir, do you reckon?" asked Red Mac.

"I'd say at the best around four to one against. And most of us have ridden winners at far worse odds."

"They may have youth on their side," agreed Melborne. "But what's that against experience?"

"And surprise," added Crossley.

"'Thrice is he armed that hath his quarrel just,'" quoted Breene. "'And four times he who gets his blow in first.'"

"So, there you are," said Grice. "That makes it evens, then."

"What sort of diversion exactly is Jock Cartwright arranging on shore?" asked Squire.

"He hopes to fix a deal with the local brothels to give free bangs to all sailors."

"After this voyage, I think we should all qualify as sailors," said Breene feelingly, glancing at Crofter.

Pugh now took over from Grice. He unrolled a plan of *Ehrenfels'* decks, which he had acquired in Calcutta before the war. When serving with the Bengal Police, he had asked a friend in the docks fire brigade to request the ship's plans from Captain Röfer on the excuse that they might be needed in case of fire. Now he pointed out the engine room, the position of the bridge, the officers' and crews' quarters, and various companionways and hatch covers which could trip a man in the dark and send him spinning across the deck.

✗ He passed the plan around each group, so that all could decide how best they should reach their particular objective.

Pugh also showed them some photographs of the ship, taken in Calcutta and later from the air when she lay in Marmagoa harbor. She appeared infinitely larger than most of them had imagined. They would have a considerable distance to cover, up and down metal companionways, along narrow corridors—all in the dark, against opposition and the clock. For they would only be able to stay aboard for a limited time in case the harbor authorities sent out police or troops to discover what was happening in the ship. They realized now why Grice had only wanted the fittest men for such a task. Some of the older ones fell silent, hoping that their muscles and spirit would prove equal to this challenge.

"One last question," said Crofter. "Do you think they'll have any idea we're on our way?"

"Of course not," replied Grice heartily. "How would they possibly know?"

No one answered.

For a moment there was silence, broken only by the thump of the engine and the beating of the wind against the canopy. And in this silence they remembered the derailment of the Cochin train.

Walter Fletcher sat reading *The Times of India* in his office in the house on Malabar Hill, Bombay. He had a free evening ahead of him, the first for several weeks, and he glanced down the advertisements for films, wondering which, if any, he would enjoy.

At the Aurora, Errol Flynn and Olivia de Havilland were starring in, "They Died with their Boots On", described as "a story of undying faith."

At the Regal, Brian Donlevy was the star of "Wake Island." "This war's greatest picture," claimed the advertisement. "What terrible odds! Yet united they stood . . . against the enormous hordes . . ."

Fletcher frowned. This was not for him on this

154

particular evening. At the Excelsior, Hugh Williams, James Mason and Michael Wilding were in "Secret Mission." That title also seemed altogether too close to reality. His thoughts strayed five hundred odd miles down the coast where *Phoebe* was beating up north on her own secret mission. Fletcher was a sensitive man. He could well imagine the thoughts of those other men aboard her, some no younger than he was, as they wondered what awaited them at the end of their voyage.

A liaison officer from Army Command came into the room, carrying a sealed envelope. He was a tall young captain, who some thought might be more advantageously employed on more martial duties. He wore highly polished brass stars on the shoulders of his immaculately pressed bush jacket, and well brushed sambur-skin boots with thick crepe rubber soles, of the type unkindly known as brothel-creepers by those who did not like them. Fletcher regarded this officer without favor. The captain placed the envelope on the desk. Fletcher opened it.

The captain explained, "It's from our consul in Marmagoa, sir. As your office requested, he's been recalled for a few days with his wife. He brought this with him, rather than send it."

Fletcher glanced cursorily at the typed lines. Then his eyes hardened. The crews of the Axis ships were taking aboard cans of kerosene with scrap iron and logs of wood. Fatigue parties had already moved a number of car batteries from the hold of one ship to decks of the others. Sacks with unknown contents had been piled around hatchways. Other members of the crew had been observed on deck carrying rolls of wire.

Fletcher could guess what these sacks contained; and in guessing he knew why the batteries and the wire were needed.

Somehow, the Germans and Italians had discovered —or made the intelligent deduction—that a raid on their ships was imminent. So they were converting them into floating fortresses, ready to blow them up rather than surrender. He was conscious of two totally separate and warring emotions. As an old soldier, he approved their action; he would have done exactly the same in their situation. On the other hand, he felt a growing horror at the thought of the massacre that could result. He had no way to warn the Light Horse what lay ahead. They were now beyond the point of no return, beyond all orders or recall. His office were deliberately observing strict radio silence in case any unknown enemy expert might pick up their signals and decipher them. The only time the Light Horse would break this silence would be after their mission, when *Phoebe* would transmit one of three code words.

The first would mean, mission unsuccessful; the second, ships seized and under tow; the third, ships sunk. According to which message they received, SOE's Bombay office would then put out a story for newspapers and radio which had already been prepared, by Alex Peterson, giving a plausible explanation for the incident in terms favorable to the Allied cause.

"What's the matter, sir?" asked the captain, looking at Fletcher's face. He hoped the old fellow wasn't going to have a heart attack or something. He was carrying a lot of weight.

"We can do nothing about it now," replied Fletcher, ignoring the captain's question. "Please thank the consul for his pains. And if he has a moment, I would be very pleased to see him."

The captain left; he had won 500 rupees at the races, held the previous week on Bombay Racecourse in aid of the Indian Red Cross, and he would spend some of his winnings that night on a girl he had also recently met. There was a dance at the Taj. He was humming to himself at the prospects ahead as he climbed into his waiting Jeep.

For a long time, Fletcher sat alone in the empty room, all thought of an evening's entertainment now driven from his mind.

How could he, a survivor from the first world war, enjoy the celluloid adventures of actors, when somewhere out on that sea of darkness beyond his window, men he had known in Calcutta—men he had done business with, played golf with, ridden against—were sailing unawares into deadly danger, and he had no way of warning them, no way at all?

TEN

Harrison climbed up the steps to *Phoebe*'s bridge. His face was grave.

"Bit of trouble with the engine, sir," he reported.

Davies looked up from his charts with a frown. *Phoebe* was already behind schedule, because of adverse currents.

"What sort of trouble?" he asked.

"Main bearing is overheating."

"Can you do anything about it?"

"If I stop the engine, yes, sir. Then dismantle the bearing and fit a new shell."

"How long will that take? Two hours?"

"More like three, sir."

Davies glanced at his watch. Five thirty in the afternoon.

"I don't like to lose power here," he said uneasily. "We are a sitting target for any sub. Can we keep going with the bearing as it is?"

"Not indefinitely, sir."

Davies nodded.

"Right," he said. "Change the bearing now." It would be even more dangerous to do so after dark.

The engine telegraph tinkled. A great gout of black smoke blew out of the funnel, and then a thin wisp trailed in the wind. The engine stopped. On the decks, squatting around the hold, the Light Horsemen and Calcutta Scottish played cards or crap. Breene glanced up quizzically as the ship slowed and began to roll heavily. The horizon dipped and rose again in an alarming way.

"Well," he said glancing at the number uppermost on the dice, "at least I know now why she's called *little Phoebe*."

"Why?" asked Melborne.

"She's hopper barge number five, isn't she?"

"Oh, I see.

In crap, number five was referred to as "little Phoebe."

"She's poor little *Phoebe* now," said Red Mac. "The damned engine's stopped altogether."

Crofter excused himself from a game and ran to the rails in an agony of sickness at the changed motion and the strong smell of oil from the engine room. Flying fish darted like dagger blades from one wave to another. Lascar engineers hurried along from the fo'c'sle, carrying metal boxes of tools.

"We are likely to be stuck here for two or three hours at least," Grice explained. "Bit of engine trouble. I suggest we all keep a lookout for any periscope."

They lined the scabby, rusting rails. Slowly, the sun moved down the western sky and sank beyond the horizon. Suddenly, it was dark. Lights glowed dimly through skylights above the engine room. They could hear the tinkle and rattle of spanners. The wind grew chill, and flattened their shirts against their bodies. For an eternity, so it seemed, they waited, while the barge dipped and wallowed and rolled.

Then unexpectedly, the telegraph rang, the engine began to thump, and they were on their way.

"We'll have to make up time," Davies told Harrison. "What's the maximum we can get out of her now?"

"Perhaps eight knots, sir. Certainly no more."

"Eight knots it is," said Davies, and pushed the telegraph lever to "Full Speed Ahead."

Down on the afterdeck, out of the freshening wind, Lumsdaine poured a measure of neat brandy for Pugh and Stewart, and turned to Crossley, who, as usual, was standing on his head.

"Do you drink like that, Yogi?" he asked him.

"I don't drink alcohol at all," replied Yogi, swinging himself down on to his feet. "I don't smoke either, and I should think this damned funnel should have put a lot of you fellows off smoking, too."

"Well, *I* drink *and* smoke," said Red Mac belligerently, overhearing the conversation, "and I think I'm a hundred per cent fit."

"Fit for what?" asked Crossley shortly.

"Anyone remember it's Saturday night?" asked Lumsdaine, almost wistfully.

The others shook their heads. In the last few days they had somehow lost count of time. They thought for a moment of other Saturday nights spent at Firpo's, or watching the cabaret at the Grand Hotel a few doors along Chowringhee after a day at the races or a gymkhana. Here, on this trembling deck, surrounded by a heaving sea, that other life seemed part of a dream, without roots in reality. Only this was real: the salt spray on their lips, hours dwindling before action, brandy running like quick fire in their blood.

"To the bright lights," said Lumsdaine, raising his glass in a toast.

"To Jack Cartwright and his bright *red* lights," added Breene, more specifically.

Two hundred odd miles to the north, Captain Röfer was making his evening rounds. Café lights along the shore reflected yellow, red and green on the oily surface of the sea. He paused for a minute, hands on the deck rail, thinking of other ports he had known on other Saturdays after dark: Shanghai, Durban, Bombay, Liverpool, New Orleans. At night, from the harbor, they all looked very much the same. Only the number of lights, and the temperature and the smell of oil or sewage or spices gave any clue to their identity.

There were the same brawls and fights between sailors of different nations or different ships. Backgrounds might change, but human nature never did. The coward remained cowardly and the braggart stuck to his boasts. Only the captains remained aloof and alone. They might be with their men but seldom could they be of them. Rarely could they show their real feelings, and never could they admit their secret fears.

He saw Pöller approaching.

"Everything all right?" Röfer asked him.

"Yes, sir. I have just checked the aft batteries and detonators. All in good order, sir."

"Excellent. I must say, I feel safer now we are ready for any attack."

"How long do you think the danger will last, sir?"

"Indefinitely. But the next 10 days will be the most likely for them to try something."

Crewman were coming up companionways, climbing over the side and going down rope ladders into rowing boats. Röfer counted 10 men leaving.

"Some sort of feast day," explained Pöller. "We're only letting half the crew ashore, of course."

"More than a feast day," said Röfer. "My steward tells me the brothels aren't charging all this week. Some kind of gesture of international goodwill and strict neutrality, they call it."

"More likely they're low on customers, sir. Our men haven't had any money from Lisbon for nearly two months."

"They make some money working on shore," Röfer reminded him, for local traders were generous with credit.

The crews of all the ships were free to seek part-time jobs in and around Marmagoa, so long as these did not interfere with their duties aboard ship. Some worked at repairing watches and cameras and sewing machines. Others helped in garages and wireless shops. Several with special skills were assisting the local authorities in their efforts to construct a canal.

A number of them had formed liaisons with Goanese girls. In some cases, the parents of these girls were strict Roman Catholics and discouraged their daughters becoming friendly with foreigners not of their faith. But the sailors discovered that many Goanese Catholics believed that their chances of entering the Kingdom of Heaven increased sevenfold for each new convert they could make. So the sailors

161

announced that they were willing and eager to take instruction, and at once, all parental disapproval vanished. Röfer smiled to himself at the ingenuity of his countrymen and the credulity of others. He lingered for a few moments more, busy with his thoughts. Then he went on his cabin. He would spend the evening alone, studying his stamp collection.

"O, God, our Help in ages past, our hope for years to come ..."

The words of John Wesley's hymn blared out on Sunday morning across the sunlit sea. Harrison had brought a portable wireless with him aboard *Phoebe* and had tuned in to the Sunday morning service from All-India Radio. He watched through the porthole of his tiny cabin as his passengers from Calcutta struggled into wakefulness. They began to roll up their bedding and then queued patiently with mess tins and shaving brushes for warm water from the galley to shave.

The sun steadily climbed up the sky. Hilliard, in shirt and shorts, was supervising a fry-up of eggs and bacon. His methodical mathematical mind had devised a system of mass production in the galley by which all the eggs were cooked in a huge flat pan, while strips of bacon grilled elsewhere. Before this, the lascar cook had cooked each breakfast individually, which took infinitely longer.

Some early risers, already washed and shaved, waited at the galley hatchway with mess tins and mugs. After breakfast there was another queue for the lavatory that hung—suspended, so Breene said, like Mahomet's coffin—between sky and sea above *Phoebe's* churning wake. Then they formed up in three ranks in the stern of the ship for Grice to give them their orders for the day.

"We are going to have target practice this morning," he told them. As he spoke, members of the crew were setting up a canvas screen on two bamboo poles on one side of the ship. It flapped and whackered

162

like a loose sail. Manners fixed two paper rifle range targets on the canvas with pins.

"First detail, get your Stens," ordered Grice.

Jack Breene and Bill Manners went to their bed spaces, pulled their Sten guns. and magazines of ammunition from their bedding rolls and came back with them. Then they faced the targets across the open hold, feet braced against the roll and dip of the ship.

"Corporal Breene, left hand target. One magazine, single shots. When you are ready. Fire!"

Breene raised his Sten, firing from the hip. His first shots went wide. Then he corrected, and the holes appeared closer to the center. Manners followed him; then Melborne, Hilliard and the others.

From the bridge, Davies looked down on men, some as old as himself, and some older, as they took aim and fired. Thinning hair blew in the wind. Faces were tense and lips pursed, muscles taut against the kick and lift of their guns. Smoking cartridge cases clattered out on the deck, to be kicked into the sea. Harrison climbed the steps to the bridge.

"More trouble, sir," he told Davies gloomily.

"What? The engine again?"

"No, the crew."

"Whats wrong with them this time? Were paying them double wages, double bonus. What's eating them?"

"They're not happy about all this firing. They think we are going into action."

"They could just be right, you know."

"That's the trouble, sir. And we cannot run the ship without them. If they get bolshie, well have to use these *Koi hais** from Calcutta—and then they won't be able to do *their* job."

"You want me to speak to them, then?"

"I think it would be a good plan, sir."

*Koi hais. This signified an "important person" from the Hindustani question: "Koi hai?" that Europeans asked when entering an empty room or bar when they wished to call a servant. It means literally: "Is there anyone about?" Only a person used to command would ask it.

"Well, get them on deck again," said Davies, "and translate what I say."

Harrison went to call the crew together and Davies signaled to Grice, who crossed behind the line of men at firing practice.

"The crew are getting a bit restive with all this firing," Davies explained. "Think someone might get hurt. I'll deal with them the best I can, but if they don't accept what I am going to say, we might have to ask your help to lock them in their quarters— and do without them."

"That means we cut down on the number of men we have for our job?"

"Afraid so. But I'll do my best to make them see sense. Thought I'd tell you in advance, just in case."

The crew stood in their working clothes outside the fo'c'sle door. They shuffled to attention as Davies and Harrison approached.

"Tell them they will be in no danger whatever. Tell them also that we had to drop our plans for the salvage job, but we are after something even better.

"We are sailing to Marmagoa. We reach there after dark tomorrow. The men who joined us at Cochin are going to attempt to board a ship where there is hidden a great treasure."

He paused while Harrison translated. Grice saw flickers of interest in some of the crew's eyes.

"I personally will guarantee each man a further bonus of 100 rupees, once we are back at anchor in the Hooghly."

The spokesman for the crew replied at length to Harrision, who turned to Davies.

"You have set most of their doubts at rest, sir. They will carry on."

"Good," said Davies approvingly. "Tell them that is what I expected. Now dismiss them of their duties."

During the afternoon, Yogi Crossley explained how PE—plastic explosive—which he had brought with him, could help them to blow open a locked metal door, or cut an anchor chain. He produced a gray, putty-like substance and explained how this could be kneaded as harmlessly as the baker's dough it so

164

closely resembled. But a sudden sharp blow could detonate it instantly. The leader of each section handled this plastic explosive nervously at first and then with more confidence.

"What are the chances of killing ourselves with the stuff before we can do any other damage with it?" asked Melborne bluntly, voicing a fear others did not like to mention.

"We have all got to go some time," Crossley said philosophically.

"Maybe so," agreed Melborne. "But I damn' well don't want to go just yet."

"At least, if you do, you won't die like Our Lord Jesus Christ.'

"What do you mean by that?" asked Melborne belligerently.

"Well, you're with friends you can trust," replied Crossley drily. "If you wanted to die like Him, you'd have to die with your lawyer on one side of you, and your doctor on the other."

That afternoon, they sewed their white identification patches on the backs of their shirts. Then they rehearsed where each group would wait as they approached their target. Space was so limited that everyone had to know exactly where he should be and what he had to do. There would be no time for questions or room for mistakes.

After dark, Grice and Pugh gave them more Sten gun practice, shooting at tin cans set up on the ship's rail. They knew when they scored a hit for the tin boomed like a gong. Then, their faces blackened with camouflage cream that Stewart had brought with him from SOE stores, they felt their way around the decks, sliding and falling on metal plates slippery with spray. At first, they could see nothing and moved cautiously, fearful of falling into the rushing sea on one side of the deck or down into the hold on the other.

Gradually, their eyes grew accustomed to the darkness and they could make out dim outlines of the deck rail, stanchions and hatchways. Peering ahead, they could just see the white circle on the back of the man in front. They followed each other in line down to the hold, up and across the sliding mountain of coal and on to the far side of the barge, and then back the other way. Already they moved as though under fire, crouched, with elbows drawn into their bodies so as to present the smallest target area. On and on they went, turning this way and that, stern to bow and bow to stern, until sweat poured from them, streaking their black makeup and the coal dust that clung to their hair, their hands and faces.

The only noise was their breathing against the thump of the ancient engine, the crash of the stokers' shovels and the constant rush of sea on either side. They cut hands and broke fingernails. They barked knees and bruised elbows as they stumbled through the humid darkness. Smoke from the funnel would suddenly choke them when the wind changed. Then, as they approached the engine room with its bright reddish glow, the heat of the boiler furnace dried the sweat on their tired bodies. Gradually, they grew more confident, and with confidence came speed and silence.

"Remember the army saying," Bill Grice told them. "Sweat saves blood—and brain saves both."

At 10 o'clock, he blew a whistle and they returned thankfully to their chalked spaces, hoping to bed down for the night. But Pugh had more training for them. On his orders, they took out their Sten guns with a magazine each.

"You may have a stoppage on the gun when we go into action, he explained. "So you must know how to dismantle and reassemble your Stens in the dark."

So men whose hands had held little more lethal than a fountain pen, sweated with concentration as they took the Stens to pieces, fitted the parts together time and again, until what had been awkward and seemingly impossible in the dark became almost automatic.

When Pugh was satisfied with their progress, Grice blew his whistle for the second time. They packed away their Stens and washed as best they could in buckets of salt water hauled up on a rope from the sea. Hilliard organized mugs of hot sweet tea. They laced these with rum and brandy and drank, leaning thankfully over *Phoebe*'s rail.

The stars rushed past in a wide emptiness of sky. Jupiter was the brightest, then The Plough, and the Southern Cross. Behind the barge stretched half a mile of phosphorescent wake. Ahead, lay one more day of firing practice and unarmed combat.

On Monday, Yogi Crossley, Pugh and Steward explained how to stab a man quickly and silently—not with a downward blow to his chest, but up through his rib cage; how to ward off an attack by two enemies simultaneously; where to press a man's neck to render him unconscious within seconds; how to use the impetus of an opponent's charge to throw him off balance in a confined space. After this, Grice explained the general plan of action.

Phoebe would sail north, past the mouth of Marmagoa Harbor, in case any lookout saw them. The fact that *Phoebe* was passing should assure him of her harmlessness. A few miles farther on, and under cover of darkness, *Phoebe* would turn and come back, planning to arrive against *Ehrenfels* shortly after one o'clock on Tuesday morning.

She would sail in on *Ehrenfels'* seaward side, so there should be less chance of any German sentry seeing them in silhouette against the shore, which Pugh explained should be well lit, with cafés and floodlights around the docks.

Ehrenfels' deck would be at least 20 or 30 feet higher than their deck, and so they would be extremely vulnerable to any downward fire from *Ehrenfels*. The Germans might also have buckets of kerosene which they could throw down with burning torches and set them alight. They would not have an easy task. Davies intended to bring *Phoebe*'s port side up against the starboard side of *Ehrenfels*, so *Phoebe*'s starboard side could be left relatively unprotected. But she would need all possible protection on her port side; this meant that the sandbags and railway sleepers would have to be rearranged.

Several of the sacks were already rotten with sea

spray, and sand burst out on the decks, streaming over their bedding rolls. They heaved the tarred sleepers, cursing splinters in their hands, and slowly built a wooden wall from the bows, halfway down *Phoebe*'s port side.

Some of the older men, who were unable to help much with moving these heavy sleepers, now applied thmselves to making the ladders or drawbridge, as Grice preferred to call them. They sawed up short lengths of bamboo, and bound these with twine and string to two long parallel poles which they would throw up against *Ehrenfels*' deck. Others checked that grappling irons were ready, with their long thin ropes neatly coiled. These irons had several hooks like huge fish hooks extending from a metal ball, and would be swung up on *Ehrenfels*' deck to grip where they could, and so hold *Phoebe* closely against her hull. By afternoon, they had attended to all their preparations.

At first these tasks had seemed like similar chores they had carried out so often before at their annual camp; simply making a pretense of war, when blank cartridges would be fired and an umpire would decide the outcome. Now, as they waited, they slowly realized, by some kind of delayed action or reaction, that this time there would be no umpire. Rehearsals were behind them; only reality remained—and the moment of ultimate action came inexorably closer with each turn of *Phoebe*'s propellers. Their future, even their survival, was entirely in their own hands. No one else could help them now. They leaned on the rail, considring this, each in his own way.

Breene was thinking how ironic it would be if in that sea, perhaps miles away, perhaps only yards from them, men encased in the steel cocoon of a submarine were at that same moment watching *Phoebe*'s progress through a periscope, or tracking them with listening devices.

With each faint flicker of phosphorescent light, when a flying fish leapt from one wave to another, he tensed instinctively, wondering whether it was only a fish, or whether he would suddenly see a periscope, then a conning tower. The wind seemed colder now and a heavy sky bore down on the darkening sea. Hilliard had organized a meal of chicken curry and rice and hot sweet tea, but no one felt very hungry. At nine o'clock, Grice called them together abaft the hold.

"Well, this is it, gentlemen," he began. "The Light Horse goes into action. The Light *Sea* Horse, if you like. Because there won't be much real light about, and our white patches can get obscured, Colonel Pugh has suggested a password. No one else can possibly know it, for it's the name of his family home in Wales. *Mathafarn.* Repeat that and remember it."

Mathafarn. They mumbled the word like the response of a prayer.

"Anyone who gives a false password is not one of us. And if he's not for us, he's against us. So deal with him immediately."

Grice now issued each man with a wad of Indian rupee notes and some gold coins.

"Put these in your back pocket," he told them. "You may have to use them, if you get ashore and you miss Cartwright. If that happens, put as much distance between you and Marmagoa as you can and as quickly as you can. Lie up tomorrow and only move after dark towards the border. This money may help to buy your way out. Now Colonel Pugh has something to say."

Grice stood to one side as Pugh faced the Light Horsemen. Two lascars carried up a wooden ammunition box with rope handles, and placed it in front of him. Pugh opened the lid.

"Right, gentlemen," he began. "I have here a quantity of German ammunition. It was captured in the western desert from the Afrika Korps, and we are going to use it in our Stens instead of the usual British ammunition.

"Everyone will leave behind in their bedding rolls all British ammunition. Charge your Sten magazines with this."

As he spoke, he handed clips of stubby rounds to the men.

"What's the point of this?" asked Melborne. "It won't fit the Stens so well."

"It fits them well enough to fire," replied Pugh shortly. "The reason for issuing this now is that if we have to leave in a hurry, and the Portuguese authorities carry out an enquiry aboard *Ehrenfels* into what happened, they won't find any British cartridge cases lying about.

"Instead, they will find German cartridge cases, and we can put out a story on All-India Radio explaining that the Germans were concealing weapons aboard their ships, and when they had some political shindy, tempers ran high and they started firing at each other. Any other questions?"

They shook their heads, and continued to fill the magazines.

"Everyone fall out, then," ordered Grice. "On the backs down till midnight. Get some rest. Then we'll put on our black warpaint and stack all the bedding rolls out of the way. Section leaders will collect plastic explosive from Yogi, and then—action."

ELEVEN

Cartwright was in his bedroom at the Gran Palacio hotel, looking at his face in the blotched yellowing mirror above the washbasin on its marble washstand. He had packed his bags and put them in the back of his car under the canvas tonneau cover. He had also paid his bill for two more days, so that if anything went wrong, and the local police tried to associate the Englishman in this hotel with any actions of his countrymen in the harbor, it would appear that he planned to stay longer than that particular night.

He poured three fingers of Portuguese brandy into a toothglass and sipped it slowly. His face in the mirror looked tired, for the strain of the last few days had been greater than he had anticipated.

That afternoon he had casually asked the hotel manager whether any fiestas or carnivals were due, because on a previous visit to Goa he had enjoyed the atmosphere very much. The manager regretted that it was early in the year to honor the saints. Later, of course, there would be fiestas to mark the days given to St. Goncalo, who helped old women to marry, and St. Sebastian, the heavenly advocate of artillery, and St. Peter, the patron saint of all fishermen. But unfortunately the esteemed senhor would not be here for these happy and traditional festivities. Then the manager's face brightened. He had remembered something. Some local café owners were making a special effort this week with a carnival of their own. There would be fado singers, who sang the old sad songs of Portugal, and he was sure that the senhor would enjoy himself if he cared to visit these cafés around midnight.

Cartwright felt relieved. So that side of his arrange-

171

ments seemed to be working. The brothels he would have to leave to the sallow-faced man, but as he was holding back one third of the sum he had agreed to pay until the end of the week, when the debts would be honored by the local bank, Cartwright felt confident the man would do his best.

Cartwright had not seen the Goanese official again, and could only hope he had been able to arrange some kind of reception for the officers. What worried Cartwright was the thought that either of these people might have told someone else who had informed the Germans than an Englishman was behind all these arrangements, but he knew that this risk was one he could not avoid. The officials would doubtless not forget his remarks about his two sons in Dehra Dun. Well, tonight or tomorrow morning would see whether his work had been successful. As his classics master at Fettes had told him so often: *Facta est alea*: The die is cast. There was nothing more he could do. Footsteps padded on the creaking wooden floor outside his room; there was a rat-tat-tat on the door.

"Who is it?" Cartwright asked, glass halfway to his lips.

"Your telephone call to India, senhor."

"Thank you."

Cartwright's relief sounded in his voice. He had forgotten all about that call, which he had placed after lunch, standing for more than an hour in the hot telephone booth near the reception desk. At first, the operator told him there was an hour's delay, then two hours' delay. Then the lines were down, then the Calcutta operator was not answering, and so the call would have to be made next day. But in the strange manner of the Indian Posts and Telegraphs system, the call he had cancelled was now unexpectedly connected.

He hurried out of his room, locked the door, followed the messenger downstairs, and shut himself in the telephone box. He picked up the receiver, already starting to sweat in the narrow, airless booth. Voices along 1,400 miles of line repeated, "Hallo,

Hallo," and then he heard his wife's voice, thin and metallic and disembodied, like a spirit speaking.

"I thought I'd ring you, dear," he said. "Everything going well at your end?"

"I've got some news, she said, excitedly, ignoring his question. "About Tim.'

"What sort of news?"

Cartwright's voice diminished to a strained whisper. He felt he was being throttled. His heart beat like a hammer, and he could see his face, sweating and pale in the mirror on the kiosk wall.

"He is safe! Alive! Oh, isn't it wonderful?"

"Where is he?"

"He's a prisoner. Changi jail, Singapore. Army Records rang me. They've just had a list of people there."

"Are you sure?"

Cartwright was gripping the telephone so tightly that his knuckles stood out white as the bones beneath the flesh.

"Of course, I'm sure. Isn't it *wonderful?*"

"Wonderful," he repeated huskily. "Wonderful."

"When are you coming back?"

"As soon as I can," he said. "Probably by the end of the week."

"Where can I ring you if there is any more news?"

"Afraid you can't," he said. "I'm moving about too much. But I'll ring you."

He replaced the receiver and stood for a moment, head bowed, trembling with reaction. It seemed too much to believe that this could be true; to know that the son he had thought dead was alive. He left the booth, went past the reception desk.

"I cannot put this call on your bill, senhor, because that has already been paid," the clerk told him pointedly.

"Take it out of that," said Cartwright. "And keep the change." He handed him two ten rupee notes.

"Thank you very much indeed, senhor."

Cartwright walked out into the street with no idea where to go, only the feeling that he must breathe open air and thank God for His mercies.

173

A white sacred cow walked along, a bell tinkling around its neck. Some Indians squatted under a veranda, sipping tea from glass jars. Across the road, beneath the shade of a tree, other Indians were selling sweatmeats wrapped in big leaves. Washing hung on strings, and wireless aerials stretched from poles above tiled roofs. Houses ended and godowns and warehouses began, and there was an open space facing the river. To the right stood the whitewashed front of St. Andrew's Church. A street lamp, with a halo of insects, shone through the deepening dusk on ornate tombstones that displayed photographs of the dead within.

The church door was open. He went inside. Candles burned on the altar, and flowers wilted in a glass jar at the foot of a wooden Christ on the cross. Cartwright knelt in the nearest pew and mumbled a few words of thanksgiving for the news about his son. Then he pushed some rupee notes into the locked offertory box, and came out again into the humidity of evening and the ever present smell of oil. A passing car slowed and stopped. White curtains were drawn protectively across the side windows. A rear door opened. The Goanese official he had visited looked out at him.

"Can I give you a lift, senhor?" he asked.

"Thank you, no," said Cartwright. "I am walking for enjoyment."

"You have seen the new arrivals in the harbor?"

"New arrivals? What do you mean?"

Concern gripped Cartwright's throat like a hand.

"The two Portuguese cruisers, *Gonzales Zarco* and *Alfonso D'Albuquerque.* From Lourenco Marques."

"I know nothing about them," said Cartwright. Could the man have an inkling of what was going to happen? Had these ships arrived to defend Portuguese neutrality? Was everything discovered?

"They had arrived with 1,600 African troops. They left Mozambique long ago, for Timor. They have now come on here."

"But the Japs have been in Timor for months."

"That is why they are here, senhor, on their way home."

"Their officers will be at your reception tonight?"

"They have received invitations. There will also be a celebration in the cafés. Do not be alarmed."

"Why should I be alarmed?" asked Cartwright quickly. Was his concern so obvious?

"It might sound like the ring of guns, senhor, but it will only be local people setting off fireworks to show they are happy. We are a happy people, senhor. There is much happiness in our hearts."

He smiled, bowed, closed the door and was driven away. Cartwright waited until the taillights diminished in the darkness. Then he walked back to his hotel. He needed a brandy.

Grice and Davies stood on *Phoebe*'s bridge. Because the need for silence was essential, Davies had instructed his engineer to disconnect the telegraph bells, which rang automatically whenever he ordered Slow or Half or Full Speed from the bridge to the engine room.

There was also a reply mechanism of bells to acknowledge this order, and on a still night at sea the clanging could be heard half a mile away. The chief did not like silencing them because it meant watching the instrument the whole time so as not to miss his captain's orders, but he had agreed, and now the only sound was a thump of the barge engine.

Through their windows, Grice and Davies could see their boarding party sitting around the edge of the hold. One or two leaned on the rails. Davies looked up from his charts.

"We should be passing the mouth of Zuari River in about half an hour," he reported.

"Will they be able to see us from the shore?"

"Possibly. With a glass," said Davies. "But we look harmless enough with this funnel. Just a small oiler or water boat. We'll sail north with navigation lights, then turn out the lights and come back."

"Ever been into Marmagoa before?"

"Never," admitted Davies. "But it shouldn't be too difficult. There is a navigation buoy at the mouth which they light after dark. I'll take my bearings from that. The position of the ships is marked on the chart here, so I know exactly where *Ehrenfels* is lying."

He handed Grice his glasses. Grice raised them to his eyes. As they passed the harbor mouth, Grice saw something that disturbed him.

"What do you make of that?" he asked Davies.

The commander turned his binoculars on the harbor and frowned.

"There's *Ehrenfels*," he said slowly.

"I don't mean her," said Grice. "I mean those ships behind her. They are not tankers, or cargo ships. They're cruisers."

"You're right. They are."

Davies saw two dim greyhound shapes, with smoke stacks and latticed masts, and the long pointing fingers of guns.

"Whose are they, do you think?" Grice asked him.

"I know whose they're not," replied Davies. "Ours."

"Can they be German?"

"Not very likely. Unless they've also sought asylum. They are most probably Portuguese."

"Do you mean we've got to go in against their guns as well? One shell from them could lift us out of the sea."

"It could do even worse than that, Bill," replied Davies quietly. "It would sink us instantly."

Captain Röfer strolled alone on the deck of his ship.

The sun had dropped long since, and the familiar evening breeze, heavy with spices and the smell of pigs aboard *Anfora*, blew past him out to sea. The bell in Vasco church began to toll. That must mark another death from typhoid or cholera, he thought. How many more would die before the sun was up?

Two officers came out of their cabins and approached him.

176

"Are you coming to the reception tonight, sir?" one of them asked him respectfully.

Röfer shook his head. He had received a rather floridly engraved card seeking the pleasure of his company there, but he had replied he would be unable to attend. He found no pleasure in these things. What had he to celebrate in years of enforced inactivity, and unknown years yet to face?

"You go, by all means."

"We've drawn lots as to who should leave, sir, so we are not diminishing the agreed numbers on duty in the ship."

"I should hope not," said Röfer. "Well, have a good time."

He would spend the evening much more enjoyably in his own room, with the reading light over his stamp album, examining smudged postmarks with the dates of peacetime, 1936, 1938, 1939, and the names of faraway ports he had visited. The officer of the watch approached him.

"Lookout reports an unidentified vessel sailing north, sir."

"Far out?"

"Possibly three kilometers from the harbor mouth, sir."

"What sort of vessel is she?"

"Has a long funnel, sir. Could be an oiler. Very small. Not much bigger than a fishing boat."

"Probably going to Bombay," said Röfer. He was not greatly concerned with ships of that kind; they dared not venture far from shore. What would worry him would be the blunt snout of a landing craft, or the sudden soaring bulk of a surfacing submarine.

"Anything else?" he asked.

"Couple of cargo ships going south, sir. Slightly closer inshore."

Röfer went back to his cabin. There was nothing in these sightings. Ships large and small constantly passed up and down the coast. The Portuguese, with their fort on the hill and their huge naval telescopes, were far better able to identify them.

The crews of all four ships had earlier drawn lots to decide who could go ashore. A carnival had been arranged in the cafés for that night and the following two nights, so with luck, all should be able to visit it. The officers were also eager to attend some reception being given on behalf of one of the port authorities. There was so little social life, so few chances of talking to strangers, that events like these, which happened so rarely, assumed immense importance. But this was no excuse to relax vigilance.

Captain Röfer called for the officer of the watch.

"Send a message by rowing boat to all the other ships," he told him. "Give the captains my compliments. Say I feel that we should maintain the fullest alertness at least until there is a moon again."

"Very good, sir."

The officer saluted.

Röfer poured himself a brandy, and then, sitting down at his table, he adjusted the reading light and opened his album.

Darkness shielded the sea like a crêpe shroud. Harrison pressed a switch on *Phoebe's* bridge and the red and green navigation lights went out. The only light now came from a dim, blue, shaded bulb over the charts and a faint red glow from the boiler furnace.

Davies spun the wooden spokes of the wheel. *Phoebe* leaned to starboard and turned, carving a crescent of foam from the indigo sea. Then she headed back towards the harbor mouth.

Grice went down the companionway to the deck. The breeze had freshened now and was almost cool. Men stood up as they saw him approach and gathered round him. This was the moment at last.

"We are going south now," Grice told them. "We are taking it easily, so we will come into the harbor around oh-one-hundred hours. All magazines charged, all guns loaded, safety catches on?"

They nodded.

"Everyone's ready, sir," reported Lumsdaine.

"Good."

Grice turned to Pugh.

"Let's get our faces blacked up while we wait."

Pugh produced round tins of black camouflage cream like boot polish. They smeared this on the backs of their hands, on their faces and around their ears and necks.

Crofter stood leaning over the rail. His retching had ceased, but he still felt a fearful nausea. Gamely, he dug his fingers into the paint and rubbed it over his face. Grice knew how ill he felt, and had proposed that he should remain aboard *Phoebe* to organize defense against any attack from *Ehrenfels*, or the other ships. He realized that after the continual rolling of the little barge, to go aboard a ship the size of *Ehrenfels* would be like going ashore. Crofter might then be seized with an attack of giddiness he could not control, and so would become an instant liability.

"I'd rather help in the assault," Crofter told Grice now.

"And I'd rather stay here," replied Grice with a smile. "But we each have our job to do. It's horses for courses."

Grice blacked his own hands and face and then went up forward to lean over the bows, peering ahead into the darkness. He saw a brief brightening flash of light that dimmed, flared again, and went out. Lumsdaine came up to him.

"Davies reckons that is a searchlight the Portuguese have in Cabo Fort at Dona Paula, north of the harbor. He is keeping in to shore as close as he dares and hopes they can't deflect it down far enough to pick us up."

"Won't they hear our engine?"

"He thinks not. We'll go in very slowly. Well, Bill, here we are in action at last."

"Yes," agreed Grice. "It's been a long time."

It was, in fact, exactly a quarter of a century since he had first felt this tightening of the stomach before an attack. Then it had been on St. George's Day,

179

1918 in HMS *Vindictive* on the Zeebrugge operation. Now it was on a March night, in a dredger's barge, approaching the Zuari River. The years, the places were different, but the smells were still the same: that sharp saltiness of sea air, sooty smoke from the funnel, coal dust everywhere, overlaid by the reek of heavy hot oil. His feelings were also the same, a tenseness of the muscles, the alertness of his mind at the prospect of approaching danger. That war had seen the first major British fleet action for more than a hundred years, and this would be the Light Horse's first action in nearly fifty.

Grice glanced at his watch. His two children would have been asleep for hours. His wife was probably either in bed or listening to a late night program on the radio, or perhaps reading *The Onlooker* or *The Illustrated Weekly of India*. Stumps would long ago have been drawn on the cricket pitch on the *maidan*, and the boats safely moored on the ornamental lake, while the *chowkidar* made his rounds with stick and lantern.

Grice wondered whether the other veterans of the First War were also remembering half forgotten experiences with him; and how the younger men would react to killing a stranger for whom, in different circumstances, and in a different world, they would have been pleased to buy a drink.

Cren Lumsdaine bent down and took something out of his bedding roll. Then he walked to the stern, where he began to untie a rope attached to the stern flagmast.

"What have you got there?" Breen asked him curiously.

"This," replied Lumsdaine. He unfolded a square of black cloth with a white skull and crossbones sewn on to it.

"Made it myself. If we're going to act like pirates, we might as well look like 'em."

And he ran up his homemade flag.

180

Bill Manners and Mark Hilliard were leaning in silence over the rail on the port side, watching the foam race against *Phoebe's* rusty hull.

"Penny for them," said Manners at last.

"If you really want to know," replied Hilliard. "I was thinking about that poor devil of a staff sergeant who'd fiddled the regimental accounts."

"I know you're keen on your job, but that's bloody ridiculous. Why think of him now?"

Hilliard was an honorary accountant for the Light Horse, and a few weeks previously he had discovered a number of chits bearing the signatures of members who were claiming a horse allowance for two or even three horses each. This might have been unremarkable if the members concerned were not miles away, serving in the Army in Burma and other parts of India, and had sold their horses long ago.

Quite by chance, one of them came into the clubhouse when on leave, and Hilliard asked him why he was claiming three horse allowances when he wasn't even eligible for one.

The member indignantly denied the charge and easily proved that the signature on the chits was a forgery. The only person who could have forged it was a regular army staff sergeant temporarily attached to the regiment as an instructor.

"I told him I wanted to see him that night," Hilliard explained now to Manners. "The poor devil immediately admitted what he had done. He had had domestic trouble back home in England, and had borrowed money from an Indian moneylender on the usual terrible terms. He knew he'd be discovered eventually, but that didn't bother him so much. He said the waiting to be found out was the worst. Now I know how he felt."

"So do I," agreed Manners softly.

Twenty feet away, Crofter was thinking about his fiancée, Marion. He hoped that his friend was taking care to post the letters he had written to her in their proper sequence, in accordance with the number on the back of each envelope. Otherwise, she would be most surprised to receive a letter dated several days after its postmark, and he did not like to think of Marion being worried or upset. Well, she certainly would be both if she could see him now, face blackened, hands on the rail blackened, Sten gun slung across his shoulder, spare magazines stuffed into his pockets. He smiled at the thought, and suddenly realized he was acutally looking forward to the moment of action. And for the first time in all the voyage he did not feel seasick. What lay ahead resembled a tribal initiation ceremony. Before it, you belonged to the boys, the youths without experience. After it, you took your place in the company of men. Then he thought about Marion again. How would she feel about this? Would she notice a change in him when he returned? And could he ever tell her what had caused it?

Up against the bridge, Crossley was going through a 15-minute exercise program. In yoga terminology, these exercises were called The Standing Forward Bend, The Bow, The Cobra, The Supine Adamant and The Face of a Cow, but they were simpler than these names would suggest.

Crossley sat on deck with his knees drawn up to his chin then rolled back slowly. Then he lay on his stomach and chest, and then he sat up on his heels with his knees together and his back straight. All the time, he breathed deeply and slowly, moving his trunk, his legs and arms with equal deliberation. He was as old as any man in the party, probably older, and he felt fit as anyone half his age. They might laugh at his exercises, at the nuts and raisins and bananas he ate for breakfast, instead of chewing eggs fried in animal fat. But the artificiality of their food and drink, their pernicious habit of smoking and using their lungs and throats as chimneys, would eventually prove the correctness of his diet, although possibly too late to help them. How foolish the West was to mock the ancient wisdom of the East! How wise Buddha had been when he wrote, "if a man conquer in battle a thousand times a thousand men, and if another conquer himself, he is the greatest of conquerors. One's own self conquered is better than all other people conquered."

Crossley became aware that Breene was near him, watching him. He uncoiled himself slowly and stood up.

"You think they'll be hostile?" Breene asked him, and Crossley heard anxiety in his voice.

"Hostile?" Crossley repeated in surprise. "Hostile? Long ago, Jack, a stranger in the Wild West was told that Big Chief Sitting Bull, who had 300 wives, wished to see him. 'Do you think he's hostile?' this man nervously asked his guide as they approached the Big Chief.

"'Course he is,' the guide replied. 'With 300 wives, he has to do it *any* style—dog style, back style, *hoss-style*.' Course they'll be hostile. But Big Chief Sitting Bull survived. And so will we—so long as we look at the funny side of things."

Pugh and Stewart, as two professionals in the company of amateurs, had gravitated together to the stern of the ship.

"Funny how we got involved in this, simply because I suggested casually we should lift Trompeta," Stewart remarked reflectively. "An odd thing, chance."

Pugh nodded. He was also thinking of the part chance had played in his own career. His father had been badly wounded in the First World War and afterwards received a very small pension. Pugh had hoped to go to Winchester, following a family tradition, but he failed to gain an exhibition, and, since his father could not now afford the full fees, Pugh went to Wellington instead because, by chance, the school offered favorable terms to the sons of disabled officers.

Later, at the Royal Military Academy in Woolwich, Pugh thought of joining the Royal Corps of

Signals, but preferred the well-cut breeches and hand-made field boots of artillery officers to the gaiters of the Signals' officers. So he had joined the Royal Artillery.

Chance had also played its part in bringing him to India. When he was first commissioned, he had served in Germany, where he learned to speak German, and then was posted back to England. He was eager to go to India, where so many of his family had lived before him, but his regiment was due to serve elsewhere.

Again, by chance, Pugh heard of a curious Army custom by which an officer who wished to go to India—not everyone's wish, by any means—could "sell his body" to another officer of equivalent rank who had been posted there and did not want to go and take his place. Pugh found another subaltern in this situation, and after some negotiation, "sold his body" to him for £50. Then this subaltern was unexpectedly posted to Egypt—halfway to India—so Pugh sportingly repaid him £25!

There were other examples of chance in his career. He happened to read an advertisement appealing for Army officers to be seconded to the Special Branch of the Bengal Police. Then surely it was pure chance that *Ehrenfels,* with Trompeta aboard, had called at Calcutta when he was there—and his fortuitous visit to the Police Superintendent in Belgaum had certainly prevented his arrest.

Could one call all this just chance, he wondered, or would it be more accurate to see a pattern in all these things and agree with the 18th-century French writer, de Chamfort, that Chance is really a nickname of Providence?

Up on *Phoebe*'s bridge, Davies now faced an unexpected hazard that filled him with unease. He knew that there should be a flashing navigation light on a buoy at the entrance to the harbor, but tonight this was not lit. Why? He called Grice to the bridge, with Stewart and Pugh, to explain his forebodings.

"There may be a simple explanation. The bulb

could have fused, or the light has just not been switched on. But I don't find these reasons very convincing myself."

"You mean the light could be out deliberately—because they are expecting us?"

"I don't know," replied Davies unhappily. "I wish I did. It just spells danger to me, and I thought I should warn you."

"Can you get into the harbor without that light?"

"I can try. But it is going to be a damned sight more difficult."

"Have you a small boat four of us could row to find that buoy and flash a torch to guide you in?" asked Stewart.

"There is a very heavy current running, and I doubt whether you'd make it. You'd have to find the buoy first in the darkness, and that wouldn't be easy."

"You feel we should call the whole thing off?" asked Grice bluntly.

"If we do that," said Pugh, before Davies could reply, "We have to sail away for another whole day, and come back again tomorrow night. That would be a bad anticlimax—and we don't know that the light would be on then, either. We must go in now as planned or lose all chance of surprise on which success depends."

"I second that," said Grice.

Davies nodded.

"Right, gentlemen," he said.

He slowed his engine as he spoke. *Phoebe* was now barely holding her own against the tide, creeping in as close to shore as Davies could bring her. Through the bridge-house windows, they could see occasional flickers, like fire flies, from houses near the sea, and faint moving cones of light from car head-lamps on the coast road.

Grice went down to the deck.

"Stand by," he said. "We are going in. And good luck to you all."

"And to you, sir," came voices from the darkness. In twos and threes, silently and carefully, for to fall now into the hold or the water would be unthinkable,

185

they moved to their places about the darkened barge.

Manners removed his glass eye, wrapped it in a silk hankerchief, and put it in the breast pocket of his shirt, and buttoned down the flap.

Crofter crouched, kneeling on one knee, his Sten gun held at the angle of 45 degrees, prepared to fire should anyone try to board them.

The ladder party stood ready, one man at each end of the two bamboo ladders. Crossley moved among them all, giving the leader of each section a ball of plastic explosive.

Harrison closed the doors of the engine room to contain the red flow of the furnace. The engine was thumping slowly now, like a heavy hammer muffled by wool. Up on the bridge, Davies strained his eyes through night glasses, trying to pick out any outline of the unlit navigation buoy. But he could only see the phosphorescence of breaking waves by the harbor bar, and in the distance the lights of Marmagoa, too far away to silhouette the anchored ships.

High on the hill, behind Portuguese fortifications that dated from the 16th century, the doors of the big house were wide open to the warm night. Lanterns had been lit above the red tiled patio, and fado singers were strumming guitars and singing their sad laments.

White-jacketed waiters expertly carried silver trays of full glasses among the guests. The chief of harbor police wore a splendid white duck uniform with medals and epaulettes and a lanyard laced with gold. He was talking to officers from the Portuguese cruisers. Marmagoa was a dull place, they said. Their return to the lights and gaiety of Lisbon could not come too quickly.

Near them, the captain of *Anfora*, handsome as ever, his eyes flitting over the other guests, discussed vintage wines with a plain clothes officer from the docks fire service. Garibaldi had been born and bred in the Chianti region of Italy, and so reckoned he knew a good red wine when he drank one. And the wine he was drinking now, he assured the fireman, was equal to the best. The fireman bowed and raised his glass to acknowledge the compliment.

Elsewhere, German officers were talking to each other and to several Portuguese and Goanese ladies, the wives of harbor officials and other local dignitaries. Some of them spoke passable German, and they were now trying to instruct their guests in the simpler Portuguese phrases.

In one corner, watching the scene, and then time after time finding his eyes drawn irresistibly to the harbor, was the Goanese whom Cartwright had visited. He had found it easy to persuade a senior official to allow his house to be used for such a reception, after certain dispositions had been made and the man's arguments gracefully overcome. Of course, arrangements had been easier because the Governor was out of town, but even if he had been present, the Goanese official assured himself, he would doubtless have approved the value of proving Portugal's strict neutrality by inviting officers of every ship in harbor—especially when the cost of this demonstration did not fall on official funds.

Dutch officers were present from a cargo vessel, and they pointedly kept away from the Germans, but no one had arrived from the British tanker. Perhaps they had not understood their invitations, or maybe they would arrive later in the evening?

The official stood for a moment, hands on the still warm balustrade, looking down across tumbling bougainvillaea, red as spilled blood in the flickering flames of the lanterns. Beyond the long garden lay other, smaller houses, and then the floodlights on the docks and the colored bulbs outside the cafés where gramophones played. And beyond them all lay the darkness of the harbor.

He was no fool, this official. He gussed that the Englishman needed a diversion for some secret purpose. But what? Not even a rich Englishman would lavish money on a stranger unless he had good reason for it. He wondered, as he watched, what that motive was—and how long it would be before he knew.

TWELVE

The wind changed, blowing out to sea a long frond of black smoke from *Phoebe*'s funnel, flecked with red sparks. It also brought to those on board a faint sound of gramophone music.

"Bet that's Cartwright's lot," said Breene enviously. "Wish I were there with him."

"Don't think I'd do the girls much good, the way I feel," said Melborne lugubriously.

"Don't think you've ever done them much good, if you ask me!"

"Why ask you?" retorted Melborne. "Ask them."

Davies moved the engine telegraph to Quarter Speed Ahead. Pugh, Yogi Crossley and Red Mac crouched in the bows, groups of men behind them. *Phoebe* dipped and rose uneasily with a nervous exaggerated movement, like the dipper on a fairground. One moment, they saw the harbor's trembling waves reflect the distant lights, the next they were pointing up towards the sky. Ahead, a ship at anchor looked like the side of a cliff because they were so close. They chugged beneath her overhanging stern. Two rusting anchor chains, growing beards of seaweed, stretched down into the sea. Peering up, Grice could just read the name: *Anfora: Triestino*.

On the deck, a gramophone was playing and lights still burned. He heard men talking. But no one hailed them; no one even seemed to have noticed them.

Phoebe moved on around *Anfora*, broadside to the shore. Ahead lay their target.

"My God, she's bloody big," said Red Mac in awe.

Everyone was thinking the same thing. They felt like pygmies about to tackle a sleeping giant. It was

188

difficult now to relate the plan that Pugh had showed them with the sight and size of the huge ship. Rows of portholes lined her side. Derricks and high masts soared up against the stars. The bridge had four storys, and the rail around her deck stretched to infinity.

Riding lights were lit, and in the fo'c'sle a dim glow showed behind drawn curtains of the crews' quarters.

"Five minutes to go," said Grice quietly.

Phoebe moved closer, turning against the rushing tide. She trembled as she met its force, and then slowly, very slowly, and with infinite care, Davies began to bring her alongside.

The second hand crept around the dial of Grice's watch.

"Three minutes," he said.

Cartwright stood on a vacant plot of land between the docks and St. Andrew's church. His arms were folded, and he watched the dark harbor, straining eyes and ears for any sight or sound of the vessel he knew should be arriving at any moment.

He was in a corner of the harbor where the tide deposited bloated bodies of drowned dogs and cats. He had seen the rocks by day, crawling with purple-shelled crabs, and had chosen this place because he guessed no-one went there at night. The smell of the foul water would drive even lovers elsewhere.

Behind him, in the shadows, his car was parked, pointing up the road, ready for a quick getaway. In the dashboard cubbyhole he had put bandages, gauze, a pair of scissors, some surgical spirit and a bottle of Portuguese brandy. The petrol tank was full, the engine warm, and he was ready to go.

He glanced at his watch. Thirteen minutes past two o'clock in the morning. The reception for the officers had been going for hours, but it was unreasonable to hope that it could continue for much longer. Soon, even the most eager revelers would return to their ships. But why hadn't *Phoebe* arrived? Had something gone wrong?

Cartwright now noticed a number of Portuguese African troops walking in twos and threes through the bazaar. He gussed that they must be part of the detachment who had arrived in the crusiers, yet he had never seen any of them before in the town. Presumably they were in a camp some distance away, so why on this one particular night were they walking around the place? Cartwright kept assuring himself that there were nothing sinister in their appearance. There was no reason to worry, either, because *Phoebe* had not appeared in the harbor, but nevertheless he was concerned and the fact that he could do nothing to help his friends accentuated his foreboding. He stood, peering into the darkness across the water, seeing nothing, fearing everything.

"Two minutes," said Grice in his clipped voice.

No hint of his feelings or the tension of the moment showed in his tones. He might have been saying grace at a Light Horse dinner, or calling up a cab in Chowringhee or Park Street. Others in the party swallowed their thoughts. Ahead of them, towering higher than any had imagined, was the tarred steel wall they had to scale. It was lined by rows of rivets, streaked by scabs of rust. Directly above their heads, like the gantry of a crane, hung the superstructure, now being blackened by smoke from their funnel.

On Davies's orders the crew had hung out old motor tires and great knotted coils of thick rope to ease the impact of collision and to minimize its noise. They were so close now they could smell rust and tar on her salt-encrusted side.

"One minute."

The men in the bows, holding the bamboo ladders, craned their necks to see the top of *Ehrenfels'* deck. All around *Phoebe*'s hold others lay silently on their stomachs in case the impact of the two hulls touching flung them off their feet.

Under *Phoebe*'s stern, her propellers churned the harbor water into a phosphorescent foam.

"Who are you?" shouted a lookout from *Ehrenfels* in German. The men aboard *Phoebe* peered up into the darkness towards the sound of the enemy voice.

"Just a harbor barge," Pugh called back in German.

"Why are you sailing without lights?"

Phoebe's hull ground against *Ehrenfels*, scouring a shining raw groove in the tarred metal.

"What the devil are you doing?" asked the German angrily.

"Now!" said Grice.

At once, the ladders came down. The tops of the bamboos scratched *Ehrenfels*' side. Pugh put his foot on the third rung and started to climb. The ladder began to tilt as momentum carried the little barge along the side of the big ship. For a moment, Pugh thought he would be thrown sideways between the two, and he reached up to grip the base of a deckrail support, high above his head. His feet left the ladder and he hauled himself up on *Ehrenfels*' deck.

The force of striking *Ehrenfels* now drove *Phoebe* out for a few feet. Instantly, the angle of the ladders changed. Part way up the other one stood Yogi Crossley and Bill Grice, leaning forwards against the bamboo poles in case these suddenly tipped backwards and threw them off.

Up in *Phoebe*'s bows, Harrison and the engineer waited, holding the ropes with grappling irons fixed to one end. They swung these like lariats around their heads and then released them. The hooks hit *Ehrenfels*' deck with a booming like giant gongs, and bit and held.

Pugh was by now up and over the German ship's gunwales, the first to board her. Everyone in *Phoebe* could hear shouts in German from the deck of the cargo ship.

"Achtung! Achtung!" someone was calling urgently. And then the whole night exploded in the blaze of a million candle power. *Ehrenfels*' searchlight focussed on little *Phoebe*.

All around the deck, Light Horse and Calcutta

Scottish stood waiting to follow the leaders up the ladders. Coal steamed in the hold. Up front, behind the railway sleepers and sandbags, other men couched ready to climb. Several had drawn bamboo screens and strips of tarpaulin across their backs in an attempt to conceal themselves. All now shielded their eyes against the aching, blinding glare of the unexpected searchlight.

The Germans stared down at them in bewilderment and disbelief. They had expected a small waterboat or an oiler, where someone had carelessly forgotten to light the navigation lamps. But instead—this. It must be the spearhead of the attack which Captain Röfer had been so certain was imminent. For an instant, no one moved, as though mesmerized by the brilliance of the light. Then Red Mac raised his Sten, took careful aim and fired deliberately along the beam. His gun chattered like a chain. Then the searchlight exploded with a blue flash and a great puff of white smoke. Darkness dropped around them.

"Come on, up the ladders!" shouted Grice, all need for concealment gone. Still dazzled, blinking blinded eyes in the sudden dark, they began to climb. Men who were in the habit of using a lift to reach even a first floor office in Calcutta now heaved themselves up the swaying, creaking bamboo ladders. Those who found the climb most difficult were the firefighting party, for each carried a red Minimax fire extinguisher. They had anticipated lifting these up a relatively gentle slope between the two ships. Instead, the climb was almost vertical. They were forced to strap the red cylinders on their backs, and they climbed slowly, for the ladders bent and curved alarmingly beneath their great weight.

The noise of the gunfire awakened Captain Röfer, always a light sleeper. He was in a small sea cabin above the tiered bridge. He switched on the light, swung down from his bunk, and pulled on his trousers. The officer of the watch burst into the room.

"Enemy boarding party alongside, sir!" he reported breathlessly.

"How many men?"

"I counted about twenty, sir. Must be the advance party."

"Sound the alarm."

The officer pulled a rope handle that hung from the roof. For a second, the siren motor whirred and then the siren blared with a bellow like a thousand car horns.

It was so loud and so unexpected that Light Horsemen and Calcutta Scottish still on the ladders and still partially blinded by the light, paused, bemused by the sheer thunder of its iron clamor. Then they went on up grimly, each to his target.

Aboard *Drachenfels,* Captain Schmidt also heard the siren and pulled aside his cabin curtain. He could see nothing but a faint glitter of water under harbor lights. That was *Ehrenfels'* siren, all right, but why weren't they showing any more lights? He began to dress as quickly as he could, moving clumsily because of his paralyzed leg. What could have happened?

Aboard *Braunfels* and *Anfora,* the officers and crews were also awake. They struggled into boots and trousers, grabbed knives and clubs and steel bars placed near their bunks for just such an emergency, and raced to their appointed places on deck. Some waited by hand pumps connected to kerosene drums. Others stood near fuses with matches and tapers in case the electrical circuits should fail. More hid in cover at the tops of companionways to deal quickly and brutally with any invaders.

Up in the house on the hill, the reception was all but over. The night had cooled suddenly and it was too chilly for the guests to remain out on the patio. But lanterns still burned there and the polished tile floor stretched, red as blood, to the white stone balustrades. Hugh moths fluttered near the lights, although the party had moved indoors. Behind wide windows edged by gilded frames, the singers were in

193

full throat. Guitarists tore at the strings, as they recalled in their traditional songs the loves and glories and memories of old Portugal. Several couples were dancing, and everywhere the buzz of conversation sounded like the drone of distant bees, over the constant tinkle of empty glasses being exchanged for full ones on the silver trays.

Through this cacophony of enjoyment the first wild wail of *Ehrenfels'* siren sliced like a sharpened knife. Officers dancing with Portuguese ladies stopped in mid-step and released their partners. Garibaldi rushed to the glass doors, flung them open, and then pushed back the heavy louvered shutters. The wind blew in, ruffling candles. Behind him, the music wailed to a stop. Ahead of him, out in the darkness, he heard the thunder of the siren.

"They are attacking!" he called.

"Who?" asked the chief of the harbor police.

"That's our warning if the enemy arrive," a German officer explained.

"The enemy? But, senhor, this is a neutral port. You have our protection. There must be some mistake. Perhaps someone has pressed the wrong button? I hear there is a fiesta in the cafès tonight. Sailors. . . . Maybe someone has had too much to drink, eh, senhor?"

"It's the British," the officer replied grimly. "We thought they'd come. Now they're here."

"Never, senhor," said the Goanese official in his grandest voice. "You must be mistaken."

"We must find out," said an officer from *Drachenfels.* "We beg your permission to leave."

"But how will you get back? There are no taxis or tongas at this hour. I have ordered cars to pick you up later on. It is a long way down to the harbor, senhors. You will have to walk."

"We'll run," retorted the German shortly. He waved to his colleagues. They all streamed out, down the wide steps, past stone urns cascading with red and purple bougainvillea and statues that stared at them with sightless eyes, down to the road. Then, instinctively falling into step, sweating in their best

194

uniforms, they began to double march toward the harbor.

Pugh and Melborne climbed up the companion-way to *Ehrenfels'* bridge, found this unexpectedly empty, but heard movements on the floor above. They went up these further steps carefully, feeling their way in the darkness, and reached a closed door. A thin strip of light showed beneath it. Somone must be inside. Pugh turned the handle gently but the door would not open. Melborne smashed the handle with the butt of his Sten. They both rushed into the captain's cabin. The scene was like a tableau. An officer faced them, one arm raised, like a strap-hanger in a suburban railway carriage, as he tugged the rope that controlled the siren.

Captain Röfer stared at them in amazement and then both men turned to seize some weapon. Mel-borne fired. Röfer opened his mouth as though to speak, and fell forward across the table. The other officer dropped and the siren stopped instantly. Mel-borne lowered his Sten. His ears still rang with the thunder of the siren and the clatter of his gun in the confined space. Through the silence, he heard the siren motor running down. He pulled out his knife, and cut the wires to the switch. Pugh ripped open the double drawers of the table, but they were empty. The code books must be elsewhere. They ran out down companionways and along the deck.

Behind them the photograph of Hitler looked down on two dead men and an open stamp album.

Crossley and Breene were crossing the deck in the other direction.

"Mathafarn!" Pugh called as they passed.

"Mathafarn to you, too," Breene retorted.

Their muffled boots made little sound; they might have been moving through cotton wool.

Crossley had seen, in the brief blaze of the search-light, a wire from the main masthead aerial leading down to a glass insulator outside a deck cabin. This would be the cabin that had contained the ship's

195

legitimate radio, immobilized on Portuguese orders. He intended to make sure that it never worked again.

He flung his weight at the door. It was locked. Breene brought up his boot and kicked a lower panel. The wood was thick and held firm.

"Shoot it out!" ordered Crossley. Breene jammed the muzzle of his Sten against the lock and fired. Then he shouldered open the door and burst inside.

A German officer crouched on the floor, surrounded by bundles of papers, and thick books with shining lead covers. He was fumbling frantically with a metal cylinder about a foot long. Crossley saw with peculiar intensity a brass clock on one wall, next to a framed photograph of the Führer.

The officer threw one of the lead-covered code books at Breene's face. Breene squeezed his trigger. The gun jammed.

The officer jumped up, fumbling for a weapon. Crossley threw himself at him in a rugger tackle, and the incendiary went off between them. A blazing jet of flame, thick as a man's wrist, roared out of the nozzle. Its intense heat scorched the ceiling, blistering paint on the walls, and lit the papers. Breene kicked it out of the way, but nothing could stop the cascade of fire.

Crossley was badly burned about the face and one hand, but the pain had not yet overcome the numbing shock of the flames. The German officer grabbed a club from beneath his bunk, and he and Breene fought hand to hand, stumbling over the blazing incendiary. This rolled to one side, and now the flame engulfed the papers and the code books. The lead began to wilt and ran like liquid silver.

Red Mac, running past the open door, saw the fighting and inferno within. He hit the German on the head with the butt of his Sten gun.

Porthole curtains were now curling and burning. Smoke and fumes blackened the ceiling. All three dragged out the unconscious German, handcuffed his right wrist to the deck rail so he could not escape and ran on. Crossley stopped to wrap his field dressing around his hands and then paused. He was not feeling any pain from his burns; that would come later, but now the nerves were still numb as the adrenalin of action poured through his blood. He remembered that photograph and the clock. He could take one but not both, for he could only use one hand. Crossley made his decision. He raised his revolver in his good hand, shot Hitler through the head, jammed the revolver in his belt—and grabbed the clock.

Up in the stern, Manners and Squire had reached the starboard anchor chain. This was wound around a stanchion and could not possibly be raised without a powered winch. They would have to blow out one link, and crouched on the cold metal of the deck to set the charge. The plastic explosive felt clammy as clay as they crammed it hurriedly between a link and the giant eyehole through which the chain ran down to the anchor. But the plastic would not adhere to the rust on the metal, already damp with spray. They squeezed it in, wedged it somehow, forgetting their fear of handling the explosive roughly in their haste to carry out their task.

"Right," said Manners. "Now the detonator."

Squire produced this. Manners set the mechanical timing device and pushed the tiny metal cylinder into the plastic. Then they both leapt up and dashed across the deck.

The explosion temporarily deafened them both, but the link had broken. With a screech and roar of rusty metal, the heavy chain disappeared down into the sea.

Now to blow the second stern anchor. Ears still ringing, eyes still dazzled by its blaze, they raced across the deck towards the other chain. And then Manners shouted, "*Wait!*"

They stopped, panting for breath, festooned with revolvers, handcuffs, Stens. They both smelled kerosene. Suddenly, the odor became almost overpowering. Manners bent down and rubbed his hand on the deck. It was slimy.

"Run!" he yelled. At that moment, near a deckhouse, a German sailor fired a signal pistol. The hissing green shell scored the deck, and in its light they caught a sudden glimpse of gray and white paintwork, a brass-rimmed porthole, a white lifebelt with the name *Ehrenfels* in black. Then the entire afterdeck erupted in a flood of flame. Manners raised his Sten and fired towards the deckhouse. He missed his target. Squire slammed a new magazine into his own Sten and sprayed the deck. The German threw up his hands, and disappeared over the side.

"Must have used your blind eye," said Squire shakily.

"Lucky for you I've got a sense of smell," retorted Manners. It was impossible to sever the second chain. Flames now engulfed the entire stern. Paint rippled into giant, bursting blisters. The white canvas cover on the lifebelt disintegrated. Even the cork beneath it began to burn.

Holding their arms across their faces to shield them from the baking, breath-catching heat, Manners and Squire ran back across the deck. No need for caution now; at least they could see their way.

Down below decks, Lumsdaine and Hilliard and Harrison found the switchboard and turned on the engine room lights. The huge MAN diesel shone with green paint. Polished brass work and copper pipes glittered beneath the bright, unshaded bulbs.

The German engineers had kept the ship's engine in first-class condition. The two men now circled it, wondering how it could be started.

"You're the engineer," said Lumsdaine.

"I've got an M.G. Midget," admitted Hilliard. "But I've never even seen a diesel like this before."

"Well, you're seeing one now. Let's get cracking."

"No go," replied Hilliard. "The injectors have gone. The Germans must have taken them. It can't run without injectors. I do know that much."

Grice came into the engine room.

"Impossible to start the engine," Hilliard reported. "They've taken out some parts."

"Don't waste any time then," said Grice. "There

should be a transmitter behind one of the bulkheads here."

"Let's have a *dekho* behind that door," suggested Lumsdaine, pointing to the louvred metal door on which Pöller had painted his warning: "High voltage ... Danger of Death," with a skull and crossbones.

Around the door's edge were six large well-oiled wing nuts. Harrison spun them open. Then he flung his weight against the door. It did not move. He pulled at the handle. It still did not open.

"Blow it open," ordered Grice.

Lumsdaine pressed plastic explosve around the main lock in the way Crossley had explained. Sweat from his face dripped on his hands as he worked in the airless room. Faintly, through layers of deck, they all heard shouts, and twice the whole ship boomed like a gigantic gong as an explosive charge was set off.

Melborne and Hilliard on the other side of the engine room had meanwhile discovered another locked door. They pressed their plastic explosive against the handle, detonated it and rushed through as soon as it swung open. On the other side stood Jack Greene, shaken by the shock of the blast.

"Open Sesame!" he said weakly. "Next time, give me warning before you do that. You nearly had me that time! I'm not insured for this."

Now Lumsdaine's charge exploded. He opened the heavy door and went inside the tiny cell from which Pöller had sent so many messages. The shelves were empty of code-books, but the radio was still bolted to the wall. The front of the set was of black crackle-finished metal, with tuning dials, plugs for earphones and a Morse key, a list of wavelengths pasted on a piece of cardboard. Hilliard ripped this off the facia and pocketed it. Then they smashed the set with the butts of their stens.

Breene arrived to report he had found a second doorway out from the engine room—and added a burst from his Sten. Smoke curled up from shattered silver-coated valves, from ruined coils and condensers, oozing wax.

Then, as they stood, ears tingling with the noise of gunfire, an explosion elsewhere in the ship threw them off their feet and the lights went out.

On shore, the Germans and Italians, breathless from running down the hill, had reached the docks. Searchlights on both sides of the harbor played on the four ships. They could see *Ehrenfels* clearly, for flames soared up above her funnel, almost reaching the top of her masts. On her decks, figures were running, and they heard shouts, and the crack of gunfire. Then came the deep sonorous boom of an explosion. The flames guttered with its force and then dimmed momentarily as the air filled with flying debris. Marble slabs, blown into tiny pieces, logs, metal bars, bags of flour erupted like rocks from a blazing volcano.

"Get a boat," ordered the officer from *Drachenfels.*

But the tide was low, and all rowing boats lay on their sides in the stinking mud. The crews waded across rocks crawling with crabs, and slid up to their knees in their frantic efforts to reach the nearest boat. But the cautious Goanese had removed the oars. Now policemen were arriving, and some Portuguese officers with a detachment of African troops who had been aboard the two warships. No one knew what was happening, except that a ship was on fire. Were they *certain* they had heard shooting?

"Of course, it's shooting," shouted the German officer angrily.

"I do not think you can be correct, senhor," replied the chief of the harbor police, who had arrived in a car. "It is our custom on Saint's days and fiestas to let off fireworks."

As he spoke, fireworks and crackers banged and fizzed from a café somewhere along the dockside.

"You see?"

"We must get out there," the German told him, ignoring this comfortable explanation. "For God's sake, haven't you got a launch, a motor boat, or something?"

"I have asked for my launch to be prepared, senhor."

"Can't you provide anything for us more quickly?"

"It is an official launch, senhor. It is not being provided for you, but for me. I will make my own reconnaissance."

As he spoke, a small motor launch puttered slowly towards a wooden quay. The official climbed down the steps and into it. He sat down as the launch chugged out into the harbor. The Germans and Italians were surrounded now by a crowd of locals, many half clothed as they had rushed from their houses. They stared in silence at the foreigners, secretly enjoying their discomfiture, grateful for any excitement in lives of poverty and routine.

The Germans looked at each other in an agony of frustration. Then one spoke for all of them.

"Scheiss," he said bitterly.

Cartwright stood by the edge of the sea, watching the harbor. Huge leaping flames lit up the godowns and other buildings along the docks; the water reflected the fire like a vast and glittering mirror.

Cartwright clenched his fists in the intensity of his feelings. His friends were out there fighting, and he could not know how the battle was going. He heard shots and shouts and explosions, and once he saw someone leap or fall from *Ehrenfels'* upper deck. In the Portuguese fort up on the headland the soldiers kept turning their searchlight from one ship to another, and back again, clearly as bewildered by what was happening as everyone else.

Cartwright lit a cheroot. Nearly everyone in Marmagoa seemed to be out on the docks. Upper windows blazed in houses, shutters were flung open as people peered out, calling to friends down in the street. Motorists parked their cars with headlights pointing across the harbor in an attempt to see the German ship more clearly. Cartwright glanced at his watch. If any of his friends were coming ashore, they should be arriving soon.

A sudden commotion from the far side of the oil tanks caught his attention. With a great rattling of anchor chains and a thump-thump of her engine, the British tanker was pulling out hastily. Stern first, she backed into the harbor and then turned towards the mouth of the river, passing on the far side of the blazing *Ehrenfels*.

Now what the hell is she doing that for? Cartwright asked himself.

THIRTEEN

Aboard *Phoebe*, Bernard Davies waited, one hand
on the engine telegraph, ready to move forwards or
astern. The windows of his bridge were pegged open
so he could order the lascars to cast off the grappling
irons if he had to leave. Above him, the long funnel
poked out its busy puffs of black smoke. The wind
spread this in a cloud, now obscuring the flames
aboard *Ehrenfels*, now drifting towards the shore
and dimming the lights on land.

The Light Horse and Calcutta Scottish had been
aboard for nearly 20 minutes. There was still no sign
of the forward anchor chain being cut, although he
had seen one of the stern chains fall away before
flames engulfed the aft of the ship. It only wanted
the troops behind the searchlight up on the headland
to focus properly on what was happening instead of
moving their light around as though it was a flashlight
in a farmyard, and they would see his barge at once—
and realize an attack was in progress. Then one round
from one gun aboard either of the two Portuguese
cruisers could end the whole attack. Even a small
launch from one of these ships, with sufficient armed
men aboard, could easily overwhelm the few men left
behind in *Phoebe*. Davies bit his lips and wished
he could light his pipe.

Down below *Ehrenfels'* engine room, below long
sweating girders, painted with red oxide against the
perpetual corrosive dampness, the inner walls of her
hull dripped and glistened with constant condensation.
Her huge rudder chains lay like slumbering serpents

alongside the vast propeller shaft with its weeping glands.

There was a faint slop of water under the feet of three German sailors who crouched by the Kingston valves. These were two large metal-spoked wheels with serrated rims so they could grip them tightly despite the rust and grease and dampness. The three men threw the weight of their muscled, tattooed arms against these wheels. Their bodies shone with sweat in the damp, dark confines. A torch propped up against a metal bracket lit the scene with a faint and feeble light.

Slowly, the valves began to open. Seawater bubbled and frothed at the mouth of a pipe in its fury to be free. The first wheel suddenly spun easily and the man gripping it slipped and fell against it, before he realized it was fully open. Then the second one opened, and the third. Water roared like a whirlpool from the pipes and streamed against them. Its pressure knocked them off their feet and swept away the torch. Almost instantly, they were up to their thighs in swirling water. Pieces of wood bashed their bare chests, as they groped, gasping towards the metal ladder, bolted to the side of the hull. They hauled themselves up and out of the swiftly rising flood, into the space beneath the engine room. Then, crouched double, trousers pasted to their thighs like a canvas skin, with feet slipping and slithering on diamond-shaped treads polished by years of use, they reached the corridor, then the companionway, and finally the open deck.

The air was suddenly cold on their panting chests, and they leaned against the rails for a moment, blinded by the sudden glare of the Portuguese searchlight, nostrils choked by the smoke from *Phoebe*'s funnel and the acrid fumes of the blaze. Behind them, they saw men moving through a sheet of fire. They rushed at them, rage knotting their muscles. The water on their bodies shielded them from the flames and they were through. A man, British no doubt, with a beard and blackened face, stood hosing the flames with a fire extinguisher. They leapt at him.

Red Mack, eyes reddened and raw with the smoke, mouth dry as a fired kiln, sensed rather than saw them. All memory of the lessons in unarmed combat he had learned at Ballygunge deserted him. They were younger than he was and bigger than he was and they outnumbered him, three to one. He raised the nozzle of his extinguisher and hosed them full in their faces.

"Got you, you bastards!" he shouted. And as he yelled, the whole deck tilted, as though gripped by a giant underwater hand. Coiled ropes slithered across shining metal plates from which wooden deck planking had been burned away. Lifebelts dropped from hooks. Life rafts cannoned into the rails, buckling the uprights.

As Red Mac braced himself, the deck rose behind him like a steep hill. His three antagonists slid away out of reach, through the flames. For a moment he thought the whole ship would turn turtle, and in that second two other crewmen leapt from behind a hatch where they had been crouching.

Red Mack turned the nozzle on them, but the extinguisher was empty. He flung it at the nearest man, who dodged it and came on, a club in his hand. Red Mac tugged at his revolver, but it was caught by its own lanyard. The German brought down his club on Red Mac's head. He staggered and fell.

Melborne saw him drop and jumped on top of the German and handcuffed him as he lay. Squire, behind Melborne, tripped the second man. He hit his head on the tilting deck as he fell and before he could crawl to his feet, Squire handcuffed him to the rail.

Down below decks, as tens of thousands of tons of seawater streamed through the open Kingston valves, the floor heaved slowly like some great beast of the sea rolling over into a more comfortable position. More lights dimmed, flickered, and went out.

"She's going over!" shouted Grice through the darkness. "Up on deck."

They began to cross the oily floor of the engine

room, feeling water rise as they moved through the darkness, hands outstretched. Finally, with water reaching their thighs and the angle of the floor increasing, they reached a handrail and began the long slow climb to the upper deck.

Davies saw *Ehrenfels* huge vertical hull sheer as a tarred wall, the height of a church steeple, and only feet away from his deck, suddenly move and tilt against *Phoebe*. The movement threw the bamboo ladders across his deck like matchsticks. He heard wood splinter on the edge of his bridge-house.

"Cast off!" he bellowed to the crew in the bows. Expertly, with the speed of years of practice, their brown fingers undid complicated knots and they flung the ropes overboard. These slapped against *Ehrenfels* turning hull and then hung out vertically, like the tails of gigantic rats.

Davies moved the engine telegraph lever to Full Speed Astern. *Phoebe's* propellers thrashed the sea like a mill race. With agnoizing slowness, she began to back off. As she moved, he pulled the cord that sounded three blasts on his siren: the warning to leave everything and return immediately—or be left behind.

Cartwright still stood on the shore, with waves lapping at his feet and the claws of unseen crabs scuttering on the rocks. *Phoebe's* siren sounded thin and feeble to him after the iron blare from *Ehrenfels*. The big ship was now blazing from bow to stern. The searchlight in the Portuguese army post up on the point played on her masts and funnel and superstructure. In its harsh narrow beam, Cartwright could see men leaping into the water as the ship began to dip slowly to one side. Against flames roaring now like a furious furnace, he could make out the barge's outline and see men on her deck. Foam churned beneath her stern as Davies tried to back away.

So they had done what they set out to do, Cartwright thought. That which had been attempted had been achieved, as his classics master used to say about Caesar's campaigns. *Ehrenfels* and her radio were out of action for ever—and of how many men on both side could the same also be said?

"Peace is better than war," that same schoolmaster had once declared, quoting Croesus to an indifferent form, eager for the classics lesson to end. "In peace, sons bury their fathers. In war, fathers bury their sons."

As a father, Cartwright thanked God he had been spared this task. But after this night's work, how many fathers and sons on both side would mourn?

Then he thought of the other side of the equation. A handful might die tonight, but as a direct result of this engagement how many hundreds or even thousands of other lives would be saved?

Up on *Ehrenfels'* deck, which was already dipping at a dangerous angle, Squire slipped a key into the lock of one of the German's handcuffs.

"You are coming with me," he told him, and gripping his arm, jumped down on to *Phoebe*'s deck. Squire's eyes were half-blinded by smoke and soot, and he braced himself for a long fall. But to his amazement, instead of being 20 feet or so, the drop was only about three feet. *Ehrenfels* was going down so fast that the two decks were now almost level. Other men were also jumping as the gap widened between the two ships. Both Red Mac and Melborne brought prisoners with them.

Lookouts with binoculars aboard the other three ships gave running commentaries on what they saw. Silhouetted against the blazing *Ehrenfels,* they could make out a small barge or other craft of similar size turning towards them. This must be an advance party of a larger British naval assault operation. Officers, despite their earlier agreement to fire their ships when any warning siren sounded, had held back in the desperate hope that there must be some mistake, some mishap that had set off *Ehrenfels'* siren. Now they admitted they were wrong. Fingers reluctantly pressed emergency switches. Blue sparks blazed across terminal gaps near fuses. Wires smoked with the heat of direct short circuits.

One by one, hidden charges exploded below decks. Portholes splintered and glass showered over the sea like confetti as crews leapt into the water. One man remained behind in each ship to make sure all the charges had blown successfully. Decks were already awash with kerosene from the split drums, and they waited bravely with boxes of matches and rolled-up newspapers, ready to light them and throw them on the kerosene if the fuses failed.

Then the explosives they had placed so carefully on hatchways and in companionways, blew up and the decks took fire. One by one, the ships heeled over and began to go down. The men who stayed behind now leapt over the rails themselves, grateful for cool salt water to douse flames which already scorched their clothes and singed their hair and eyebrows.

The harbor was not deep enough to allow the ships to sink completely. They settled on their sides on the bottom, funnels, masts and superstructure sticking up at an angle out of the sea, still burning furiously. And between ships and shore, the sea was dotted with survivors striking out desperately for land.

Grice turned his binoculars on *Drachenfels*, then *Braunfels*, and last of all, *Anfora*. Here he was astonished to see a complete garden, with bushes, trees and trellises, slither slowly sideways into the sea. Hogs squealed in fear as they began to swim clumsily for the shore between floating shrubs and wooden spars.

"Well done, the Italians," he said to himself. "Late as usual."

He lowered his glasses and turned to Crofter.

"Everyone aboard?" he asked.

"So far as I can see, sir. I have counted them."

Grice ran up the steps to the bridge. Davies turned the telegraph to Full Speed Ahead. The heat from the burning *Ehrenfels* was still so strong that when the wind changed it dried the breath in their throats and the streaming sweat on their blackened faces.

Everyone looked for friends, shaking their hands warmly, slapping each other on the back in a general euphoria of reaction and relief. Bottles of rum and brandy were passed around. They drank greedily. They were all alive, and they could so easily have been dead. Relief poured through their blood as intoxicating as the alcohol. The three German prisoners sat dejectedly in the stern. Above their heads, the Jolly Roger waved briskly in the wind.

The heat was now intense. Thick oily smoke carried sparks and blazing strips of fabric out into the darkness beyond the burning ships. Parts of *Ehrenfels'* hull glowed red hot. Metal pulsed with heat, as wind fanned the flames. But within minutes, with luck, they should all be safely out beyond the harbor bar.

Lumsdaine and Pugh marshalled several men with Bren guns in the stern. If any boat put out after them, they were to fire below the water line, to try and sink them. But if either of the Portuguese cruisers made one hit on *Phoebe* with even their smallest gun, they realized the barge would sink like a stone.

"Wait a minute!" shouted Melborne suddenly. Someone's signaling!"

Davies idled his engine. *Phoebe* began to roll. Pugh, Grice and Stewart peered back at the burning ship. Showers of sparks, burning pieces of wood and cloth soared up against the sky. At the base of the flames, to the right, they could distinctly see two figures standing against the rails, frantically waving torches towards *Phoebe*.

"Maybe they're a couple of Deutschers who can't swim," suggested Red Mac.

"Give 'em a burst, and let 'em learn," advised Melborne.

The distance was too great for a Sten, and there was no need now to worry about leaving British cartridge cases. Someone lifted a Bren from its stand in the stern and fired. Tracer bullets soared like red stars, spattering the decks around the two figures. But the wind was strong and *Phoebe*'s deck was rolling badly. The torches went out for a moment and came on again.

"You've missed," said Melborne in disgust. He took a long swig of rum and threw away the empty bottle.

"Here. Give me the bloody gun."

He reached out for it, jammed on a fresh magazine and took aim. The two men aboard *Ehrenfels* were now holding their torches under their chins. The light shone up on their faces like turnip lanterns.

"Hold it!" shouted Red Mac suddenly. "They're not Germans! They're our blokes! Charlie Wilton and Harry Breene!"

"My God!" said Melborne slowly. "You're right!"

He lowered the Bren and his hands were trembling.

Davies began to maneuver *Phoebe* up against *Ehrenfels* for the second time. As she came alongside, Wilton and Breene threw away their torches and leapt down on the deck. Hands stretched out to steady them in case they overbalanced into the hold as *Phoebe* reversed at full speed away from *Ehrenfels'* incandescent hull.

"What the hell happened to you?" Stewart asked them angrily. "Didn't you hear the siren?"

"Of course we heard the bloody siren. But we were trapped below decks. The only door I could see jammed as the ship heeled over. If it hadn't been for Wilton who found another way out, we'd have had it. Quite apart from you idiots shooting at us!"

"First time in your life, Jack, the joke wasn't on you," said Manners soothingly. "Here, have a drink, both of you."

He splashed the remains of a bottle of Portuguese brandy into two enamel mugs. They drank thankfully.

Davies asked once more for Full Speed Ahead. The whole harbor now erupted like a firework spectacular as drum after drum of kerosene caught fire. In the reflection of the flames, water glowed and glittered like a sea of gold.

Down in *Phoebe*'s boiler room, the stokers shoveled furiously, their bare bodies burnished by sweat in the white heat of the furnace. In the engine room, the needle on the pressure gauge climbed steadily up the dial until it stood against the danger stop.

The tide was turning now and waves punched and pummeled *Phoebe*'s blunt old-fashioned bows, soaking the Light Horsemen up on the forward deck. Grice saw the stokers flag and pause, and stripped off his own shirt.

"Come on, lads," he said. "Let's give 'em a hand."

So, working in relays, bankers, accountants, insurance agents and jute merchants, their bodies blackened with coal dust and streaked by sweat, flung shovel after shovel of coal into the roaring mouth of the furnace. As one group wearied, others took their places. Everyone knew it was essential to make the best possible speed. And although they could probably shoot up a pursuing motor launch, that must bring political retribution, for they would be attacking sailors of a neutral country, and traditionally England's oldest ally.

Davies kept *Phoebe* close inshore so that the Portuguese army unit with their searchlight could not bring it to bear on them. The closest it came was about 50 yards to their left, but all it revealed to the watchers in the Fort were breaking waves on the harbor bar, and the black trail of smoke from *Phoebe*'s long funnel merging with the smoke of the burning ships.

Cartwright, still waiting on the dark side of the harbor, heard shouted orders and counter orders along the docks. In the blaze of car headlamps he could see men staggering up out of the sea soaking wet, some half clothed, others naked, save for underpants. A platoon of Portuguese soldiers had arrived in a truck and were being detailed to line up the survivors as they landed.

Cartwright would have liked to have walked closer to this activity, but he did not wish to involve himself too deeply in case his nationality was recognized and his reason for being there at all was questioned. He glanced at his watch: 03:15 hours. He waited until dawn lit the sky and the flames, which had seemed so bright in the darkness, paled against the power of the rising sun.

Explosions still rippled the morning air. Showers of

sparks still cascaded occasionally over the sea, as though from some marine display of fireworks. Cartwright guessed that the ships would burn for several days.

None of the swimmers had headed for the oil storage tanks, so he assumed that all the Light Horse and Calcutta Scottish had sailed safely away in *Phoebe*. It was therefore time for him to leave. He climbed into his car and drove slowly out through Vasco da Gama, up the hill and along the road that lay like a long spine above the paddy fields. Already, groups of local people were going to work, jogging along with bundles on their heads, and in the case of the women, babies on their backs. The events in the harbor must have disturbed their sleep, thought Cartwright, but he had not even been to bed. All night he had stayed on his feet, waiting to help his friends, but it was only now, when the excitement was over and the sun was in his eyes, that he felt tired.

Perhaps his wife was right. He wasn't so young as he had been, and what years ago he could have taken without a thought, now became an effort. Perhaps they should have a brief holiday somewhere, a few days' rest away from work, to celebrate the news about their son? He would suggest it to her as soon as he reached Calcutta.

Behind him, the harbor fell away and soon the hills hid the view of burning ships, ringed in by the sweep of headland. Cartwright did not look back.

Harrison climbed the steps to *Phoebe*'s bridge.

"Sorry to say it again, sir, but that bearing's giving trouble."

"To hell with the bearing. We can't stop now."

"It's getting very hot, sir."

"And the heat's on for us, too," replied Davies. "I'll ease up as soon as I dare, but if we are caught within the three-mile limit, none of us goes free until the end of the war. Think about that. And if you want to try your luck in a Goanese prison indefinitely, I don't."

The nagging worry in Davies's mind was that before his passengers had destroyed *Ehrenfels'* transmitter, her radio operator might have managed to send out a last message to all U-boats in the vicinity warning them that she was under attack. These U-boats could now be converging at speed on the harbor mouth in the hope they could rescue their own countrymen or else deal with their attackers. With the sun growing steadily stronger, it would be madness to stop. If they did, and a U-boat did not intercept them, then almost certainly a Portuguese naval vessel would put out after them. So he pressed on as speedily as he could, and hoped his guardian angel was looking after him.

Pugh asked his permission to send a signal over *Phoebe's* radio transmitter. He tapped one word on the Morse key: *Longshanks.* This had been chosen because it was inspired by Stewart's long legs. It meant that the Axis ships had all sunk at their moorings. Pugh repeated the word for a second time. Then he turned the dials and listened to other men's messages. He could recognize the groups of numbers and letters used in British and Allied codes. But most of the signals he heard now were using German groups and codes. Occasionally, German voices spoke in clear, but the static was too great for him to do more than pick up isolated words.

Walter Fletcher, waiting in his office in Malabar Hill, Bombay, put out his hand to receive the sheet of paper which the messenger handed to him. He read the single word typed on it and at once went into the next room. Alex Peterson was sitting at his desk.

"Longshanks," said Fletcher briefly. "They've done it."

Peterson opened a buff file and took out some previously typed press releases that he had prepared. The first claimed that morale was so low among the Axis crews in the ships in Marmagoa harbor that they had set fire to their own vessels. The next

213

elaborated this, and declared that a dispute between Nazis and anti-Nazis was the underlying cause. He would submit these reports to the Indian news agency, Associated Press of India, which would transmit them to English language and vernacular newspapers throughout India. Other countries would also pick them up and print them.

Over the next few days, other reports would appear, as though from Nova Goa, the name sometimes given to Panjim, the capital, to differentiate itself from Old Goa, the original capital, a few miles away, now in ruins and overgrown by jungle. He had acquired several photographs of the ships at anchor before the fire, and he had made arrangements for other photographs to be taken within the next few days.

All that day, *Phoebe* steamed north at full speed. The main bearing, although showing increasing signs of wear, stood up to its task. The members of Creek Force shared out the remains of their liquor ration. They fed the prisoners. They tended Crossley's burns, and the cuts from nicks by bullets and knives which others had suffered in the fighting.

Crossley bore the pain of his injuries with patience and stoicism.

"It is just mind over matter," he explained. "Anyone can minimize pain, if you give your mind to it." Then he upended himself and stood on his head and gave his mind over to meditation.

Red Mac reported with some embarrassment to Bill Grice that one red Minimax fire extinguisher had been left behind aboard *Ehrenfels*. Grice told him not to worry. These fire extinguishers were exported to India and Goa in considerable quantities; it was unlikely that the Portuguese authorities would consider this evidence of British involvement. There was no sign of any ship in pursuit or of any U-boat. When darkness finally fell, they sat around the deck, backs against the uprights of the rails, certain now they would make home base safely.

Gradually, they began to sing the songs they used to sing at pre-war concerts, around the fire in camp,

214

and after rugger matches. The words—defiant, rude, belligerent and masculine—drifted out on the evening wind. Mission accomplished, they thought. But none of them guessed at the real magnitude of their achievement.

FOURTEEN

Fifteen miles to the west and several hours later, Lieutenant Lüths U-boat No. U-181 shook off her weight of water and soared like a giant seal from the sea. The conning tower hatch opened. Lüth and another officer climbed down the slippery steps to the long narrow deck space. Under their feet, the U-boat's generator began its task of charging storage batteries. Above their heads, the radio antenna pointed to the stars like a wand.

The last instruction Lüth had received had been to surface at 01:15 hours on March 10 at a certain bearing. He was well on time. At half past one he climbed back inside the U-boat and approached the radio operator. The man removed his headphones.

"Nothing, sir."

"That's odd," said Lüth. "Wavelength all right? No interference?"

"Everything's perfect, sir. I am picking up all kinds of other signals, but not what we want."

"Give it another half an hour then," Lüth told him.

In fact, they gave it another one-and-a-half hours, but still no message came with the peculiar and distinctive tapping of the wrist that U-boat radio operators across the Indian Ocean had come to recognize so well.

At three o'clock, Lüth, much puzzled and perplexed, gave the order to submerge. Within minutes, the sea closed over them and it was as though they had never been.

All across the Indian Ocean that night, and on night after night thereafter for the next few weeks, German U-boats surfaced, and operators listened for that familiar tapping of a Morse key. But they would never hear it again. They had received their last instructions, and one by one, as fuel and stores dwindled, they asked their base for other orders, and dispersed for Rangoon and Singapore, and in some cases were ordered round the Cape.

Without their detailed instructions, they were like blind men without guide dogs, eyeless hunters seeking an elusive prey across millions of miles of empty ocean.

At six o'clock on that same Wednesday morning, *Phoebe* arrived off Bombay. Davies anchored her well out in midstream, feeling disreputable and scruffy alongside naval ships in their camouflage, and freighters being loaded. He hoped that a representative of the Port Commission or the Customs or the Police might wonder at the arrival of such an unlikely vessel and come out to enquire their business, so they could ask for instructions. But no one came near them.

"I am going in," announced Pugh at last.

"I'll come with you," said Grice. "Just in case there is any trouble."

They hailed a rowing boat with two Indians, who were carrying out some maintenance on a buoy, and were rowed in to a muddy creek. They gave the boatmen a tip and picked their way through the filthy mud, among scuttling crabs, until they came to Colaba Causeway and hailed a taxi.

Pugh gave the driver the address of Army Headquarters, Bombay District.

It was now nearly eleven o'clock and the British sentry, smart in whitened belt and gaiters, looked dubiously at these men in dirty uniforms who claimed to be officers and who sought an urgent interview with Colonel Freddie Hutson. This was the officer Pugh had telephoned from Belgaum when he was with Trompeta and his wife. They were passed from the sentry to the corporal of the guard, to a sergeant major. Finally, they were shown into the colonel's office. He roared with laughter when he saw them.

"What the hell have you been up to this time?" he

asked Pugh. "Well, sit down. Tell me all about it."

"You've probably heard some rather extraordinary story about Goa?" asked Pugh.

"You're right," said Hutson. "I have indeed heard some extraordinary stories."

He pushed across a copy of *The Times of India* and another of *The Statesman*. Both had two news items ringed with pencil:

AXIS SHIPS IN GOA GUTTED

—

Low Morale Of Crew

◆

FROM OUR OWN CORRESPONDENT.

NOVA GOA, March 9.

In the early hours of March 9 the crew of the interned enemy ships in Marmagoa harbour are reported to have set fire to three German ships, the BRAUNFELS, the DRACHENFELS, and the EHRENFELS, and the Italian cargo ship ANFORA, which had been interned since the outbreak of war. The fire could not be controlled and the ships were burnt down.

It is believed that the crew have been leading a wretched life owing to lack of absolute necessities of life. The Portuguese authorities have taken the ships' men and officers to Nova Goa under a police escort.

GERMANS SCUTTLE SHIPS

—

INCIDENT IN MARMAGOA HARBOR

NEW DELHI. Mar. 9—A number of German cargo ships, which have been lying in Marmagoa port since the outbreak of war, were recently scuttled by their Nazi crews, according to a report received here.

They took this desperate step in order to scotch a plan which they feared other members of the crew might carry out to elude the guards and make a dash for Singapore or some other Japanese-occupied port.

The 2 groups are reported to have engaged in violent fighting and some of the Germans set fire to a few of the ships, which were burnt out. The men escaped ashore where they were rounded up and detained—API.

"Did you do it?" asked Hutson bluntly.

"As a matter of fact, we did," replied Pugh. "With a lot of help from some *koi hais* from Calcutta."

"Well, I'm damned," said Hutson, instantly serious. "That's about four and a half million pounds of enemy shipping gone down. "How did you get there?"

"In a hopper barge."

"A *hopper* barge? I don't believe a word of it."

"Have you got a car?" asked Pugh.

"Yes."

"Then let's get in it and we'll show you."

They drove down to the marsh where they had come ashore. A hundred yards out, *Phoebe* lay at anchor, a wisp of smoke playing around the blackened mouth of her preposterous funnel.

"You see that craft out here?" said Pugh. "Well, that's our hopper barge. Little *Phoebe*."

"Good God!" said Hutson. "Doesn't look as though she could sail more than 50 yards."

"Well, she has," said Grice. "She's sailed a long way, and she still has a long way to go—to Calcutta. But we can't sail back aboard her. There just isn't room."

"How can I help you?" Hutson asked him.

Pugh explained that they would like reservations on that evening's train to Calcutta. This could be difficult to arrange, for with drafts of troops taking over most of the available accommodation, all trains were heavily booked. But if they had to wait in Bombay for several days, that could be detrimental to the security aspect of their trip.

Hutson promised he would do everything he could to arrange this. Grice asked him whether he had heard anything else about events in Goa.

"There was an oil tanker in Marmagoa at the time," replied Hutson. "And as soon as the firing broke out, she up-anchored and came hell for leather back here, not knowing what had really happened, except that the whole port seemed to be ablaze and ships on fire and sinking. The testimony of her crew fully bears out the newspaper stories."

"A bit of luck for us," said Pugh. But was it luck, or chance—or providential?

By lunch time, Hutson had acquired his reservations and Creek Force were ferried ashore in a harbor launch. The German prisoners were also taken off for interrogation and then to an internment camp.

The Light Horse and Calcutta Scottish dumped their kit at Army Headquarters and crowded into the Taj Hotel. This stood near the Gateway of India and was Bombay's most elegant hotel, with a magnificent view across the sea. Then, as they saw themselves in the huge full-length mirrors in the foyer—unkempt, with faces blackened and bruised, their clothes filthy and torn—they realized what embarrassment they would cause to other guests in the hotel. Worse, what possible explanation could they give to any friends in Bombay who recognized them? So out they trooped before the welcome luxury of the place overcame these scruples.

Some belonged to the Bombay Yacht Club, so they took friends there for a wash and brush-up—to the visible if silent horror of their fellow members who looked the other way rather than see them.

"I hope you're not thinking of putting any of these fellows up for the club?" one old member asked Melborne in a stage whisper.

Others went to the Gymkhana Club to take advantage of their facilities. A few booked rooms in less salubrious hotels, where they washed and bathed and shaved. And those whose firms maintained branches in Bombay presented themselves at their offices and demanded baths and clean clothes.

In the harbor, Davies was already preparing to take *Phoebe* out to sea. Soon he began on his 2,500 mile trip back to the Hooghly as unobtrusively as he had arrived.

That night, the Calcutta mail left on its long trans-India journey, and as dusk deepened into darkness, *Phoebe*, navigation lights now lit, was preparing to beat steadily south again, keeping well within sight of the coast. A new bearing was in her engine and her crew were happy about the bonuses they would collect on arrival in Calcutta.

By the end of the week, the Light Horse were back in their homes and offices.

As soon as Crofter arrived, he had a bath and a change of clothes and went to see his fiancée.

"Thank you so much for your letters, darling," she told him. "I *did* appreciate them. It was very kind of you to write so fully when you were so busy. I really felt I was there by your side."

Crofter smiled contentedly; his deception had been worthwhile and was undiscovered.

"Only one thing puzzled me a little," Marion went on, with the deliberately deceptive ingenuousness of a wife-to-be. "Why didn't you answer *any* of the questions I asked in *my* letters to *you?*"

When Hilliard came into his office, his superior nodded a brief greeting.

"I managed to get that audit done myself when you were away," he told him with the satisfaction of a professional martyr. "But there's a stack of new stuff waiting for you. Do you good to get your back into something after all that fooling around, eh?" He paused.

"You did say it was Ranchi, didn't you?" he asked.

"Yes, sir. Why?"

"Must say, you look damned sunburned. If I hadn't known where you were I'd have said you'd had a few days by the sea."

Jack Breene also returned to his office to face a

pile of letters. He made a face, then pressed the bell for his Bengali male secretary to come in and take dictation. But before the man arrived Breene's partner put his head around the door.

"I wanted to see you, Jack," he said. "We've had a bit of bad luck while you've been away."

"Oh? How?"

"Hell of a big claim's due."

"Go on? From whom?"

The partner put a newspaper cutting on Breene's desk. He read:

Inquiry Into Fire On Axis Ships In Goa

FROM OUR OWN CORRESPONDENT.

NOVA GOA, March 13:-

The Government of Portuguese India are investigating the causes that led to the fire on three German and one Italian ships in Marmagoa harbour. The hulks have not sunk, owing to low water, but the harbour is navigable and has not in any way been obstructed.

Government have provided accommodation for the crew. It is reported that some Germans have disappeared from Goa. One or two have died in the hospital, but the rest are all right. Life in Marmagoa harbour is quite normal. The German ship BRAUNFELS had merchandise worth about Rs. 70,00,000, consigned to merchants in British India. The other two German steamers, DRACHENFELS and EHRENFELS, had very little merchandise on them. The Italian ship ANFORA had merchandise worth about Rs. 12,00,000. It is understood that some of the merchandise was sold by the crew to maintain themselves.

Since the disappearance some time ago of the Nazi chief, who was supposed to be their leader and who was helping them financially, the Germans were becoming disorderly and there was no discipline among them.

"What's that got to do with us?" asked Breene innocently.

222

"Hell of a lot. Didn't you know I'd insured the damned things? They're worth over £4,500,000. There'll be a claim as long as your arm."

Suddenly Breene started to laugh.

His partner looked at him in amazement.

"What's so funny?"

"Nothing, really. Just that, at last, I think the joke's really on me."

For the British and the Allies, the silencing of Trompeta's secret transmitter produced a dramatic and almost immediate decline in shipping losses from German U-boats. Without this urgently needed relief, war in the East could well have taken a very different course.

During the first 11 days of March 1943 three German U-boats, U-160, U-182 and U-506, accounted for 12 British, American, Norwegian and Dutch ships, a total of roughly 80,000 tons. Of these, U-160 alone sank 10.

But without the radio messages to give precise details of speed, destination, cargo and other material factors, U-boat commanders now had to rely only on luck or chance for their kill.

During the rest of March, the 13 German U-boats operating in the Indian Ocean only sank one ship, the Panamanian *Nortun* of 3,663 tons. Throughout the following month of April, their total was only three.

So the immediate advantage went to the hard pressed Allies. They could continue their build-up of men and war material on India's eastern frontier. The Japanese armies, poised to sweep down triumphantly on Calcutta and Delhi in the dream of Subhas Chandra Bose, had to postpone their attempt for another year. By then, it was too late. The Rising Sun was beginning to set and their armies advanced no more. Bose's dream had became his nightmare.

For the Germans, the benefits of the action were delayed, but no less valuable for that. On the morning of March 9, while their ships still burned,

Portuguese army trucks drove them north through Panjim, to Fort Aguanda on the coast. This was an ancient Portuguese fort originally built to defend the colony from overseas attack. Here they were interned for the rest of the war.

They bore what seemed like humiliating defeat with dignity and courage—an example in adversity not lost upon the Portuguese or the Goanese or the Indians. They still worked part-time in garages or mending cameras and radios and watches. In so doing, a number formed permanent friendships with local families. At the end of the war, not all Germans elected to return home, and some stayed on in Goa, where they married, raised families and started businesses of their own or worked for local firms.

Those who did go back to Europe spoke highly of their treatment in Goa. As a result, when West Germany's financial institutions began to seek new areas suitable for overseas investment, it was remembered how their countrymen had been treated in Goa, and West Germany invested largely in that colony. This investment increased when India annexed Goa in 1961.

The old Fort Aguada has now been transformed into one of the most luxurious hotel complexes in the East—the Fort Aguada Beach Resort. German families are among their most numerous and popular guests.

Many of the Germans and Italians who formed the crews in 1943 are now extremely rich and successful men. So it is with the contingent from Calcutta. Several have been knighted for their services to commerce in India; others have received honors and awards of other kinds. Pugh retired from the Army after a distinguished career in which he was awarded the D.S.O. three times. But of them all, Yogi Crossley is the only one who still lives in Calcutta.

Colin Mackenzie returned to Scotland to his business interests. He later became chairman of the Scottish Council, FBI, and then chairman of the Scottish Arts Council.

Alex Peterson went back to teaching, and then

served in Malaya during the 1950's emergency as Director General of Information Services. He was subsequently appointed director of the Department of Education at Oxford University.

Walter Fletcher was elected Conservative MP for Bury in 1945, and remained in the House for 10 years, latterly representing Bury and Radcliffe. He was knighted in 1953, three years before his death.

Nothing has been heard of Trompeta and his wife. It is not known whether they returned to Germany after the war or stayed in India. Some evidence points to this second possibility.

The authorities kept faith with the Light Horse over one particular promise. They would have no credit for what they volunteered to do, and there would be no medals. So closely was this last pledge adhered to that the men who had willingly risked their lives and careers, at their own expense, to carry out a task which produced unparalleled benefits, were categorically refused the right to wear one of Britain's humbler issue medals of the Second World War, the 1939-45 Star.

This was given to many who had been in no physical danger, including, ironically, ticket collectors at Howrah Station in Calcutta, from which the Light Horse and Calcutta Scottish had set off on their long journey. The ticket collectors' claim was allowed, because they had been embodied to prevent the risk of any labor dispute slowing the essential flow of rail traffic. But the Light Horse never publicly complained. They remained true to their regimental motto: Defense not Defiance. Denied any official recognition of their services, they designed their own private memento—a sea horse. This appeared in subsequent issues of *Gallop*, their regular regimental magazine, without any explanation. Several members of Creek Force gave brooches of this design to wives and girl friends, without telling them its special significance. Now they know.

Possibly the man who achieved most for himself individually and hence for his country, is a Goanese, Vasudev Salgaocar. As a young man, he owned a small shop in Marmagoa, and had supplied the Axis ships with food and vegetables during the long months they were anchored in the harbor. He had also arranged football matches between the crews and local teams.

When the crews were interned, with no possessions apart from the clothes they wore, Salgaocar advanced money to them against their signature on a chit, without much hope of repayment. Weeks and months afterwards, when they disposed of cargo that seawater had not spoiled, he successfully bid for it to resell. After the war, once money was again available from West Germany, and the crews came to him to pay their debts, Salgaocar told them, "You have already repaid me many times over."

From this small beginning, he built up what is now known as the House of Salgaocar. This is a vast international organization concerned with such diverse interests as mining and shipping iron ore; the manufacture of chemicals and industrial gases; ship building; civil engineering and bulk carriers.

But possibly Vasudev Salgaocar, who was left fatherless at 10, and so could not finish his own primary education, draws most satisfaction from the fact that his wealth has enabled him to found and endow Goa's Law College for 500 students.

So what began as a desperate wartime operation, using for expediency middle-aged members of a part-time auxiliary cavalry regiment, was completely successful in a military sense. Even more important, this last action of the Calcutta Light Horse, the only amphibious operation in their long history, has produced remarkable economic consequences involving India and Europe.

In so doing it has surely disproved the Duke of Wellington's melancholy opinion that "There is nothing so dreadful as a great victory—excepting a great defeat."

Here, victory has been shared by all concerned.

When India became independent in 1947, there was, of course, no place for such anachronistic auxiliary units as the Calcutta Light Horse, and in November of that year they stood down for the last time.

It had long been the custom for the Viceroy of India to be their Honorary Colonel, and Earl Mountbatten of Burma, the last Viceroy, recalled his own association with the Regiment when he contributed the preface to their official history.

"One of my saddest duties in India in 1947 was to give the order for the disbandment of the Calcutta Light Horse, of which Regiment I was then Honorary Colonel," he wrote, and went on to trace the Regiment's long career in India.

"But," he added, "It was not in this country that the Calcutta Light Horse was to fulfil its destiny. . . ."

Mountbatten was, of course, referring to the 286 members who had joined the fighting services in the First World War, and the further 383 who had served in the second. But of all those who had gone to war, and those who had to remain in their civilian jobs, the 14 members who traveled to Goa in March, 1943, felt that for them his words held a secret and special significance.

I know nothing—
absolutely NOTHING
about anything

INDEX

posed Light Horse operation, 75; and transport problems, 96–97, 100–1; and Cartwright, 97, 99–104; on operation, 111; on board *Phoebe*, 159, 165; shipboard training, 167; in assault, 183; withdrawal, 209

ABOUT THE AUTHOR

JAMES LEASOR, who was educated at the City of London School and Oriel College, Oxford, is the author of many other books, including the internationally acclaimed Dr. Jason Love series. His most recent book was *Green Beach*, a story of the Dieppe raid in 1942 which was published in ten countries.

RELAX!
SIT DOWN
and Catch Up On Your Reading!